INCREDIBLE VOYAGES

Self Discovery Through Travel

Klotsche, Charles Martin
First edition. Hardback

ISBN 0-9673890-4-6

1. Non fiction. 2. Travel adventure. 3. History. 4. Ecology.
5. Philosophy. 6. Spirituality.

FRONT COVER PHOTOS
Clockwise from left:
Breakers Hotel, Palm Beach, FL; Wine Country in Mallorca;
Jetting to Nantucket; Crew of the Enola Gay prior to dropping
first atomic bomb; Sailing in the British Virgin Island; Sky
City in Acoma, NM

BACK COVER
Author photo courtesy of Casey O'Connor, Palm Beach

PAN AMERICAN PRESS
New York
All rights reserved

Printed in the United States of America

Distributed in Canada and the United Kingdom by Ingram Books.

OTHER BOOKS BY THE AUTHOR

The Real Estate Revolution: Acquisition and Development Concepts

Real Estate Investing: A Complete Guide to Wealth Building Secrets

Real Estate Syndicator's Handbook

Color Medicine: The Secrets of Color/Vibrational Healing

Omega Point: An Apocalyptic Parable of Spiritual Transcendence

Journeys: Self-discovery Through Travel

The Silent Victims: The Aftermath of Failed Children on Their Mothers' Lives

Crossings: Self-discovery Through Travel

Passages: Self-discovery Through Travel

How Wall Street Makes Money The Old-Fashioned Way: They Steal It.

Travels With Charlie: Self Discovery Through Travel

2012 Dire Cataclysmic Events Predicted

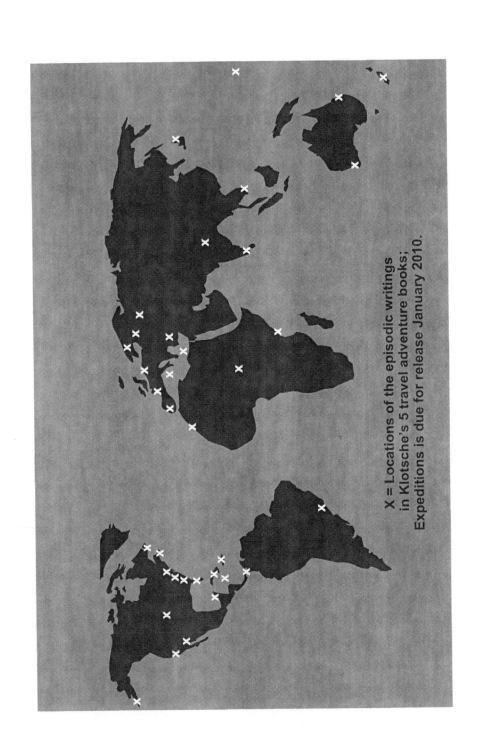

X = Locations of the episodic writings
in Klotsche's 5 travel adventure books;
Expeditions is due for release January 2010.

INCREDIBLE VOYAGES
TABLE OF CONTENTS

SECTION I
Playgrounds of the Rich and Famous

SECTION II
The World is a Book

SECTION III
Iconic Moments from the Past

SECTION I

Playgrounds of the Rich and Famous

A s Aristotle Onassis, who certainly knew what he was talking
about, once noted, "After a certain point, money is
meaningless. It ceases to be the goal. The game is what counts."
For a small but powerful segment of society, where you live, or
where you spend a season, is an indicator of who you are, and of
how much wealth you have accumulated. In places like Monte
Carlo, Cannes, Monaco, and the Bahamas, people are there
primarily to see and be seen, to flaunt their wealth, and to enjoy
the better things in life. In this section I take a look at Nantucket
and, over two chapters, at Palm Beach. In both places, there is an
unmistakable tension between the Old Guard, who have lived there
in luxury for several generations, putting down strong roots, and
the newer arrivals, desperately trying to show off their success and
their wealth, and to establish that they belong to the upper crust.
Busy with expensive and extensive renovations, the *nouveaux-
riche* have little connection with the traditions of the past, and little
in common with the Old Guard. Fortunately, in both places, a
sense of history and heritage prevails, but the contrast between the
two affluent groups, who have different aspirations and values and
different ways of showcasing their wealth, is an indication of how
much the concept of success has changed over the last century.

THE PLATINUM ISLAND REVISITED — PALM BEACH NOW WITH CONSPICUOUS CONSUMPTION

Several years ago I wrote about the "Old Guard" in Palm Beach, those aristocratic men and women whose ancestry could often be traced back to the courts of the European monarchs. They were people with impeccable genes, and their long-established bloodlines were accompanied by a quiet and unassuming sophistication that set them apart from the crowd. Their families had maintained time-tested traditions, considerable fortunes, and a certain elegance for a great many decades.

As the twentieth century came to an end, there was a noticeable change in the mentality of those who traditionally wintered here in Palm Beach. They seemed far more preoccupied with the idea that here, it was money that paved the way into high society. An old, respectable family, or long-standing traditions, they rationalized, could easily be substituted with ostentatious living standards. They believed that money can buy anything, including social standing and inclusion in a traditionally closed society. "Having arrived" here, in the Old Guard sense, took on a new meaning than the one established for generations by the elite, who had adhered to a specific social code of ethics and had created a clearly defined position for themselves in American society. In the 1970s, there was a new trend in the air: self-made executives with prominence and some independently acquired social graces were readily accepted into some of the A-List circles. Their wives were frequently called upon to head up some of the more prominent charitable events as well.

The newcomers came out in droves, and were not to be outdone. Sometimes they had little in the way of social graces. They assumed they would be worshiped because of their bank accounts and their pricy toys which the Old Guard had to take notice of, not only due to their abundance but also because of their outrageous price tags. Sometimes, even before or shortly after their arrival, this new group, whom some refer to as the "newly affluent," needed an introduction to this dignified, long-established group that constitutes the leisure class. This usually meant that even before their homes were decorated and fully occupied, they hired a publicist to get them some exposure in the society magazines and the appropriate sections of the *Palm Beach Daily News*, hoping that they could then easily obtain their much-needed introductions to those who orchestrated the more prestigious charity balls and other high-profile events in the city. Of course, this practice seemed completely foreign to the remnants of Old- World aristocrats who had come here after carefully cultivating other like-minded people of a similar heritage and background. They had moved here from traditional places in the east and Midwest such as Lake Forest, Grosse Pointe, Philadelphia, the Hamptons, and Greenwich, to mention a few.

No longer was it necessary, the new arrivals reasoned, to spend endless seasons and decades bonding with the Old Guard and cultivating a comfort level. Historically, the road to acceptance had been paved, to a large degree, by those already living in this elite setting. For the Newly affluent, the instant gratification that they associated with their newly found riches led them to believe that their entry into high society could be equally instantaneous, even though they had usually obtained their wealth in places and settings far less chic than those where the Old Money crowd had cut their teeth.

What some of the new arrivals failed to realize was that much of the Old Guard were groomed over many generations in the grand ballrooms in places like New York and Newport, where they blossomed under close supervision. They were observed and guided by those who had had to jump through the same hoops decades before, but the new arrivals, in their haste to fit in, thought they could simply bypass this process of learning and initiation. Many newly affluent came to realize that the term *cotillion* was not some four-legged creature that darted in and out of one's hedges here. They found that to muscle one's way in here, one did not need sharp elbows, but a more genteel demeanor, and a series of interlocking friendships, introductions, and proper connections that often took quite some time to cultivate.

Prior to this recent period of history, it was virtually impossible to penetrate this closed world of the elite. Many interlopers came, but departed in frustration after a few seasons, and went off in search of other wintering and watering holes more to their liking. They sensed that they would be more comfortable in places that were receptive to their habits, manners, and spending methods. It seemed as if here in Palm Beach, instant gratification was not part of the equation. Without a well-thought-out and well-documented game plan, it was easy to get trapped in the quicksand, and before long, your life could turn into some sort of Shakespearian-type tragedy. The sheer numbers of new arrivals, unassociated with those who have long-established roots, today represent a permanent shift in the course of the island's occupants. This new tide might prove difficult to reverse, at least for those who cling to the traditional, old and established ways.

Now it is cash, the coin of the realm that springs eternal from Wall Street, that seems to be driving a wedge between old and new. Money, at least the old, quiet type, has never been a sticking point here; however, without having some sense of style, it is difficult to get accepted. Even some of the old-time, so-called "spendthrifts" are wearing the carpet thin, those who are at the end of the runway with their trust funds, but still get a "lift" from the more fortunate and prudent of the Old Guard here, with whom they have cultivated friendships for decades. Conversely, the new kids on the block often openly discuss their net worth figures and spending patterns, if not in person then through their publicists, who spread the word like wildfire. It is not so among those who are attempting to preserve the social scene here, with their passed-down inheritances, even if they now have had to quietly accept a coupon-clipping lifestyle.

One might easily sum up this incoming tide, these less-than-desirable characters and their toys that are washed ashore. The troubling social shift was particularly evident during the hijacking of the Red Cross Ball, which formerly was the premier social event of the past, attracting all of the local blue bloods for an evening of elegance. The ball brought back the splendor of the Gilded Age, and the excitement of the Roaring Twenties—back in those days, things were, of course, flaunted without shame. Large waterfront homes, lavish parties, expensive chauffeur-driven cars, and opulent lifestyles with servants galore were just part of the fabric of life in Palm Beach. Back then, Old Money did not show off to the outside world, but inwardly, in the confines of elite society, there was no bashfulness about enjoying and displaying what you had. It was a bit like the old European royalty, who conducted and achieved their social standing in the privacy of their courts, and performed their roles as elites with subtle style and grace. No need for a publicity agent, thank you. In effect, one got one's standing "incrementally," so to speak, in a variety of ways, not exclusively by clawing one's way up the economic ladder, but through marriage, respectable bloodlines and schooling, or through the slower process of inheritance.

Herein lies the difference that separates the two vying, sometimes diametrically opposed social groups on the island. Some of the new arrivals are attempting to move up to the high water mark of acceptance here, without the traditional laying of the necessary ground work. It seems that a certain percentage of the new arrivals are mainly motivated by the mentality that one can float in on the high tide in short order here, with their publicists and toys in tow. They adhere to the old saying that "it is better to be Nouveau Riche than not rich at all." Being rich without a doubt has its merits, as well as its constraints. After all, there are only so many social slots that money can buy here or in the other desirable parts of the world. And money has a whole new significance now, in a world that seems so flush in cash these days, where the multi-millionaires of the hedge funds and private equity firms seem to have devised ways to generate great wealth in a very short order.

So some reasoned that moving up to the upper rungs of the social ladder here could be achieved by pledging large amounts of money at the many highly publicized charitable events—there are literally dozens each month of the season. The apparent goal of these upstarts, supported by expensive publicists that make the dream come true, is to get "ink," either in the society magazines or in sections of the newspapers—this is something that the Old Guard totally abhors, as is evidenced by the fact that the most exclusive of clubs here still do not permit photos, or even the passing around of business cards: in fact, many of the old residents don't even bother to have them printed up, since one's word and reputation travels here through contacts and references.

When the new kids on the block hijacked the premier event, the Red Cross Ball, the results were exactly as the Old Guard had predicted. The newly appointed chairman of the event, interestingly enough a convicted felon with a splashy lifestyle who supported a bevy of publicists and several widely publicized charitable events, set the tone for things to come. The capstone of the evening of the big event, his so-called grand entrance into what he though was the apex of Palm Beach society, was less than glamorous to say the least, and was of course hushed up by the newspapers that he traditionally showered with cash. Unbeknownst to the readers in the days to come, it turned out that when he was poised to make his final speech of the evening, the crowing glory of his achievements, everything fizzled in a heart-beat. Some who observed his behavior that night said he was only one step away from a self-induced coronation. Reliable word has it that as he attempted to mount the stage into this stratified world of society, he stumbled and fell off the stage, and had to be taken by ambulance to a local hospital by the 911 crew.

This fiasco of an evening was all prefaced by the fact that those who had regularly attended the Red Cross Ball in the past boycotted the event because of the new leadership, which meant that both he and his checkbook had to reach far and wide to "paper the house" with attendees, giving the artificial appearance that the event was still the Old Guard personified, at least in terms of numbers.

A dramatic shift took place during the last quarter of the last century. Those people with household names who wintered here season after season, many of whom had been associated with founding companies on the Fortune 500 list, began to decline.

And their offshoot, who either lacked the leisure time or the disposable income, or had found other watering holes more to their liking, seemed to disappear. With the changing of the guard, values evolved that were a bit foreign to the Old Guard, who cherished the old relationships and rituals that were cultivated here over the decades. The old order blood lines were being thinned out, in part because of the newly created wealthy class who showed an indifference to the island's culture. So in effect, those who traditionally had been on the outside looking in found that they could now open the door a crack or two, and make their way towards the upper echelons of society on the island. Palm Beach and its demographics have changed dramatically in the last decade. The island used to be jokingly referred to as "God's waiting room," since over 70% of the population was over 65. But in recent years, there has been a rapid growth of arrivals from the younger moneyed set, who are attracted to the prestige and the heritage of the island.

My extended family and I had wintered here in earlier days. I attended Kindergarten to Eighth Grade when we were here during the season. Back then, it seemed the financial equation for social acceptance was easy enough to manage. It was not uncommon for a family to have a moderately sized winter home here, and a summer residence on a much grander scale, usually without the encumbrance of a mortgage. You would need a small household staff that worked both homes equally, and a minimum tangible, liquid net worth of, say, five million dollars, would do the trick. A membership to the Bath and Tennis or the Everglades Club was the icing on the cake, and would place one on or near the A-List, assuming you had the correct lineage, and had been to the proper boarding schools and Ivy League colleges. Such people were assured a place at the table for the entire season, and their prestige increased even more when an inheritance followed.

Sure, the rules were strict and the openings were limited, but Palm Beach was always a community that catered to the idle rich, those who came into their prime at about the time they reached middle age, which often coincided with the transfer of wealth through inheritance. Going to the proper clubs, doing extensive traveling, studying abroad, having parents with large estates and live-in staff members, having anglicized names, at least in former generations, and adopting extra curricular activities such as sailing, tennis, bridge and especially polo were not prerequisites, but certainly helped one to be accepted. The equation had to be well balanced: you not only needed massive amounts of cash—the number of zeros in your bank and stock holdings had to be notable—but at the end of the day, you also had to be respectable, balanced, polished, and totally above board.

Those who had formerly been "ingrained institutions" here have slowly become somewhat marginalized because of the massive amounts of money that have arrived here, money that needs constant attention, I am told, to preserve its status. The Old Guard and their descendants really weren't interested in soiling their hands, unlike the new arrivals, with their electronic ways of keeping in touch with their businesses. As a way of preserving and not flaunting their wealth, many of the long-time elite have taken to downsizing their homes, or even parting with the splendor of the past by quietly disposing of jewelry or rare antiques or works of art, or even letting their mansions fall into a state of disrepair, or just cutting back on high-ticket items found on Worth Avenue; they now limit their visits to this high-end shopping area, which features boutiques like Gucci, Chanel, and Louis Vuitton. Some of the wannabes even host their own charity balls, taking perks at other events for their efforts, or provide guided tours of faraway lands to preserve their independence and purchasing power. Once the place gets into your blood, it's amazing how creative some people here can get when they are looking for ways to stay here, and to continue living in the style to which you have grown accustomed. It's hard to give up your inside position on this most prestigious of tracks.

Gone are the servants of old, in their white dresses and waist coats. Now the members of the Old Guard, when opening the doors of their secluded properties for specific occasions, often rely on outside bartenders and waitresses from a few well chosen catering companies, or staff members from the most exclusive clubs. Many find it more convenient to simply entertain at the best clubs in order to maintain the dignified lifestyle that they are known for and used to; private sections of the clubs can be reserved for cocktail gatherings before dinner, and are acceptable to those who are used to intimate entertaining.

All of this so-called shedding of some of the former trappings can be rationalized by the fact that members of the traditional elite are becoming somewhat eccentric with time, though some eagerly adopt an aura of eccentricity, and in lieu of spending lavishly, they proclaim that they are no longer tied to the expensive traditions of the past. After all, they reason, once you have made the A-List, you have no need whatsoever to impress the rest of the less seasoned public. Why keep up with the splashy newly affluent? Especially when this has been our territory for so many generations?

Nevertheless, the old habits die hard, and are still ingrained here. The Old Guard still forges out to lunch destinations that are much sought after relics of the past, such as the beach side cafeteria at the Bath and Tennis Club. This strikes the new arrivals as a bit of an antiquated idea, and they prefer to lunch at the pricy restaurants on the island. Nevertheless, both groups enjoy the concept of seeing and being seen. The Old Guard still passes the afternoons at their cabanas, around the adult-only salt water swimming pool at the Bath and Tennis, or on the golf course at the Everglades Club. These traditions haven't changed much at all in the last seventy-five years or so. And the old elite go about their business without cell phones, Blackberries or ipods, making them somewhat oblivious to the outside world of those who must toil for a living.

Instead, they nap, and have an early cocktail before dressing for dinner. They put on the standard blue blazer, chino trouser outfit, or a tuxedo, depending on the nature of the event they are going to. Life on the island, for them, involves an endless stream of dinner parties, many sponsored by members of the A-list, all of whom intend to retire early, certainly by 10:00 pm, so they can get their beauty street and get ready for a repeat performance the following day. Needless to say, it is non-stop fun for those who are regularly included, and they burn up the telephone lines the next morning, chronicling the prior evening's events.

In the past, the overriding rules of the game here did not change easily, and were monitored by a well-known and fully rehearsed committee of the ruling elite, mainly comprised of women with long-standing reputations here and in their summer communities. Formerly, these "grand dames" always decided who was acceptable and who was not, at least on the social scene, which dominates the playing field in season. So in this world of high intrigue and sometimes total exclusion, a few elites would always determine who would play and get invitations to the top-tier charity balls. Today, however, it seems that even a bank teller can get on the invitation lists to many of the main-line charity balls. The elegant black tie events at the clubs and inclusion in the A-List dinner and cocktail circuit are the brass ring everybody strives for. Being financially successful or well bred are the keys for inclusion, and there is simply no middle ground between being included or excluded, at least in my estimation. For that reason, it is a common fact that many of the Old Guard find it below their dignity to work, at least during the season here. They will do nothing more than checking their stock portfolios and occasionally contacting their lawyers and trust officers.

Over the years I have found it interesting to observe the so-called A-List and its changing composition and requirements. The term A-List was originally used to designate the most bankable celebrities in the Hollywood movie industry, but in popular usage, it simply refers to anyone with an admired or desirable social status. In Palm Beach, without a doubt, being on the A-List or in close proximity to it is the most coveted prize on the island, no matter whose definition one relies on for inclusion. It is, indeed, quite a subjective list—many people are certain they are on it, but others around them would say they are not. It depends to some extent on what clubs you belong to. Certainly as a start, one can say with some degree of authority that about half of the members of the Bath and Tennis Club, and half of the 2000 members of the Everglades Club, an 18-hole regulation-length golf course built in 1932, would belong to the A-List. Palm Beach is a town whose people rely heavily on club memberships to achieve status and recognition, and of course these clubs are ideal and upscale venues for entertaining.

The A-List consists of roughly 1500 people, plus or minus depending on which circle of friends you talk to. But as the Old Guard here likes to say, "fruit doesn't fall far from the tree." They believe that their children and their children's friends, and all of those that they have accepted into their elite circle, are worthy, and should be included on the A-List. The Old Guard certainly never advertise themselves to the outside world, or blatantly promote themselves through society magazines, as the new arrivals do. The new arrivals would have you believe, for self-serving purposes, that the A-List is much greater in number. They never stop hoping that, at least some day, there will be a place for them in the higher echelons of island society.

This separation between the Old Guard, who are wealthy but do not work, and everyone else irks some of those who have made it on their own. Some of the newly affluent, unlike the power elite, seem to want to tell the world that they have arrived on their own steam, and want plenty of recognition for their achievements in the commercial world. The rule used to be that soiling one's hands in the workplace in this most prestigious of environments was totally inappropriate. Even the mention of "gainful employment" during the season sent shivers up the spines of the Old Guard. But now that rule has been softened or compromised quite a bit.

There was an old saying in Palm Beach that I often heard when I was younger: "It's not what you do from 9 to 5 that matters, it's what you do from 5 to 9 that counts!" The exclusive clubs, well-connected lunches, and A-list cocktail and dinner parties are still the venue of choice for those who have established a beachhead on the island. In the current environment, gone are the days when chauffeurs crisscrossed the streets and waited patiently on Worth Avenue or at the clubs while the idle rich socialized, shopped, lunched and cocktailed. Where the butlers ironed the morning newspapers so their masters would not get ink on their hands. Where household staff members were subservient and strictly on a last-name basis with the family members, including the children, whose first names were often preceded Mr. or Miss when they entered their teens.

The real shifting of the tectonic plates started to erupt around the turn of the 21st century. Much of it was associated with the advent of the hedge funds, private equity managers, and to a lesser degree, of the sub-prime mortgage market. In addition, numerous corporate CEOs that have helped themselves, sometimes undeservingly, to the shareholders' funds through questionable stock options and golden parachute contracts have taken a foothold here. I wrote about this topic in a series of articles for the local *Palm Beach Daily News,* and incorporated it at a later date into a full-length book on the subject entitled *How Wall Street Makes Money the Old-Fashioned Way: They Steal it."*

As could be predicted from this almost "manufacturing machine of money" that these people designed for themselves and their cronies, a new class of opulent people arrived here, with the instant gratification principle ingrained in their psyches. Many had had very little exposure to the traditional social circles here, having spent their waking hours in all-night trading rooms in New York and other strategic parts of the world, looking to find a niche in which to make a killing. They didn't realize that here, a different set of rules apply. And of course, this is the bone of contention that the Old Guard looks on unfavorably. Those who created the likes of ENRON and Tyco, to name a few are always in the shadows here, so unfortunately, all with newly acquired wealth are not beyond suspicion.

These new arrivals whom some refer to as the "working super-rich" are quite abundant here, as of late. Most had upbringings that are reflected their middle-class lifestyles, in which the stainless steel spoon was replaced by the silver one only in later life. These are the guys who worked in the trading rooms of Wall Street, making millions a year capitalizing on a fraction of a point in some highly leveraged bond market, or by using sophisticated computer models that traded duratives that were little understood beyond the trading rooms. Much of these activities take place in the unregulated world of investing money for those who are well-heeled, or for various forms of pension funds.

A quick look at the "Forbes 400" list sheds a bit of light on the subject. The new cutoff point for making the list is now $1.3 billion, $300 million more than the year before. In effect, if you did not increase you financial portfolio last year by $300 million, you lost ground. According to the local newspaper, the *Daily News*, two dozen of these people live on the island part or full time, and the majority of them appear in the upper half of the list. Two brothers are both in the top ten of the list, and a third brother is down the list a bit.

These are people who run their homes and private lives like a business, managing their lifestyles with a sophisticated staff that controls their every move with spread sheets and computer models all combined with the instant knowledge found on the Internet, which many of them have on 24-7. These are people who often make tens of millions a year or more, who have sold out to multinational companies or just retired with tens or even hundreds of millions, and in some cases billions, in stock, from an idea that found its time in the world of globalization and high-speed technology.

There are no longer as many of the household names that evoke the quiet wealth and leisure of the past, those elegant families who used to spend their winters here: the DuPonts, Mellons, Rockefellers, Annenburgs, Vanderbilts and Fords. Nowadays, you can forget that whole WASP image, the traditional boarding schools, the Ivy league colleges, the prestigious memberships to important clubs passed down from generation to generation. To the newly arrived, moneyed types, the time-tested traditions here can just take a back seat, since their bank accounts can easily buy and sell a half a dozen of the Old Guard at a crack. I should point out, though, that there are, in fact, many newly affluent who are lovely, educated, decent and refined people. There are also the many prominent longtime achievers who might not make the A-List at first, due to a lack of genes, or blue-blood documentation, but many of them end up contributing greatly to the ambiance and stability of Palm Beach, and head up many of the worthwhile charities.

One of the other significant changes over the years is the length of the social season here. Back in the days before there was air conditioning, the season ran a short six weeks, from New Year's to the middle of February. Now, with the easy accessibility by aircraft, the season takes on a much different character. For one thing, those who are new to the scene always seem to want to start a new charitable gala or two each year, to stroke their egos. Back when Palm Beach was in its prime, you could count the A-List Charitable events on one hand; the top three were the Heart Ball, the Hospital Ball and the Red Cross Ball. Today there are literally a dozen each month, and this has had a great effect on the nature of entertainment in Palm Beach.

The Old Guard is not delighted with the new instant gratification crowd, to put it mildly, especially since their share of the financial pie is steadily decreasing. Currently, only 10 % of Palm Beach's "truly wealthy" have inherited their money. The Old Guard tend to view some of the newly affluent as interlopers in this traditional town. Many of the new arrivals have yet to approach middle age, and have a lot of room to run on the racetrack, and the Old Guard knows it is losing the high ground at an alarming rate of speed, so there is natural resentment on both sides.

The new arrivals are bidding up property values here to the point that those who were comfortable a few decades ago (with, say, the $5 million liquid net worth yardstick I mentioned earlier) no longer have bragging rights today. In many instances, on almost every block it seems that they are purchasing and renovating adjoining properties, right next to the Old Guard. They are willing to pay prices, sometimes just for the "dirt," that would put a sizable dent of the savings of those who have been here for generations, especially when you consider that many have placed substantial portions of their assets in trust for future generations. Today, the average home in Palm Beach is selling for $5.3 million.

A not-so-typical example, but one that highlights the trend, is that when a recent hedge fund and private equity manager bought a multi-acre site along the intra-coastal area, he immediately declared that the old signature home on it had to be totally renovated. The property sold for $50 million and was one of the grand homes built by one of the power elite from Detroit—a fairly pricy so-called "tear down," at $50 million. Such stories seem to rub salt in the wounds of the Old Guard. To add to the annoyance, the construction process will no doubt go on for years. In the past, construction was limited to the off season, but now it appears that the rules have been adjusted or in some cases waived by the architects and those on the City Council who are friendly with the new arrivals. This, like other large-scale purchases, seems a bit excessive, even though most of the Old Guard and their ancestors have long favored the mega-mansions along the ocean or inland waterway. After all, this lavishness is precisely what made Palm Beach so grand and impressive in the early days.

A fact overlooked by many is that over half of this country's wealth has been created in the last fifteen years, much of it garnered from technology. Developments in technology have taken place at the expense of those with fixed incomes and relatively fixed investment portfolios, who are just the type of people who have historically taken refuge here during the season. A large percentage of these people are world travelers, in the recreational sense, and given what the Washington politicians have done to the greenback lately, they also feel the pinch. This explains their considerable resentment when they leave Palm Beach after the season for other popular watering holes around the globe. For instance, there are more millionaires in North Carolina than in all of India (about 100,000), the second largest country in the world in terms of population. Who knows about southeast Florida? The numbers must no doubt be staggering.

Nevertheless, many of the newly affluent here develop, sometimes shortly after arrival, a sense of insecurity, a weakness that even their large pools of cash does not seem able to offset. The obvious "quick fix" solution is to wrap themselves in a security blanket of high-visibility homes, and water and airborne toys that are beyond the reach of most here, and certainly far beyond the concept of "basic" necessities. The Old Guard, on the other hand, has always tended to measure things on the basis of quality as opposed to quantity, and they are unimpressed by the quickly growing McMansions, as they are referred to here. These homes, with 20,000 square feet of living space or more, provide security and status to the new arrivals, and give them the illusion of fitting in to their new surroundings.

These gaudy, ostentatious houses are frowned upon by those who have enjoyed the quiet, sophisticated lifestyle of the past in Palm Beach. The newly affluent can't be satisfied with just settling into their McMansions. They hire extended staffs, dozens of people, some of whom are totally devoted to showing off the household and impressing those established here with the owners' lavish lifestyle, which generally goes far beyond most people's imagination or comprehension. And keep in mind that this extravagance, this excess, is taking place in a setting that was already extremely wealthy, where most of the inhabitants were always used to luxurious lifestyles with everyone at their beck and call. In the past, the staff was seen at meals, cocktail time, and occasionally passing in the corridors. But now they are an integral part of the entire daily routine. Somehow there is a feeling that whatever they have, the part-time residents, that is, it is not enough, even though they cannot possibly spend even a fraction of what they have recently accumulated. Often they depend on their staff to show off their lifestyle and their household. Many of the staff simply provide menial services, but are kept around so that they can play one-upsmanship with the other new arrivals, who think they have the only game in town.

Palm Beach's residents today have an average yearly household wealth of $500,000. Some of these glamorous homes actually resemble five-star hotels, in both size and staffing, and require constant renovation and design work in order to maintain a high level of excellence. Frequently, professional part-time staffers are hired on to do the job and to bring about endless enhancements. Many of these homes are nothing more than an extension of the Newly affluent's offices and places of travel, with full secretarial and concierge services; often a well-trained staff member manages their wine cellars, which can contain in the thousands of bottles, or else their tightly controlled and humidified cigar inventory. Someone is also needed to oversee their stock portfolios, and on a more mundane scale, the hourly pool temperatures often are provided in computerized spread sheets, to ensure that every detail is nothing short of perfect.

Even the closets in their various homes are arranged in identical fashion, with duplicate sets of clothing, selected on the basis of seasonal needs. The closet contents are actually videotaped for quality assurance so that the occupant can scan his or her wardrobe with comfort and ease, regardless of the location. It is not uncommon, a lady friend told me, for a few of the ladies to fly to New York to shop Fifth Avenue, get picked up in a limousine, and go for an hour or two of shopping followed by lunch, then back to the shopping bonanza, and then finally back to Palm Beach, all in time for dinner. With a private airplane at their disposal, it makes for a pleasant and easy day of shopping.

Their yachts, of course, create a requirement for further staff. Some people have more than one yacht, and keeping them on the radar screen and arranging for transportation to and from them can be demanding when large families or businesses are involved. Owning an aircraft seems to be the easiest way to schedule things in short order, since the arrival and departure times of their guests are of extreme importance. Finding a way to transport them in a pampered setting both in the air and on land is a must for some whose image needs constant polishing. One finds that on the way up the social ladder here, one absolutely needs to foster a larger-than-life image.

Management of these large household staffs, including those associated with the toys—the yachts, airplanes, race horses, and art collections, not to mention the other homes and vacation spots—makes running a household a much different enterprise than it was in the past, at least from my somewhat limited perspective. I recently got an inkling of the combined effort of all this at a lunch with a few women friends, one of whom enjoyed almost all of the perks that a billion-dollar net worth could afford. She was telling us about how overseeing the staff amounted to at least a full-time job. It seemed that at a minimum, a double-digit residential staff was required. (This, of course, does not include the minimum wage gang that makes the beds and mows the lawn, or the more pricy security personnel.) Just keeping enough people hired and trained and in line was an extremely time-consuming activity, according to this very wealthy woman.

One of the newly affluent's favorite ways of accommodating their guests who come to visit their enormous households is to send their private jet to fetch them. Alternately, a limousine is sent to the airport to pick up guests for weekend stay or a cocktail party. When you toss in the yacht's captain and crew, the airplane pilots, the computerized and necessarily tech-oriented household staff, the outlay for back-up services can very easily approach the million-dollar-a-year range. And this figure becomes even greater when you factor in the costs of the second and third homes, which must also be decorated and staffed and maintained. The whole exercise of keeping track of their elaborate households and lifestyles and the ongoing costs is downloaded onto their personal computers, so that at a moment's notice they can supposedly can get back in touch with reality, although many of the Old Guard here think they have totally lost track of it.

The need for security here, whether real or perceived, can also take on vast dimensions, sometimes escaping even the imagination of the most sophisticated. Several women I have met here over the years have twenty-four-hour live security people. These security agents spend their time monitoring all forms of activity on all corners of their properties, including the beach or lake frontage. Some are even told to monitor the small boats that fish the shores at night for possible intrusion, and they are asked to go as far as scanning the registration numbers on the hulls. Another woman living on the south end of the island has double security gates. Upon your arrival, you have to pass through one door, and then be locked in between the two while you are scanned; only then can you pass through the second door. It reminds you of some of the more exclusive vaults in the banks.

Some of these homes have wall-mounted key pads that permit only those with the combinations to move from one wing of the estate to another. In many Palm Beach homes, movement sensors light up the grounds like a Christmas tree, even if just a tiny animal crosses the sensor. Many of these security measures are merely reflections of the opulent residents themselves, who without thinking go in search of the very best of everything. Having spent a fortune on their large ocean- front homes, water toys and airplanes, it seems logical that they wouldn't scrimp when it came to security measures. And of course, a high-end security system and the accompanying staff is yet another way of protecting your wealth, and underlining that what is inside the doors of your mansion is highly precious and well worth stealing. Needless to say, the society magazines pick up on these larger-than-life performances, as I will discuss in the next chapter of this book.

Even dying takes on a new dimension here. Usually the death of a prominent person on the island is commemorated by a wake following the church service that cuts a wide swath among Palm Beach's elite. The gathering is usually held at one of the more prominent mansions or clubs during the season, and is a celebration of the long-lasting friendships and privileged lifestyles that have often extended over many decades. Also, after an off-season death, a memorial service some months afterward is often scheduled, to include those who have returned for the season and to ensure the friends of the deceased are not inconvenienced by having to go to his other residence for the funeral.

As an example, and believe me there are many deaths during any given season, a friend of mine died at the St. Edward's Church. He died right in a pew, as he was writing out his weekly check for the collection plate. His head simply collapsed onto the pew in front of him and he was gone, without any hope of resuscitation. Being good Irish Catholics, the family held an impressive wake at the Bath and Tennis Club the following weekend, all in season, of course. Literally hundreds of people celebrated his life over drinks and a marvelous seafood buffet that lasted for hours; it was a truly spectacular event, to say the least. Throughout his entire life, he had traditionally socialized in the late morning and early afternoon, like many others on the island. He was especially fond of lively

Irish music and great companionship, and so the wake was definitely one he would have approved of. I also had another friend, much younger, who collapsed after a practice round of polo in Wellington; his family rolled out the red carpet at the Everglades Club for his wake.

Not to be overlooked are the society pages and their ever-present photos, all taken with soft lenses that hide the years of aging. There is a never-ending stream of willing participants who are happy to strike carefully rehearsed poses in front of the camera, perhaps after having practiced in the privacy of their mirrors at home. The women wear their most elaborate gowns when they know they will be photographed, and the men, likewise, bring out all of their sartorial finery. This need for publicity and exposure has reached the point where during the season, many people reach for *the Palm Beach Daily News* first thing in the morning, as they enjoy their morning cup of coffee. As soon as they wake up, they need to open the paper and find out whether photos of them were included, and to catch up on any news or gossip they might have missed at the event the evening before. Needless to say, inclusion in the *Daily News* is an absolute necessity for the new arrivals. It is their favorite way of making a statement and emphasizing their own worth and importance, and of course their publicists also play a crucial role in this image-building. The newly affluent consider that they have succeeded if photos of themselves, or gossip about them, appears in the *Palm Beach Society Magazine* and the *Shiny Sheet*, which are publish weekly and daily, respectively, throughout the season.

One publication I find a bit pretentious, and just a bit over the top, is the book featuring the pets with the best grooming and pedigree on the island. By necessity, it also includes details about the owners and sometimes their partners and children as well, who are often featured in photos, standing next to the pets, which are forced to become fluffy four-legged versions of the social climbers who purchase and flaunt them. I assume that one must pay dearly for inclusion in this prestigious book, which commemorates the animal for life, but also acts as an indicator of one's elevated social status. That being said, pets are ridiculously idolized here. I admit that from time to time, I myself have taken my two parakeets to the annual blessing of the pets at the Bethesda By The Sea Church, which is a unique event in itself. One must overlook or accept the horrible yapping of grouchy pets, who are stuck inside the church for an hour or so; even though it is a most elegant place, the animals resent being enclosed, and don't care about being blessed. Like everything else on the island, the blessing ceremony is followed by an outdoor reception. One time a woman in an adjoining pew commented to me on how my birds sounded better than those in the choir. I will leave that for others to decide!

Another publication that seems to be a must for filling up one's dance card here is one that mimics the so-called socially solid "Blue Books" that are found in most mainline communities elsewhere. Some here conclude, most with some degree of distaste, that these publications are a slicked up version of the traditional social registers, and thus are a sort of an "illicit read" for those who are curious. The idea is to get some form of recognition early on; it marks a departure from the original idea behind the "Blue Books," which were designed be able to keep in constant touch with those of like heritage and mindset. Blue Books were a vehicle to be used for inward communication among those who cherished their privacy and hid themselves away behind their large-hedged properties and private clubs. Back then, the registers focused on those who had attended the right schools, clubs and organizations, and often listed the most eligible bachelors so that the proper families could discretely scan the horizon and find acceptable partners for their children among peers of their own pedigree. But now almost anyone can pay to play.

Currently the book of choice, and one that must certainly be read and discussed by those who want to be noticed and included in the best social circles, is *Palm Beach Facts and Fancies*. The work is a bit of a tongue-in-cheek effort to describe those who have the "Passions, Possessions and Pleasures of the World's Richest Society," as the back cover puts it. At the moment it is the island's best-selling book, bar none, except for a few works by local authors who distribute worldwide. Published by the Palm Beach Society Magazine, *Facts and Fancies* was brought into being by the late James Sheeran, a delightful and talented man who observed the social scene here for decades, and who decided to put pen to paper. The book makes for entertaining reading, and Jim's cutting and often cynical style and subtle sense of humor seem to take on an almost Harvard Lampoon style, at least in my estimation.

Facts and Fancies, a kind of insiders' guide to the Palm Beach lifestyle, lists literally thousands of names, from the past and the present. Most are lumped into categories that people find delightful to be included under. The book was first published in 1994, but of course, it must constantly be updated. Each time a revised edition comes out, it seems there is a run on the bookstores. Many give it to their friends and guests as a gift, since it paints a lively picture of the happenings and the people who are on the island for the season.

Some of the more colorful groupings of individuals, topics, and events, taken from the table of contents, are as follows:

The Merry Widows, Dance Masters, Social Lions, Sugar Daddies, High Ticket Togs, Nips and Tucks, Palm Beach Narcissism, Bank Rank, WASP Codes, Money and Power, and the Haves and the Have Nots, to mention just a few. They even have a classification for what is called "Moustache Panache," in which I find myself included in the latest edition. So there is something for everyone here; the book is a great beach read from cover to cover, especially for those who do not take themselves too seriously.

I have spent many seasons at this playground for the rich, ever since my early childhood. Today it caters more and more to those who wish they had been born into wealth and prestige rather than having to accumulate it on their own. Like James Sheeran, I have seen many changes in Palm Beach society over the years, and I try to accept them; I still come here for the season, every year, because it is a very nostalgic place for me that reminds me of days past. The Old Guard are a dying breed, and a few decades from now, who knows if their habits and lifestyles will only be a thing of the past.

Today there are far more year-round people—whereas in the past, staying here year-round was almost unheard of. But there is some consolation in the fact that Palm Beach is constantly reinventing itself, with each new season. It may be hard to accept that the traditions of old are falling out of favor, but the fact remains that Palm Beach is still a place of privilege and comfort, even though nowadays, new traditions and values have established themselves. The old and the new have a sometimes uneven coexistence, but at least all of the people who settle here share an affinity for the finer things in life. It is still a wondrous place, an active community that is based mostly on wealth and prestige, and I hope that the rich heritage of this place will not soon be forgotten.

THE TOYS ON PLATINUM ISLAND:

HOUSES, YACHTS, AIRPLANES, ART, HORSES, WARDROBES AND MUCH MORE

The true extent to which the super-rich spend is difficult to know. Often, the actual figures are only known to the accountants and bean counters who keep the books updated. Needless to say, the very wealthy are unique in the way they view the finer things in life. But what exactly would you do, where would you start, if, say, a hundred million dollars was dumped on your doorstep and you didn't have a clue how to fit in gracefully with those around you, who were born with a silver spoon in their mouths? Wealth can be extremely empowering, as we all know, but those who are not accustomed to the importance and influence it brings, both to present and future generations, need to rein it in and keep a level head. As we shall see here, the sudden arrival of recent wealth can cause one to try and buy one's way out of reality.

Here in Palm Beach, the types of toys available to those who don't have to balance their checkbooks on a regular basis has changed substantially. When my family started wintering here (my grandparents bought their first house in 1936), half of the family came by train and the other half flew down in the old DC-3s, the funny shaped planes whose tails sat on a small wheel in back; you had to walk up an incline to find your seat. We traveled separately because back then, many thought airplane travel was unsafe. My immediate family has been a continued presence in Palm Beach for the past seventy years, and we have witnessed many, many changes.

Not too long ago, I had a conversation with one of the super-rich new arrivals, a delightful woman, I might add. She had everything imaginable under the sun, and then some. At the gathering where I met her, I was informed that there are actually schools offering advanced technical and professional degrees for those who want to wait hand and foot on the new wealth here, and in other places. I was told that a college degree is usually a forerunner to employment, but it is also possible to be hired if you are computer savvy, with a good presence. Apparently, some who take these positions view this as a glamorous lifestyle, and don't mind temporarily setting aside their aspirations to be upwardly mobile in the corporate world.

Estate Management

These schools, and there are several, teach "household management" to young people who aspire to becoming an Estate Manager, which is currently a buzzword on the island. The mission of the school is to train a young person to become not a traditional English butler, but his modern-day counterpart, a high-tech, 21st-century character who can deal with the complexities of running a series of homes, oversee air transportation and executive toys, and acquire in-depth knowledge of the Internet and its research capabilities, in addition to an extensive understanding of spreadsheets and accounting capabilities that probably exceeds the capabilities of the average small business in this country. Most often, these positions are filled by women, given the importance of the social season down here.

Recently, out of curiosity, I contacted one of these institutions, and after a brief conversation with their placement services, they seemed convinced that I, with my Palm Beach zip code, had potential as an employer. They definitely had a snobbish attitude on the phone, although I suspected that they were as wet behind the ears as their graduates must have been. Nevertheless, after stroking them a bit, they agreed to send me a brochure with the full range of their graduates' services. They seemed to care little about my personality and lifestyle, so I embellished, wanting to match their insincerity. I told them I was clean-shaven, filthy rich, and somewhat articulate in the English language, and that I purchased my clothing at Brooks Brothers. With only this sketchy overview, they assured me that they could find someone to fit my bill, that is, if I was willing to pay 23% of the first year's salary to them as a finder's fee. The starting salaries, I was informed, were in the $80,000 to $100,000 range.

As I opened the FEDEX package from them the next day, I doubted whether the Old Guard in Palm Beach would ever take on one of their graduates, given the brevity of their training. After all, those who served here historically were tutored under the watchful eyes of their ancestors, or were trained by the principals as in-house servants for decades. Nevertheless, the school told me that as an employer, I should limit my scope and focus on three categories in which I required help, so that they could set me up with the most appropriate player to manage my estate(s). I was a bit tongue in cheek when I spoke with them, since their courses only last 4 to 8 weeks—not exactly an eternity for those who have spent generations honing their social habits with dedicated servants. Not to mention the fact that I had absolutely no need for what they offered.

Here is a sampling of the various categories listed in their brochure. I present them with some skepticism, especially the first specialty on the list, Wine Cellar Management. Now, in my estimation, this is not something that is learned in a month at a vocational school. I, for one, have consumed a fair amount of wine over the decades and have been invited to several international wine and food society functions, and yet I would not claim to even scratch the surface on the subject. In any case, here are the two dozen other specialties in which the graduates are proficient. I include them to satisfy my own sense of humor, and possibly that of the reader.

They Are as Follows:

Service etiquette and protocol, Entertainment and event planning, Estate security and protection, Architectural and construction consulting services, Domestic staffing and human resource needs, Culinary and nutritional consulting, Household administration and maintenance, Transportation and travel, Personal care (sub-categories: Elder, Guest, Child and Pets), Service standards in the household, Household inventory skills, Household budgeting, current and future (all on Excel spreadsheets), Boundaries with your staff and casual acquaintances, Recognition of the various luxury products, Landscaping and grounds maintenance, Care of fine linens and bed turndown instruction, Closet and wardrobe advice and organization, Designer clothing recognition, Care of fine art and other collectibles, Fire protection, Storage and refrigeration techniques, Menu planning, Marriage of food and wine, Personal shopping, Working with charities and non-profits, Trip packing and unpacking, Selection of appropriate gifts, Etiquette and international protocol, Invitation and RSVP services and seating arrangements, Working with caterers, Holiday event planning and, last but not least, Music consultants.

I stopped reading when I reached 40 of their services, but as you can see, you might need a few players for each category, though some would definitely overlap. It's easy to see how a hundred or so household staff would be required, just to keep the household and the toys in order. Add to that the airplanes, yachts, art collections and jewelry, and suddenly you have a small cadre of paid disciples that can easily run into a seven-figure annual payroll. If you're not yet overwhelmed by the number of services this set requires, you would be if you saw the thousand-page manuals listing services. One interesting skill listed therein is being proficient in snuffing out candles at the end of a dinner party "with style."

McMansions

Palm Beach has always been considered the playground of the old-line aristocratic members of American East Coast society. Traditionally, oceanfront mansions were reserved for the elite, often with household names attached to the great fortunes of this country. Today, increased home sizes are a contentious part of the ever-changing Palm Beach scene. The new kids on the block seem to need a minimum of 10,000 square feet for a starter home, which usually means acquiring a tear-down on certain older parts of the island. The new arrivals focus less on ample yard space and maximize their structures at the expense of open space. Their lifestyle is totally different from that of the Old Guard, who relish the outdoors and usher in the arrival of the mild winter weather, dressed to the nines.

For some new arrivals, multi-car garages are a must, given the vast assortment of automobiles they collect. Many of these are immaculate and even air-conditioned. Some car collections are priceless, such as a nearby collection of antique Fords that includes fire engines, ambulances, and police cars from the early past of the last century; it is second only to the Ford Museum in Dearborn, Michigan. Even though some garages are well over 10,000 square feet, it is not uncommon for people to leave their pricy vehicles conveniently parked in the driveways, to let those passing by know that they are part of the island's elite. A family down the street from me leaves their $250,000 Bentley in their driveway for weeks on end, even when they are absent. In the old days, these types of vehicles were kept garaged and were regularly washed by the chauffeurs. Today, however, cars are flaunted, and are used to promote image and status.

Since the new super-rich generally come from backgrounds with no live-in servants, they must go to outside consultants and head-hunters to find people who can offer guidance. High-priced assistants offer hands-on supervision of the endless numbers of maids, yard men, chauffeurs, nannies, travel planners, landscape architects, security guards, and household maintenance people. Having this huge collection of players is the best way to impress the neighbors.

Some gigantic homes here have dozens and dozens of revolving staff who also take care of the family's second, third, and fourth homes. Sometimes travel to these homes on private aircraft can approach $100,000 a month, especially when the big, $40-50-million-dollar Gulfstreams are in play. Owning property here is like having an endless string of pearls that need constant polishing, but that never fail to impress.

For some of the working rich, leisure in Palm Beach takes a back seat to the working environment. Often, supporting people are located and housed in adjoining buildings a stone's throw from the main residence, and either travel everywhere with their "principals" or are in continuous contact with them. Those who keep track of the various companies, portfolios, investments, and the string of advisors such as lawyers, accountants, money managers, deal finders, and communication experts are always close by. Not to be forgotten are those who set social schedules, keep track of charitable foundations, monitor fine art and jewelry collections and attend the high-end auctions on their principal's behalf, as well as endless numbers of world- wide realtors who are constantly on the prowl for new opportunities in the hot spots.

A few years ago, a dot-com character, before his company went south, leaving many investors holding the bag, thought Palm Beach would be the ideal place for his start-up operation. So, he purchased a large oceanfront estate and immediately informed almost two dozen of his top executives that they should relocate here and partake in the festivities. He showered them with cash, and they immediately went on a buying spree that elevated housing prices to an all-time high. Of course, when the company failed, the reverse took place, and all the young geeks had to dump their leveraged holdings at fire sale prices. But that is the way for some of the new super rich—they not only have to have it all at once, but it must be high-profile, as well.

The list of vendors who serve these well-heeled people is longer than one can imagine. There are people to measure the moisture content of the soil in their greenhouses for their orchids, or to observe the health and feeding habits of their tropical fish, birds, and other exotic pets. The room temperature in the wine cellars and reflecting pools must be recorded on an hourly basis on computerized spread sheets. Some extremists even go so far as to have various wardrobes stored with vendors in central locations through out the United States; these can be sent by FEDEX to any location that they might choose the next day, and then re-shipped to the central storage area to be dry cleaned and recycled for the next occasion. I am told it costs about $500.00 a suitcase round trip to the European countries for such a service, plus tip, of course.

It seems that in this electronic age, everything the super-rich possesses must be logged in and tracked. Their linens, food and wine supplies, individualized menus for children and aging parents, business and social schedules, and holiday events must all be itemized and recorded. It's the modern-day version of the wealthy man sitting at a table counting his gold coins, I suppose.

A New Type of Butler

The old money of the past had competent household staff members who performed repetitive functions that required little high-tech training. These staff members could be hired for a fraction of the cost now paid by the new super-rich, with their sophisticated needs. The new arrivals' upper-end staff members, at least those in a professional capacity, are considered to be almost be on an equal footing with their principals. No longer do they remain on a last-name basis, as the Old Guard did for generations. Some are "almost family," since they are, according to their job description, so fully involved in overseeing the family's day-to-day lifestyle. There are endless decisions to make, and the household's butler now plays a crucial professional role. It is a far cry from the days when butlers were recruited from England. Back then, they just had to have the proper look and demeanor, and knew to keep a respectful distance from their employers.

Most "household managers" are young, computer-literate college graduates. Many have attended schools specializing in culinary arts or hotel and restaurant management. Their activities are often governed by computerized lists and manuals that are required for maintaining the lifestyles of the super wealthy. Countless hours are spent keeping track of such things as the principal's medicine and sporting equipment, the movements of their children, the inventories of their other residences, and the humidity levels in their cigar humidors and greenhouses. Household managers also have to keep track of local social events and, for instance, of international fishing tournaments; they must have at their fingertips details about the deadlines for entry, the types of prizes, and the names of all registered participants.

Some household managers keep track of the nearby big-game fish, and are called upon to report on their movements with the warm water, and on where they are biting and what types of bait are being used. The staff download fishing reports and forecasts from the Internet which are updated hourly in some cases, so the captain of the fishing boat can move the boat to where the action is, just in case the principal should desire to jump in his private plane for a day or two of high-tech fishing. Purchasing fish-finding equipment, hiring the appropriate captain, and renting multiple docking locations can add six figures to a boat's yearly expenditures. Since dockage is becoming quite scarce here in Palm Beach, it is not uncommon for a boat owner to spend $5,000 a lineal foot for a condominium in, say, the Bahamas. (Let me do the math for you: a 100-foot yacht @ $5,000/ft equals a half a million before common area assessments and utilities at one location.)

I occasionally attended big-time fishing tournaments when I lived in San Diego. Most were held in the lower edges of the Baja Peninsula in Mexico, where it was not uncommon for the individual boat entry fee to be in the range of $25,000 for a week's fishing. Prize money often totaled over a million dollars for the well-recognized outings. In addition to the captain and crew's salaries, you had to secure a top-notch fishing guide, who would come at a premium, especially for the major tournaments.

Worth Avenue and Its Female Inhabitants

A dichotomy exists here between the Old Guard and the new super-rich, each of whom compete for the limited A-List slots on the winter social circuit, and fashion plays an important role, since first impressions definitely count. However, with all the recent activity brought about by the new arrivals—the expanded social activities and high-visibility galas—the market for social standing has taken on new breadth. Supply and demand for the coveted social slots and recognition have become more elastic, which is not exactly to the liking of the Old Guard.

Some gain a leg up by having a "trophy wife" in tow, and believe me, they are abundant, with their facelifts and reconfigured bust lines, driving around town in their expensive, often leased, open-air automobiles. There is never a shortage of "arm charms," as they are known, in town. These enterprising women are brought along to restaurants, galas, clubs and parties. I am told that when it comes to their husbands, the key is not necessarily how much they have in their portfolios, but how much they spend on the ladies. Some here are tightwads, even with millions in the bank, and the arm charms easily sift out the wheat from the chaff.

Many of these ladies are quite attractive and interesting and add a lot to the scenery, which has become a bit aged over the passing decades, even though the old dowagers pay little attention to them. The younger women are former models or dancers, or were once connected to the theater or the television world as celebrities; many have strong public presence and engaging personalities. Most of them have now become "serial charity ball goers," spending large sums of their oftentimes older husband's money in order to get into the array of events such as the pre-ball lunches, dinners and cocktail parties as well as the post-ball gatherings that generally do nothing more than flatter the egos of those who worked diligently on the events.

For the women, fashion elevates the financial crossbar to new heights. The men usually get a pass card in this department with a few well-chosen sports coats and a dozen well-tailored and monogrammed shirts. The blue blazer is still the standard, as is a well-used tuxedo. The names of the popular designers here are quite varied, and far beyond the comprehension of people like myself, who stick to the old standbys: Bill Blass, Oscar de La Renta, Calvin Klein, and Pierre Cardin. For the ladies, it's Pierre Balmain, Galanos, Serge and Real, Steven Stolman and Badgley Mischka, to name just a few. And if the outfits are not enough to lighten one's wallet a bit, the accessory stores on the Avenue with shoes and handbags—the Chanel, St. John's, Jimmy Choo, Ferragamo, and Gucci—do a respectable job as well.

Some of these women spend upwards of $100,000 a season—around $1,000 a day on dresses, jewelry, accessories, and charity ball tickets. Add to that the cosmetic surgery and style consultants, the limousines, the off-night trips, when not included in the A-List events, to expensive restaurants, and things can get quite pricey. But clothes and accessories are the showy and influential tools of the trade for those who think they are on the path of upward mobility here. It can be an exorbitant figure, especially for those of serious intent, considering that the season is only about three months long. First impressions can make or break a situation for some who have not made it to the upper stratosphere of society, and a little dose of the plastic now and then seems to do the trick for many.

Worth Avenue, indisputably one of the finest shopping areas in the world, is delightful because of its relatively modest size. The whole street has a wonderful scale—the small court yards and low-slung buildings have dimensions not found in other parts of the world. The classy area used to be mainly patronized by the leisure class, who would arrive at any hour. It was their way of showing off that they had little to do from 9 to 5 and loved every moment of it. They walked the Avenue in style, the men rarely without a sports coat and slacks, and the women in their Lilly Pulitzer outfits. At day's end, the Old Guard would climb into their sometimes decade-old, Detroit model cars, with or without a driver, and go prepare for the evening's entertainment.

It was simply their way. They'd go to Taboo and the Patio for late afternoon drinks. They were elegant and moderately opulent, and spent most of their time among their close circle of A-List friends. Never were they extravagant or showy, or trying to impress the unwashed public, so to speak. Impressions were formulated for those who counted, and certainly not for the second tier of social magnates accompanied by their self-promoting publicists.

But today, in contrast, many of those who walk the avenue, shop and dine in the restaurants arrive in their $250,000 Bentleys wearing shorts and a polo shirt. They often go without a jacket in the evening. The women seem to dress up a bit more, it seems, probably to show off their Worth Avenue possessions, from stores that the old money would no longer think of entering, except to sneak a look or two. The new arrivals, the working super-rich, are people with well- cultivated middle-class ethics and tastes. However, they arrive with a separate set of opulent standards; they embrace showmanship and have conversations that are only designed for the outside world to take in. Many of them fail to realize that they are entering a terrain where "understated elegance" and "quiet memberships" in the right clubs and "the dignified displaying of wealth" have more meaning than the outer trappings of wealth.

On Worth Avenue, the old and new money people often find themselves on a collision course. For example, at the west end of Worth Avenue is the Everglades Club, one of those establishments where membership is not easily obtained, regardless of the size of one's bank account. On the other end of the Avenue are the high-ticket stores that cater to the fashion- conscious who need big-name designers to compete for attention on the social circuit. Somewhere in between is where the two groups often meet. But this is what Palm Beach is really about: it's a blend of the Old Guard and the newly affluent, and of course the rare people who are able to fit in with those on either end of the Avenue.

The Elusive A-List

The old money people are simply skeptical, and rightfully so in some cases, concerning these new players with tens and sometimes hundreds of millions at their disposal. They reason that some have either made it in haste or in situations that the Old Guard considers suspicious at best. Some have a paper trail that is less than opaque, or a sub-standard provenance, as they say in the art world. They reason, with some degree of accuracy, that some of these people are cut from the same cloth as those who ran the likes of ENRON, Adeplhia and WorldCom, disasters they are reminded almost daily in the financial sections of their newspapers.

Rarely does a month go by without some well-heeled character who bought a home in the estate section finding himself adversely in the news. Many, when exposed, simply skip town, as is the case of a couple in today's *Shiny Sheet*, who were indicted for receiving kickbacks for appraisal work, as well as for income tax evasion.

Earlier in the week, a Wall Street hot shot who lived in a large 7,200 square foot mansion with a private jet, was sentenced to 18 months in prison for hiring underage prostitutes. And Canadian media mogul Conrad Black, a part-time Palm Beacher, was just sent off to the slammer for bilking the stockholders. But this in some respects is southeast Florida. It all goes back to the early land rush days, where land was sold by the quart. Florida has always attracted more than its share of unsavory characters.

So it's easy to see why the Old Guard is leery, and slow to invite relative strangers to the A-List parties and the more exclusive clubs. Again, here, breeding and bloodlines are equally as important as pots of money, when it comes to the Old Guard. It's all quite contradictory, since many of the Old Guard's ancestors, generations back, made their fortunes in less-than-respectable ways as well, and were never exposed. But in a way, that is the American way of life. Money in many communities does buy respectability, and Palm Beach is no exception.

This is why some newcomers are elbowing their way into Palm Beach—to find the type of recognition that money alone cannot buy. Often they start in communities like Boca Raton and other upscale communities south of here, where new money and questionable reputations tend to be glossed over, and where one's past can be whitewashed if necessary, in both the financial and social circles. Sooner or later, they move to Palm Beach to see if they are now respectable enough to be accepted by the elite.

One couple occupied a Palm Beach estate mansion on the ocean for a few years. They arrived with a high-profile publicist in tow, and were supported by rumors of substantial, recently acquired wealth. Instantly they received coverage in all the society magazines and newspapers, though I might add that the Old Guard doesn't read these, or at least doesn't admit to it. Their publicist leaked the number and cost of several of the wife's evening gowns to the *Shiny Sheet*, and this information later found its way into the columns. The party I attended at their ostentatious home was packed with glamorous young women, and a lesser amount of men.

The host and hostess seemed almost secondary as the evening moved on and the liquor flowed. This was not a crowd that builds ongoing one-on-one relationships; they were strictly the see-and-be-seen types. The women, mostly with some help from the cosmetic surgeons, were literally falling out of their dresses, something that tends to raise the eyebrows of the older, more established women here.. The owner was then and still is under the delusion that he had "arrived" socially in Palm Beach. He now describes himself to those who ask, and often to those who don't, in the following fashion: "The papers tell me that I am A-list. I don't know for sure, but that's what they tell me". End of quote.

Of course, most of the A-list on the island don't even know his name, nor would they be caught dead with him in tow at one of the more exclusive clubs or the private parties hosted by the elite. The crowning event of the party was when I walked through the living room to the tented area outside to refresh my drink. Spread out there for all to see were four pole dancers in short costumes, climbing phallic shafts that extended to the ceiling. It was like something you'd expect to see at a West Palm Beach strip club. Since then, the city of Palm Beach has put an end to this type of gathering, and the host in question must get a permit before hosting any other events.

Another often-touted prerequisite for achieving A- List status, for some, is to tie one's heritage to European royalty, something the former titans of U.S. industry at the early part of 20th century did. Many of the early Wall Street barons married European aristocracy to cement themselves in the footings of New York society. Currently, the A-List has expanded considerably, to include CEOs of major companies that are publicly held and respectable. Interesting enough, many of these types find the whole social exercise here boring, especially those with wide circles of self-made friends. When it comes to the charitable galas, they look the other way, since the phoniness of some of these gatherings has become more than evident.

The methodology of seeking the Holy Grail involves three narrowly defined steps. (1) Invitation to an event. (2) Jockeying for position at the starting gate. (3) (As is usually the case), still staying in the stables, (but at least, they rationalize, they have made it to the track). The rest of the people are summarily assigned to a lower level, known as the B-List, and reaching its upper end is quite an achievement. The loud, unrefined, brash leftovers seem to drop to something I would call the C-List, which nobody fesses up to knowing anything about. It is strictly too mundane and broad for those who are on the climb to consider.

But perception is the important thing. Even those who occasionally sit at home on evenings when the big parties and top-tier charitable events are held feel the need to come up with a bevy of excuses to explain why they weren't present. To avoid the embarrassment of being excluded, they hurriedly mention health problems, prior commitments, or the old standby, house guests. The cross-island telephone communication that follows a big social evening in Palm Beach is truly amazing. Lucky invitees can't wait to tell those on the outside looking in that they were included in the top-drawer festivities. Phone calls like this are a fact of life for those who swim just below the rough waters here.

What do you have to do to be included on the elusive A-List? Having a large oceanfront or intercoastal mansion does not guarantee one's inclusion by any means. In fact, the 60,000-square-foot palace on the beach called Maison de l'Amitié, owned by a now-bankrupt, cigar-smoking, Bentley-driving corporate healthcare baron, is the largest house on the island. It's a place that Michael Jackson considered purchasing from the bankruptcy court, until the locals got up in arms and the newspapers crucified him. It went for $45 million at auction, and recently was sold by my traveling companion, Carol, for $96,000,000, to a Russian fertilizer magnet. But the current owner will never be included on the A-List.

Rarely does a season go by that the rug is not pulled out from under some of those who have bought the splashy oceanfront homes hoping for immediate acceptance. Some are convicted felons, and some even have kidnaped their children after messy divorces. Many have left town under cover of darkness, leaving their trophy homes to the creditors. But in a way, Florida encourages such activity, since a castle here is often a safe haven from the creditors.

To offset this glass ceiling, there is a growing, viable subculture here among the newly affluent, who are determined to establish their own A-List, devoid of the refinement of those who are at the helm. They want their own list for many reasons, one being the fact that they view a large part of the old establishment as less-than-self-made, and this denies them access. In a way, those who are self-made in the financial world take a dim view of the coupon clippers, of those who inherited their wealth, and of people who have never had to face the harsh realities of survival in the outside world. According to the newly affluent, those with inherited wealth hide behind their exclusive clubs and long-established relationships. There is some truth to their reasoning, I suppose, and the pendulum seems to be shifting in their direction.

The Galas

The style of galas we have here originated in New York City, and was exported to Palm Beach in the early part of the last century. The nature of the charity balls has radically changed since the early days of the Red Cross Ball in the roaring 1920s, where inclusion was denied without a proper introduction. Today, however, even a bank teller can get a ticket or two. The days of the grand dames of old taking charge are no longer, and those in positions of authority seem only to lend their names to the events as honorary chairmen, leaving the day-to- day operations to those who want the recognition that goes with being attached to some committee.

Historically, the grand dames decided who was acceptable and who was not, and therefore, who was included in functions and who would get the ongoing recognition that went with attending. Since the early days, an elaborate competitive environment has developed among the women associated with these events. Rivalries and cruel gossip abound, whereas such behavior was kept to a minimum when the former grand dames were at the helm. In the old days the hoi polloi sat on the sidelines, trying to pick up the pieces that nobody else wanted. Now they vie for slots in the ever-expanding number of events, which in my estimation is about as exciting as requesting a frontal lobotomy when you go to your physician for an annual checkup.

Many view gala-going as a necessary means of entry into this island's privileged social scene, and work diligently and contribute large amounts of money, unaware whether they will eventually rise to the top, like cream on coffee, or sink to the bottom, like lead and burnout. Their posturing and social ambitions are sometimes simply beyond the understanding of their friends and the time-tested and proven aristocrats here, who were born into their social status and never had to work to achieve acceptance. They just put in their time and paid their dues, like the ladies of old who wore pinstripe dresses and worked the Junior League scene in many prominent American cities.

Until recently, the status of the old money group came from genetic inheritance, from proper grooming and a gracious upbringing in which the rules of high society were passed down from generation to generation. The opposite is true of the corporate world, where instant recognition or gratification can be achieved by, say, being on the right side of the stock market at the right time. But interesting enough, both groups are tolerant of each other, and have come to accept each other's presence.

I, for one, have given up on most galas. Normally you are seated at tables of ten and you can barely be understood across the table. Having to make small talk for hours on end with complete strangers, to the tune of $500.00 a ticket, makes little sense to me. But many people here have tremendous amounts of discretionary income, and some feel obligated to be seen at high- visibility events, so the galas seem to attract the right numbers of participants each season.

To show the shifting values demonstrated at these events, I was invited to a rather uninteresting gala last season, a dinner dance at one of the private, exclusive prep schools on the north end of Palm

Beach County. It was billed as a black and white party, and I assumed that meant black tie. But many of those attending showed up without a tie, and in some cases without a jacket, even though the tickets were quite pricey. As we moved into the dining room after a large number of cocktails, I assumed that we were in for an evening of elegant dining, dancing and quiet conversation. But I and others of like mind had a rude awakening: as soon as we sat down, a live auction began. We all know the drill, with the abrasive auctioneer growing louder and louder as each item is sold. This silly performance went on non-stop throughout the entire two-hour dinner, to the horror of those who thought they were in for an elegant evening.

What was particularly interesting, and a bit repulsive to me, was the type of items being auctioned off. One of the most absurd was personalized parking spaces—throughout the upcoming school year, students whose parents bid the highest amounts would have parking spaces with their names prominently displayed on them. As for the parents themselves, if that were not enough, they could buy a placard with their name on it, a sort of "reserved sanctuary" in front of the main entrance for when they came to pick up their children after school. The grand prize for personal recognition and economic standing in the school community went for $15,000 and permitted the donor to have the loop street in front of the entrance named after him. This whole system is a throwback to what corporate guys do with baseball and football stadiums—hardly typical of the way the Old Guard used to operate.

This sort of bragging-rights game doesn't sit well with people here, and it went on and on. Somehow, these characters thought they had hit a home run that evening, but in my estimation they never got to first base, and I'm sure many of the Old Guard would say they had struck out. At parties, some of the more showy characters carry their hefty contributions, of which they are very proud, in their inside pockets to indicate to others their great commitment to charity.

Fine Art, Polo and the Equestrian Scene

Fine art can be another toy of the newly affluent. The Old Guard
tends to turn up their noses at this superficial effort; the newly
affluent are not considered serious collectors since according to
their more traditional counterparts, their holdings are based on
value and are not purchased with the idea of eventually giving
them to a museum or hanging quietly in their homes. Of course,
there are exceptions, like long-time Palm Beacher Ron Lauder,
who recently spent a record $135 million on a painting, which was
really pushing the envelope, even though the ownership trail of the
seller is now being questioned in the courts.

It seems that when you have all the toys—the jets and yachts, the
second, third, and fourth homes—art has to be the next logical step
in the process of consuming and making an impression on others.
The new Wall Street breed of billionaires, with their hedge funds
and sub-prime mortgage packages, acquire art to gain notoriety,
and because they enjoy quickly flipping it. Trade is part of their
professional mentality, and the art market is seen as no different
from any other business, except that it has the added bonus of
implying a certain cultural sophistication that is required here.

Most of the crowd in the fast lane has little time to do research
connected with collecting fine art, and little inclination for
developing a discerning eye, so they hire art consultants, who
generally keep an eye on the art indexes for their clients. These
contain pricing guidelines, just as the NASDAQ Index does for the
more speculative stocks. These indices are devoted to the
speculative side of the art markets, and through computers and
hands-on managers they keep track of the cost of works mostly by
contemporary artists.

These works, depending on their size, are sometimes priced and
sold by the square inch. The consultants follow various artists and
keep track of works that have been sold to the public two or three
times in recent history; unlike the Old Guard, they are not willing
to wait generations for the right piece to surface. It's all about
instant gratification.

Both physically and financially, polo is not for the faint of heart. Wellington has a bevy of polo fields second to none, I am told. A respectable team is one that travels in the off season to other parts of the country or internationally. Fielding a good team can easily cost seven figures, without bating an eye. Here there are many respectable teams, with families behind them like the Busch family of Budweiser fame. Teams consist of five players and a half a dozen polo ponies per player; since the talent often has to be recruited from places like Argentina, it can get pricey. Imported players are paid based on their goal ratings, ten being the best. Salaries are in the low six figures for the high goal scorers. To enter the prize matches, held in late winter, you often need to have several of these top-notch players just to enter.

Horses can be at the top of the list for those who have everything. I have a friend who has won the Kentucky Derby twice, and another who, with her traveling companion, owned a racing stable with hundreds of thoroughbreds that they brought to compete in places like Hong Kong. They even won the most prestigious steeplechase in England a few years back. I even have a friend who owns two homes: one in Wellington for the horsy events, and the other a signature oceanfront mansion, even though it's a half-hour drive in her chauffeured Rolls Royce between the two dwellings.

Since they moved the most prestigious U.S. horse shows from Madison Square Garden to Wellington a few years ago, the ante for bragging rights has been upped considerably. Black-tie dinners and ringside galas are a sight to behold. Endless miles of magnificent estates all surrounded by white fences seem to set the tone in Wellington, which has established itself as one of the premier places to show jumpers and dressage horses. Many are brought in by FEDEX airplanes for these top-of-the-line events, from as far away as Europe.

Floating Palaces

Next on the list of things the newly affluent are not to be denied are the yachts. Here, for many, the only thing that seems to count is the size. A reverse "form" over "function," as the architects of

the world would say. The magic number separating the men from
the boys seems to be 50 meters or longer, about the size of a half a
football field. (The bigger boys draw the line in the sand at 80
meters, and some of those mega-yachts even contain indoor
basketball courts). What is unique is the instant information
collected by the yachting community on the toys of the other big
boys. One's yacht is no longer measured as the biggest or best in
the "neighborhood," and instead it has become a world-wide
bragging rights contest.

I was on a mega-yacht last year in Newport R.I., where if you are
so inclined, you can pull up on your computer the call signs of the
registration of most mega-yachts in the world and plot their exact
location and movement at any given point in time. So, if you need
to enhance your cocktail conversation a bit, keep track of the big
boy toys and you'll be able to name-drop and discuss the
movements of yachts thousands of miles away.

Since the Palm Beach City Marina dates back a half a century,
many of the bigger, newer yachts simply won't fit into the slips
here. Often the new money is so eager to get into the game that
they first purchase a pre-owned yacht from some character who
just can't live without an additional 50 feet. As a result, the bar for
everyone is raised in a heartbeat.

There was an interesting character down here a few years ago who
had a hidden platform covered with artificial turf on the aft deck.
When it was elevated into position, he could drive his golf balls off
the fantail. Members of his crew, to his delight, were stationed in
their tenders conveniently placing floating flags, like those you'd
find on putting greens, at distances dictated by his directions over a
two-way radio. It was certainly a unique way of livening up his
game.

I equate some of these unique waterfront scenarios to when we
were children, and played endlessly with our erector sets. I have
fond memories of those days, when it seemed that the size and
scale of the finished product were the key factors in determining
who had the best toys. Many of today's Newly affluent grew up

with few resources and ordinary toys, and it could be said that they are now making a statement with the size of their yachts instead of their erector sets.

Recently I attended the annual Fort Lauderdale Boat Show, where numerous people were lined up to spread their cash around. Twenty yachts at over $15 million sold the week of the show, according to some of the less inebriated yacht brokers there. Apparently, there are about ten miles of mega-yachts over 100 feet long, either on the drawing boards or in boatyards worldwide. Ten miles might not seem like a long distance—it's about the length of the island of Palm Beach, if you include the high-rise condominiums on the south end. But ten miles times approximately 4500 lineal feet per mile is 45,000 feet of product, a substantial amount of inventory when you consider that these well-equipped bathtubs sell for around $100,000 per lineal foot (150 feet x $100,000 = $ 15,000,000). You do the math. (It's in the hundreds of billions—unfortunately, my calculator doesn't have enough zeros). In any event, the number is larger than the Gross National Product of many developing countries. A great many of these yachts can be found in southeast Florida and the Caribbean during the season.

Sometimes one yacht is just not enough. In that case, a companion yacht becomes a sheer necessity; a standby yacht can be kept for friends or in the event of a spillover of business associates. Most require their second yacht to be a minimum of 75 feet in length to make a statement. When the need for a second yacht is a little excessive for one's budget, it's not uncommon to charter a back-up vessel in some remote location to take care of the overflow.

Maintaining one of these puppies is not for the faint of heart either. Starting with the initial investment of, say, $15 million, just the "lost cost" of having money tied up can fall in the 10% range, or $1.5 million per year, a tad over $100,000 per month. At least Uncle Sam pays for up to 40% of their vacation time, depending on their income bracket. (When I worked on Wall Street, I thought I was getting away with murder on the two-martini lunch circuit). The expense of the crew, provisions and insurance can tag on another half-million. Ongoing repairs, fuel and dockage fees, and condominium slip costs another half million, and annual haul-out and movement to remote parts of the world, with helicopter and pilot, is yet another half-million. So parting with three million a year (20% of the value) is not unusual for this investment in one's image. Based on, say, five weeks of constant usage per year, the cost comes close to $10,000 a day, not accounting for depreciation.

One of the most far-fetched fairytales I ever heard highlights the idea of taking no prisoners in the game of one-upmanship. Aristotle Onassis' yacht *Christina*, a must-see, I'm told, went a long way to impressing Jackie Kennedy, who was a part-time Palm Beach resident. She was thoroughly fascinated by the man and his toys. (Incidentally, I remember my mom dragging my brothers and me down to Hamburger Heaven during the season, in the hopes of catching a glimpse of Jackie and her children (which as far as I know never happened). However, Jackie was a remarkable woman I've heard. Her interesting prenuptial agreement with Onassis was partially based on some of the rumored events that took place on his yacht. Christina I'm told the agreement detailed her intended sleeping arrangements with Onassis, which I will leave to others to authenticate.

Other Water Toys

Another often forgotten toy is what is referred to as a shadow boat around the circuit. These are vessels that most newly affluent will not be caught dead without—they are multi-million-dollar separate ships that trail the mother ship just close enough that the other yachts on the fringes know who the shadow ship belongs to. They carry the wide array of toys: the smaller boats and cars that are needed when the owners go ashore and the well-equipped limited-range fishing vessels. Not to be forgotten are the private submarines, jet skis, and dry areas to store the owner's seaplane, so that guests can drop in from time to time without having to take up space on the mother ship where the owner's helicopter is parked. Some of the new mega-yachts we see here in southeast Florida have such things as indoor fresh-water swimming pools.

In Palm Beach, many of these yachts can't be displayed properly, sometimes to the dismay of their owners, so they have to be stowed out of view. This is certainly a self-defeating situation for those who crave high visibility. Since some yachts are so large, such as Tiger Woods's 150-foot mega-yacht which is often berthed in Old Port Cove, far from the action, they temporarily lose their effectiveness as status symbols. (Not that Tiger cares or needs to impress anyone). For some, the lack of visibility of their $10,000-a-day toy takes the wind out of their sails.

Decades ago, I had the opportunity to see, up-close and first hand, how these people live day to day when I purchased Howard Hughes's 1927, 60-foot mahogany-planked motor yacht. I lived on it and chartered it for several years in the early 1990s during the America's Cup Races in San Diego. The docks were full of exciting yachts, as one can imagine, who had come for this big-ticket event; there were yachts belonging to the likes of the wife of Ray Krock, founder of McDonald's, or Mr. Gucci of fashion fame, who was a sponsor of the *Italian Syndicate*, which was on the same dock as I was that year. It was a real eye-opener into the discretionary income that these larger-than-life people have at the fingertips and how they spend it.

As a final parting shot, however, it was interesting to view the crews on these two yachts, who were dressed in their pressed whites and who stood at attention when the owners appeared. I have it on good authority that Gucci had a multi-million-dollar Old Masters' art collection stowed onboard. It is truly amazing how much wealth can be accumulated and displayed by those top 3 to 5 percent of the world of affluence.

Aircraft

Palm Beach International Airport is unique in that two-thirds of the landings and take-offs are associated with private aircraft. Many here use fractional ownership to gain access to the thousands of airports to which commercial carriers offer limited service. The largest of these time-shared fleets have around 600 jets, with over 3,000 pilots, and book close to 400,000 flights a year to over 150 countries. Many of these airplanes are available with an hour or two's notice, and the type of aircraft and its flying ranges give great flexibility to those with the inclination and the resources to use them.

The cost of the aircraft varies from the small $5,000,000 Cessna to the top-of-the-line Gulfstream that approaches $50,000,000. The economics are something else, and one company even offers a pre-paid card from which you deduct hours as you travel, like telephone companies sell for long-distance service. The pre-paid card starts at $230,000 for 25 hours; this accommodates six to seven people in a smaller version of the Citation, but the range is only up and down the east coast—Palm Beach to NYC, for instance.(The cost is about $5,000 per hour of use, for 6-7 people.) The larger capacity Citation X can travel coast to coast, 3500 statue miles (costing about $9,400 per hour for usage) and the card sells for about double that of the small Citation. So if one takes a trip from Palm Beach to Los Angeles, depending on head winds and so on, it will take almost four hours each way, and cost a cool $75,000 round trip. It's a great way to beat the Homeland Security drill, if you can afford it.

Interval ownership is a better situation if you have the where-with-all to put down a $1,100,000 for a 1/16th ownership of the Citation. With the ownership goes the privilege of paying $13,000 a month for maintenance, and you can lease the aircraft for about $4,500 an hour. There are some tax benefits if you use the aircraft for business. Assuming you are in the 40% tax bracket, Uncle Sam can pay for part of the fun. Of course, catering services are available on the aircraft, as is any other desired perk within reason.

The Publicists, Consultants and Private Banks

One must obviously have more than a presence in the real estate market here to be considered a player. Dozens of books and articles have been written about the overextended "basic residential requirements" of this new crowd, so I will leave that to others. After one gets past the multi-million-dollar houses and their hefty payrolls, it would be delinquent to overlook some of the other fine points of expenditure that are so much a part of the winter scene here.

Dining can be an expensive proposition in Palm Beach, to put it mildly. For instance, some of the newly affluent leak stories, sometimes discretely, through their publicists, about dropping $300 or $500 per wine bottle at a place like Chez Jean Pierre. And of course, when it comes to paying the bill, a few have been known to broadcast the final tab amount. Recently, the man hosting the party next to our table forgot his credit card, and asked his wife for hers, at which time she commented that her credit line was a certain amount and that he would have to increase it if she turned it over to the waiter. The amount was quite sizable even by Palm Beach standards, and their publicist got wind of it and leaked it to those who write the social columns.

The publicists also have a way of leaking the net worths of these newly affluent, who pay them will for almost any kind of exposure, something the Old Guard would never seek out. Publicity is often linked to some highly publicized charitable event, where the pledges are not always honored after the alcohol clears the next morning.

Like the rest of us who must from time to time assess our spending habits, sooner or later, the super-wealthy must take stock of their expenditures. Moderation, as strange as it might seem, is starting to find its way into the newly affluent's vocabulary. More and more, after the initial splash, are scaling back to preserve for their children's sake some form of balance with the outside world. After all, many of these privileged children eventually go off to colleges where they will interact with others of lesser means, and the parents don't want their offspring to develop a Paris Hilton image. The Old Guard dealt with this problem by only making the luxuries of life available to their children after they graduated from college or when they matured, and were able to appreciate the significance of their wealth and how others would react to it.

Consultants come in all shapes and sizes. To show you just how

NANTUCKET NOW AND THEN

If there any pin on the map with a central theme attached to it, it the great whaling industry of the past on Nantucket. The location fits the image perfectly: the crescent-shaped island, with its protected bays and inlets, is thirteen miles long and seven miles wide. Thirty miles out to sea you can see lower New England closest land mass to the Gulf Stream, with its vast inner harbor that once sheltered an impressive fleet of whaling boats. In the harbor, a series of basins flow into each other as the tide rises and falls, moving in a circular fashion unique to this part of the planet. Not much remains of the ancient historical industry of whaling, though the quaint cobblestone streets of Nantucket still boast some 800 well-preserved buildings, which today house numerous trinket shops. A sense of history remains in the air.

There is no doubt about what initially brought settlers to this unique setting. The Indians arrived around 300 A.D. and prospered off the land as well as the sea. By the late 1650s the island became a settler colony when a small group of Massachusetts men formed the permanent English settlement there, purchasing a large part of the island from a gentleman named Mayhew for thirty pounds and two beaver caps, one for Mayhew and the other for his wife. Thomas Mayhew, a wealthy Massachusetts merchant, was given a deed to most of the island by Charles I of England, even though he had never set foot on the island. The early settlers wished to escape the strict Puritan lifestyles in the colonies, and its ever-present, irritating watchfulness. They survived initially by raising sheep, although they were men of substantial means, a tradition that still permeates the island today.

As the English population expanded, it became apparent that Nantucket was very close to the migratory routes of the sperm whales, offering a great advantage over the mainland fleets, and the weather was much fairer during the season, permitting the men to go out to sea when many of the other harbors were frozen in. Initially the whaling efforts consisted of the small-time industry of drift whaling, which concentrated on whales that were old or incapacitated and had washed up on Nantucket shores. The Indians had long capitalized on these whales, retaining their blubber for their personal consumption.

With the advent of the white settlers, with their larger ocean-going ships, the next step in the evolution was offshore whaling. The Indians played a role here as well: Wampanoags were converted to Christianity and used for heavy lifting on whaling ventures. These inexpensive laborers, often given only a percentage of the profits, helped to land the whales, each of which would produce around 200 barrels of oil, which was shipped off and used to light the lanterns of New England. As Nantucket turned the pages into the eighteenth century, there were about 300 Englishmen and 800 Indians on the island, a demographic that fit perfectly into the labor equation for offshore whaling.

The Indians received a cut of the profits at less than the white crews' cut began dying off from traditional European diseases. As the Indians disappeared, the settlers acquired much of the prime waterfront acreage that is so valuable today. The imported blacks, many bought at higher prices than the southern plantations could afford, were the next group to do the heavy lifting. Now the whaling industry took on a life of its own: great ships set out to sea, sometimes for a year or more, and returned with a cargo of oil that could be worth millions of dollars. The captains of those ships and their investors soon became the wealthiest men in the colonies. The industry was transformed almost overnight. The profits from a good-sized whale would provide a crew member who propelled the dangerous, small boats that harpooned the whales with an amount equal to six months wages of the second-tier employees working on the land. Soon, the glamour of this lifestyle attracted young men in droves; they were treated like rock stars.

The sperm whales were the catch of the day, since they provided the most refined oil, but they were only found well beyond the horizon. They were the mammoth beasts, according to folklore and to the novel *Moby-Dick*, that decimated and sank many whaling ships; they could be over 60 feet long and weigh some 50 tons. Processing the various parts was tremendously lucrative, though the dangers were obvious: the whales could dive down thousands of feet when threatened, and their skin was in parts often more than a foot thick, making it difficult for the whalers spear to penetrate their vulnerable spots, except at close and risky distances. Their jaws and tooth structure could easily snap a small whale boat in half in a matter of seconds, especially if the whale was antagonized.

The whales bones were made into corsets and petticoats for the well-to-do. But the ultimate prize, after considerable refinement, was the spermaceti candle, and this industry flourished for decades, catering to the discriminating American colonists, the Europeans, and the settlers in the Caribbean Islands. Benjamin Franklin was impressed by this new kind of candle whose clear, white light enabled him to read in the evening. The trade was so lucrative that a monopoly was formed. The largest candle manufacturers on Nantucket formed the Spermaceti Trust, which some consider the world's first energy cartel.

Many of the sperm whaling voyages set sail for years, often to such faraway places as Greenland and the Falkland Islands. The Nantucket fleet grew to over 300 ships, comprising roughly half of the entire fleet in the colonies. Whale men became prominent citizens of the Nantucket community, building massive homes in the highest part of town, far from the seedy wharf areas. Many of these homes still stand, and have been beautifully renovated. The whale men were viewed by society women as great catches, and many of them became pillars of society, with all the newfound wealth attached to whaling.

The American Revolution and the War of 1812 devastated Nantucket. The English enemy ships often blockaded the important ports along the eastern seaboard. As a result, over 80% of the whaling industry was destroyed, and many of the seamen were incarcerated. Those on Nantucket have always been a hardy, independent group. They rebuilt after the dust settled, using new technology that allowed the ships to store and process whale blubber while at sea. These large, floating whale-processing factories permitted them to undertake voyages for extended periods of time.

Next came the Civil War, which sounded the death knell for the whaling industry and Nantucket for the next 100 years. A surprise development unfolded in Pennsylvania, where oil was found, and soon a way was invented to produce kerosene as a byproduct, inexpensively. Previously, kerosene had been derived from coal, but on a very limited basis. Almost overnight it replaced the need for whale oil, and the whaling fleet became obsolete. Many ships were sold to the Union Navy to help blockade Confederate ports. The idea was to take the now somewhat dilapidated whaling fleet south across the Mason-Dixon line, with the idea of sinking the practically worthless fleet inside the Confederate harbors, thus barring passage of the ships that were supplying the Confederates with household goods and weapons from England and France, in places such as Charleston. After the war, the ships that had survived were converted into human transport ships, for those wishing to go to the California Gold Rush. Few of them returned after making the dangerous trip around the tip of South America, since often no worthwhile cargo was found on the other end to pay the return expenses.

To add more misery to the decaying economic picture, much of Nantucket was destroyed by the great fire of 1846, and for many residents, this was the straw that broke the camel's back. By 1875, two-thirds of the population had left Nantucket, leaving only about 3,000 die-hard souls. Adding fuel to the fire, the Industrial Revolution simply bypassed Nantucket, and things were status quo for the next hundred years. In the 1950s things started to revive when the wealthy people of the past, and some from the mainland, recognized the island as an ideal vacation destination. They renovated the old town and salvaged the architectural gems of the past.

Those who undertook the project restored what was standing, rather than demolishing and then rebuilding, as happens in many urban renewal programs. The zoning standards were preserved, and historic designations were reserved for much of the downtown area. As it turned out, people began to appreciate the historical significance of the island, and the island came to life once again. Renovators preserved the shake shingle and white shutters of the past, and updated the quaint cottages along the wharf, rejuvenating the downtown area. The established homes in the historic district were returned to their former splendor. Although the construction went on for decades, it was done in the spirit of maintaining the unspoiled historical identity of Nantucket.

The quaint improvements that reflected New England's rich history soon attracted visitors who came over on ferry boats from Woods Hole, at first on day trips and then on a more permanent basis. As a result, perishable goods were in ready supply, building materials became competitive, and limited airline service from Boston and New York became available. The population, which had remained constant at 3,500 for a hundred years after the Civil War, now exploded.

The rebirth took place in the 1950s and 60s, around the time when I attended Babson College in Wellesley, near Boston. Occasionally we would go to Nantucket, realizing that a major transformation was taking place. Our prime motivation was to escape from the harsh winters, and as soon as the spring arrived and the sun finally came out on a consistent basis, we were on our way. It was the same thing, to a lesser degree, in the fall, which featured wonderful football weekends. I never spent the summer months there, unfortunately, since I returned to Milwaukee for employment, which usually amounted to life-guarding on the beaches of Lake Michigan.

In the 1960s, summer people began to replace the full-time residents in numbers and in purchasing power. On a long-weekend trip to Nantucket in 2008, I had the opportunity to see what the island is like now, and to marvel at the changes. I was surprised to learn that the year-round population now hovers at about 12,000 and swells to 55,000 during the summer. The summer population makes up roughly 70% of the economic base, much as in Palm

Beach, where I currently reside. The cost of living here is very high, whereas in the late 50s and early 60s, one could maneuver around town on a shoestring.

The late 50s were special nevertheless. We went to old hangouts like the Club Car, and then bummed around in a somewhat inebriated state to other watering holes, staying on our limited budgets in rooming houses that are have now blossomed into upscale bed and breakfast operations. Back then, we though we were chic, the guys from Boston in their fancy duds, with plastic money that seemed not to end until we went home for the summer and our parents brought us back down to reality. But today, people arrive on private jets, and lodge in multi-million-dollar homes. The price of a meal in an upscale restaurant today probably exceeds what we spent on an entire weekend back then. Since then, offshore money has poured in, the yacht basins were expanded considerably, and the old, rotting docks and piers were replaced and are now the site of elegant restaurants and pubs.

Wealthy residents have built summer enclaves of stylish homes on the limited land available for residential development. Their plots of land are manicured to the nines, not quite in harmony with the rugged openness of the marshes and fragile ecosystem, but nevertheless quite picturesque. As the 60s unfolded, Nantucket took on a degree of civility that had not found its way to its shores in over a century.

My companion Carol and I arrived for a long weekend as guests of a couple we knew who wintered in Palm Beach. They put together a small group for the weekend, including some from Palm Beach and others who summer on Nantucket. The guests all stayed at the magnificent White Elephant Inn, which dates back to the early days of the island and was recently totally renovated into a first-class seasonal resort. All the charm of the past was incorporated into the new structure; there was superb cuisine and a bevy of young summer interns catered to everybody's whims. Our suite, which overlooked the harbor, had a small balcony for reading as we enjoyed the constant movement on the water of the private yachts and the massive ferries from the mainland. On the first day we were privy to see the fleet from the New York Yacht Club that had stopped for the evening to recharge their batteries and to party at a lobster bake on Jetties Beach. It reminded me of a few years earlier, when I, too, participated in the week-long cruise. I went on a special year, the 150th anniversary of the event.

Carol and I arrived on our guest's Beech 400, an eight-passenger corporate jet dispatched just for the two of us to Palm Beach. After a light lunch and a bottle of wine, we circled Nantucket for our landing approach, giving us a bird's eye view of what had taken place there in the last three decades. Much of the island, up to 40%, is a protected wilderness, since the Town of Nantucket assesses each real estate sale so that 2% of the purchase price which is matched by the State of Massachusetts to acquire land that will never be developed. The conservation groups here take their work very seriously and have ample funds, over $100 million to land bank key pieces.

From the air you got a feel for this unique island in the ocean. The tiny roads extending out of the Historic Village area begin at the wharf and fan out like spider webs to other, more remote enclaves that the well-to-do patronize. Places like Sconset, eight miles to the east, epitomize the island's windswept openness. Located on the eastern tip of the island, Sconset is known for its upscale living and its decorative floral arrangements in season. Other small villages have the same appeal and solitude three miles to the south, and Madak, six miles west. From the air we could see the 260-acre Milestone Cranberry Bog, one of the largest in the United States. However, raising cranberries is a fading industry on the island, partly due to escalating land prices. On our final approach we passed over the harbor area where the Brant Point Light House announces the entrance into this majestic place, which looks like a fairy tale come true. Most of our stay was confined to the immediate downtown and the wharf area.

Some 800 pre-1840 structures are at the core of Nantucket Town, and have been preserved and rebuilt into a nationally recognized landmark district where property rarely changes hands, and when it does, prices are quite lofty. Intentionally, there are no stop lights, shopping malls, or fast-food franchises, or, for that matter, chain operations that one normally finds in resort locations. We looked at a beach shack on pilings; it could not have been over 1500 square feet. It was overlooking the harbor and its asking price had just been reduced to around $4 million. It a bit absurd, to say the least, but they seem to justify this hyperactivity as a drop in the bucket compared to the mega-mansions in the outskirts.

Each sale here sets the bar higher for those who need to have a presence. Lately the Who's Who of Wall Street have invaded, and the sky's the limit, in terms of one-upmanship. Even the children who play along the endless miles of public beaches reflect the grand nature of the homes in their elaborate sandcastles, which reflect the attitude of those who raise them.

The Historic Area is a marvel to behold. I doubt there is anyplace in this country with so much concentration of restoration in such a small area, and with such diversity of shopping. Literally hundreds of buildings haven't changed externally since the whaling days of old. Diversity is the order of the day: you can find needlework and goldsmith stores, kite shops, basket weaving, book establishments, sweets and ice cream parlors, pillows and hooked rugs, hand-loomed shawls, wood and candle boutiques, and stores catering to ceramics and European silk shoes. There are art galleries galore; it a paradise for those who like to shop til they drop.

I found the scrimshaw venders unique. They still practice the traditional art of carving images into whale bones or teeth, the latter being the most prevalent. In this community the early settlers took that medium to the highest levels, even though its origin dates back to England. The whales teeth are rough and must be sanded down first, and are then polished with a fine file before the artisan starts carving, usually with a jack knife, or in some cases with a more sophisticated tool that resembles a doctor scalpel. Most carvings depict ships of the day or famous people. After the cuttings are in place, a dark ink is placed over the etchings and rubbed deeply into the recessed surface; then the tooth is buffed to a glossy shine.

In my youth, I knew Nantucket as a fun fall and spring playground for me and my friends, who were in the early stages of making the transition from being moderate to fairly well-to-do people. Those who summered there came from all over New England, bringing their servants with them for the entire season. It was a place that the hippies, with their off-beat lifestyle, also found fascinating and irresistible. The increased ferryboat activity and limited air service started to bring a new crowd of people who stayed for shorter durations and came mostly with the idea of letting off a little steam in the downtown area, which was often a bit distasteful to others. Some used recreational drugs non-stop and crashed in hotels and rooming houses, and Nantucket got a bit of a reputation as a place for derelicts. During that timeframe, as I recall, the old wharf area was a disaster, to say the least, having been built in 1725 and having not been fully kept up since the whaling days. The noise, the rowdiness, and the displays of immaturity forced many full-time residents to move from the downtown into the less congested outlying areas.

During that period, not many outside of New England had even heard of the island. However, the sinking of the *Andrea Doria* brought some notoriety to Nantucket, since at the time, the disaster was billed as the greatest maritime event since the sinking of the *Titanic*. The *Andrea Doria* collided with another ship in dense fog off of Nantucket and quickly went to the bottom. Many of us in college took a different interest in Nantucket, especially on weekends: the powers-that-be rarely enforced the Massachusetts Blue Laws established shortly after the Pilgrims arrived, which prohibited the serving of liquor in drinking establishments on Sundays. This was a true blow to those of us who enjoyed partying and needed a bit of the hair of the dog after a strenuous weekend schedule.

The local police looked the other way, even when the Governor and Attorney General of Massachusetts attempted to enforce the strict provisions on the mainland. Of course, we all loved it, beating the rap and having fun at the same time. It doesn't get any better, with the possible exception of hearing the Kingston Trio play *Charlie and the MTA*, a favorite song in the Boston area that was a tribute to the inept management of the Metropolitan Transit Authority. Nantucket was a grand place to forget reality for a while, not that college in Boston didn't accomplish the same goal, with its dozens of colleges and universities spewing out thousands upon thousands of us on the prowl, up and down Beacon Street and Massachusetts Avenue, at almost any time of the day or evening. For those spending their years in Boston attempting to attain a higher education and at the same time achieve a more advanced degree of maturity, it was grand!

Nantucket was an extension of the Boston party scene. There were watering holes all over the Historic District, and the drinking age was rarely enforced, and if it was, ample false IDs were given out at the doors of the saloons and returned as one was leaving, just in case the authorities had to perform their token duties. I remember the White Elephant Hotel, a popular spot back then, and I was told that it sold sometime during that period for $150,000. Today, with its adjoining properties developed for condominiums, it would probably fetch in excess of $50 million. Our rooms back then cost a pittance, whereas today, with hotel and consumption taxes, it bordered on $1,000 an evening.

We would journey back and forth to Nantucket on the ferry from Woods Hole with our trusty hip flasks, arriving well lubricated and ready for more. Back then, places like the old Opera House were in vogue; its light piano music mixed in with the spirit of those there to have fun. It was, in my recollection, a place on the front burner for the college crowd, where writers and celebrities like Gloria Vanderbilt mixed with the happy-go-lucky college students from Boston.

During breakfast, on my most recent trip at the White Elephant, I met a man named Henry, who filled me in with great detail and enthusiasm on the happenings in the thirty-plus years that I had been absent. He had been a long-time staffer at the Elephant and a native of Nantucket, and like most locals he enjoyed talking about the unique history and the changes that have taken place on the island. Most local residents take great pride in there lifestyle here, even though during the height of the tourist season it gets a bit crazy.

Henry said that at an earlier time, the island was in transition. The wharf had been downsized, due to the collapse of the fishing industry there, and many of the dilapidated old wooden shanties were torn down; they had belonged to scallop fishermen who no longer made a viable living off the sea. As a result, the commercial yacht harbor began to surface. Upscale retail shops replaced the old wooden shacks and both seedy rooming houses, bars and restaurants and upscale rental properties took hold along the waterfront, appealing to the new short-term summer residents. The removal of most of the unsightly gas stations and the major lumber yard paved the way for what Nantucket has become today. In the 60s, fashionable shops began to appear, featuring New York and California-style merchandise with a distinctive Nantucket touch. Pleasure yachts replaced the old fishing vessels, and many, including Henry, attributed this transformation to the efforts of one man, Walter Bienecke, owner of Sherburne Associates.

The seventies, Henry said, brought on the hippies. After the Vietnam issue was resolved, they seemed to take haven here to further advance their various causes. As often as not they could be found sleeping on the beaches, using heavy recreational drugs; their presence contrasted strongly with that of the clean-cut college students who were there to party. Partly because the hippies congregated at the run-down rooming houses, the Historical District Commission extended its roots deeper into the community and set development standards and growth limits, and began to enforce the code violations that were so prevalent during that time.

The glamorous younger generation of Kennedys were always within eyesight either here on Martha's Vineyard, and added excitement and a touch of tragedy to these towns. Teddy's folly was Chappaquiddick; Joseph Kennedy III also had a misfortune on Nantucket when his jeep overturned, paralyzing a young woman in the process, Henry told me. The seventies were rounded out with the hardships associated with the Arab Oil Embargo, where gasoline and fuel oil were rationed here, leaving many homes in the dark for extended periods of time. But the people of Nantucket are independent, to say the least, and survived. This was never more apparent than in the 70s, when the powers that be drew up Articles of Independence in an attempt to succeed from the state of Massachusetts, supposedly after receiving a proposal for inclusion into the state of New Hampshire, and according to Henry they even designed their own flag. The idea was quashed in short order, when the then-Governor of Massachusetts threatened to install a nuclear power plant on the island, or at least that's how the story went.

The profile of the island rose when Peter Benchley, a long-time resident of Nantucket, wrote the book that became the movie JAWS, which was filmed on Martha's Vineyard. As the decade closed Nantucket became a place for minor and major celebrities, and a place for change. There were big- time parties and galas at the yacht club as the town started to shape itself around the moneyed gentry set. With the renovation of the historic district, affluent day-trippers from the mainland began coming in droves, just as they do on summer weekends today.

Again according to Henry, the 80s further paved the way for the wealthy and influential who congregate here today. They pushed land and home values skyward, and subdivisions came into play for instance, the 200 residences on 5,000 square-foot lots like Naushop Village emerged as buyers from New York, Texas and California appeared on the scene. The era also ushered in million-dollar homes, even though the average house on the island still hovered around $100,000. The old cobblestone streets were replaced with a modern-day replica that most residents, like Henry, think adds a feel of phoniness to the area.

As the decade ended, Nantucket felt the financial pressures that the rest of the country was experiencing. At the time, I was in the real estate development business in the southwestern part of the country, and for a while the entire residential and commercial real estate market crashed, partly due to the Tax Reform Act of 1986, which eliminated many of the tax deductions associated with owning second homes in resort areas. That was followed by the collapse of much of the savings and loan industry, which made

financing virtually unavailable for many years. According to
Henry, it also dovetailed with the five-year cap that Nantucket
placed on building permits. The stock market crash of October
1987 added fuel to the fire as well. So, it was back to the old days
of hardship, inexpensive rents, and falling property values.

Old haunts like the Opera House, formerly the place to see and be
seen, gave way to the wrecking ball, and other gems like the
Backside Motel morphed into a 100-unit condominium. By then,
the old lifestyle had begun to change dramatically; for instance, the
once-prosperous farming community was now reduced to three
farms in total on the entire island. Much of the farmland was
scooped up by developers who were not pulled down by the
savings and loan fiasco. A buyer's market developed as the decade
closed. It was somewhat similar to today's tragic situation, caused
by excessive and unjustified lending in the sub-prime mortgage
market.

However, a deep wind from offshore was blowing over the island,
sweeping up some of the important major industries and
transferring ownership to the mainland. First to go was the
newspaper *The Inquirer and Mirror,* which fell to a chain. Next
was the major developer Sherbourn Associates, which was
purchased by First Winthrop and later by Steven Karp, whose
yacht we charted for an afternoon of sailing on Nantucket Bay.
Next, the electric company was absorbed by a mainland public
utility company, which extended underground cables to the island
that replaced the old generating system, and finally, the main
commercial bank, Pacific National, an institution for close to 150
years, was sold to a Boston banking operation.

High-profile characters began to arrive, people like Tommy
Hilfiger, who built mega-mansions, creating a need for things like
the Nantucket Golf Course and other high-end forms of
entertainment. The Clintons traveled here during the height of the
Monica Lewinski scandal, apparently with the idea of getting away
from it all. As I recall, it looked as if Bill's dog was the only one
that had a good time. And of course, with all the people came
automobiles, by some estimates 10,000 of them, that choked the

two-lane roads, just as they do today.

As the new century unfolded, Henry said, the island took on the appearance of a summer place for the super-rich. The private jets on weekends here sometimes outnumber the commercial flights at Logan Airport in Boston, just as they do at Palm Beach International during the season. The Hamptons, it appeared, no longer captivated the super rich of Wall Street, having become too showy and pricy with all the newfound fortunes. Now the mega-yachts glided into the expanded yacht basin, and the ever-growing ferries maneuvered for docking space. Currently, house values have risen to astronomical heights; for instance, it is not uncommon for a large estate home on the water to fetch $30 million, a truly amazing development when one considers that the total assessed valuation of Nantucket in the early eighties was $32 million.

Much of the Historic District has remained the same for decades, at least from the exterior standpoint. This nice touch makes one feel in tune with the past, which is what Nantucket is all about. The interiors of many of the old houses in the Historic District have been gutted to make room for the endless varieties of merchandise that is offered for sale. Gone are the large hearths that used to warm the main rooms and acted as meeting places for the families of old, but nevertheless the merchandise is diverse and high-quality, although a bit pricy. Nantucket is no longer the small, sleepy town I remembered from my college days, but remains a very special pin on the map.

One of the more interesting events that weekend that Carol and I went to Nantucket was when our hosts chartered a Sparkman and Stevens 71-foot sailboat named *Sleighride*, owned by one of the prominent families on Nantucket. Steven Karp was a Boston-based developer whose real estate holdings were vast, including many fine hotels, one of which was the White Elephant, and a considerable amount of the retail space in the historic district. We were fortunate to have chartered the yacht, since normally the family keeps a tight reign on her, but an afternoon's use was auctioned off for the local hospital several weeks before and our hosts were the high bidders. We ventured out with twelve aboard, six of whom were from Nantucket, two from Martha's Vineyard, Carol and me, and a couple from New Jersey.

Our skipper was a delightful New Zealander, and we passed the afternoon in style, with wonderful food and wine served and replenished by the second mate as we cruised Nantucket Sound, following the shoreline of the crescent-shaped island on a light wind. From time to time we used an auxiliary 2000-square-foot foresail in an attempt to increase our speed, which averaged at about 5 nautical miles per hour. As a special treat one of our fellow passengers, Robert, a multi-generational native and local realtor, pointed out all the luxurious homes overlooking the ocean, providing a who's who of those who have put down their stakes over the past decades.

From here, with a little imagination, one could picture, but not quite see, where the Pilgrims first laid anchor just north of our route on the northern tip of Cape Cod. The sun shining off the ocean surface sparkled like diamonds, captivating us and holding our attention. The movement of the water was therapeutic and I found my mind drifting back in time; I could almost visualize Nantucket during the whaling era. The home fires would be burning along the wharf for those who remained behind, and the men would be at sea on the massive whaling vessels, fighting the elements, hunger, thirst and the powerful whales, all from their tiny rowing craft. They'd return to the ship if successful, exhausted, and then had to carve up the blubber, after a strenuous day. Retiring at dusk to their small, airless and darkened cargo holds, they'd gather around a pot-bellied stove, dine on the less-than-desirable whale parts that could not be sold at market, and with their trusty cup of rum, try hard to forget the day and their families back home.

One must wonder how they navigated in those days, without the assistance of electronic global positioning devices. They glided over the Atlantic in search of their bounty, without I am sure an ample supply of fresh drinking water. The officers lived fairly well, I was told, and likely instructed the crew to bait the circulating birds with whale meat on the decks so that they could dine in style in their private ship quarters.

We read so much about the North-Easters, who were also depicted in the movie the *Perfect Storm*, which showed the blinding rain storms with such great winds that churn up the ocean with violence, putting the men and their boats at the mercy of Mother Nature. You wonder what those below deck thought of the waves constantly crashing against the hull, wondering how much punishment the infrastructure could take. As for those on top, one wonders how many years or even decades it took to get sea legs to stand watch, even though at times, not much could be done to prevent a catastrophe. The soothing sounds of the waves that we hear and see from *Sleighride*, our chartered yacht for the afternoon, take on a whole new meaning when you're in trouble, with no perceivable way out of your fix. I am always amazed at the consistency of the wave patterns, the way they break like a herd of wild animals charging the beach in uniformity, and then suddenly, as if frightened by some magnetic force, form a retreat, for no apparent reason except to give the next grouping its turn.

Certainly, many boats back then must have been washed up on the shoals for lack of proper directions, or were unable to get their bearings. Looking at the debris that collects on the beaches, one wonders, over a century later, if some of it contains remnant parts of the ships, still in the process of breaking off. Surely some of the driftwood souvenirs sold in Nantucket's gift stores were once attached to sunken hulls. Who knows how many homes have pieces of driftwood that hold significant meaning in relation to those fateful voyages?

It hard to imagine the terror these men felt as they floundered for days or even weeks, with nothing more than a compass, unable to fix a position with the stars, or on land, or in some cases unable to navigate at all, just being stuck with the deck of cards they were dealt. Drifting, ever drifting over the restless seas. But those who take to the seas accept that challenge; after all, our bodies contain about the same amount of water as the oceans do compared to the land masses, and roughly the same saline content. Still, what a helpless feeling it must have been to have to rely on old charts showing only partial findings of the New World as your only hope for survival.

From the yacht, we watched the shore. I was especially taken with the funny little birds with long, skinny, out-of-proportion legs scampering back and forth looking for a morsel, until a wave would come and inundate their hunting grounds. When the tide recedes, the sands soak up the thirsty water, replenishing the small creatures that live just below the surface, and washing away any signs of life on their way in. The breakers are also special, changing the color of the water from blue to green.

As far as I know, the women and young children back then rarely ventured over the tide lines into the vast expanses of the open sea. This sacred hunting ground was reserved for the men and aspiring young boys. The men went to sea at their own peril, and many, most likely, washed up on the shorelines, torn apart and bloated just like the dead whales, whose carcasses were stripped of their flesh and cut adrift from the mammoth whaling ships. One wonders how many boats sought in vain the refuge of the Brant Point Lighthouse, a make-or-break destination that has now been reduced to a tourist attraction. How many captains neatly wrapped his ship's log in a watertight container as the end approached and dispatched it for posterity? I assume that only a fraction of these ever found their way to attics or museums.

We did a leisurely sail that afternoon along the pristine beaches. Of course, there are no divisions on the beaches, which are in the public domain; here, there are no claims of ownership. The beach belongs to man and nature, equally, unlike the developed tracts of land, where man has staked his claim, and where no others can intrude unless invited. The miles upon miles of shoreline seem mostly barren, almost like a desert on the edge of the ocean. And one wonders how the sailors of old picked out navigational points along these shores with the ever-changing bluffs of sand piled up, which constantly must have shifted their landmarks through the motion of the winds. I have tried celestial navigation, the method of choice in days gone by, but soon switched over to modern-day satellite navigation.

And yet I have always been attracted to the heavens. I have sailed
for many decades, in my early days on the Great Lakes, in midlife
in the Caribbean, and most recently in the Florida Keys and on the
southeast coast of Florida. I sense that the seas are somehow
anchored to the heavens in some mystical fashion. If you take a
timed-release photo with a wide angle lens for, say a four-hour
period at night, you see the streaking lights of heavenly bodies
stretched out for tens of thousands of miles. It seems they are
reaching out for something, a cord of light, so to speak, trying to
connect with us, though only through our imagination can we can
bring it down to earth. It like those who studied the skies in, say,
the Mayan culture, and were able to control others by
understanding the growing cycle of crops and predicting the future.
The sand ripples on the beach and in the dunes are equally
fascinating for those who can connect the dots with the shifting
weather and wind patterns. They are tea leaves that we need to
read, as painstakingly hard as it might seem. Just like the heavenly
bodies, the seasons are relevant, and the snow drifts can be read
too, when the sand is no longer visible during the winters here.

We returned from our afternoon on the water covered with salt air
and filled with happy thoughts. The wind had finally picked up; we
had spent most of the afternoon going under 10 knots. We came in
a bit early, but did get a look at the windswept beaches where we
would spend that evening for the Nantucket Cottage Hospital
charity event, featuring cocktails and dinner on the beach, with the
Boston Pops full orchestra providing a perfect backdrop.

We returned to the hotel for a quick glass of wine before preparing
for the evening's events, and lo and behold, we encountered a
somewhat nefarious relic from the past, seated in the hotel's
elegant beach bar. This disheveled dock master, who had drifted in
from the docks for a bit of grog, seemed totally out of place in this
environment. We all know the type weather-beaten and unshaven,
with a rough, unsophisticated voice, sunken cheeks in a face that
looked like a sail that had been stretched to its limits and then
shrunk, and should have been discarded years ago. Intent on

impressing others with his importance, he spoke into his two-way radio, expressing his displeasure at some mega-yacht owner who wanted a berth that he did not have. He was stooped over from a hard life, and sour as rotten grapes, and too depressed to do anything but to demonstrate his authority over his little assistant on the dock. This old salt, who I met in passing, brought to mind the hardened sailors of a hundred and fifty years ago.

The beach party concert, supper and fireworks were grand. The event has been going on for a dozen summers, attracting 10,000 people to Jetties Beach. Those on the beach itself had umbrellas, lawn chairs, coolers and a bevy of toys for the younger generation. This event builds momentum from the start of the season, and is without a doubt the premier evening on Nantucket. The drawing card is the Boston Pops full orchestra, flown in just for the evening; the group set up on an elevated stage with a formidable acoustic system that involved many speakers being installed on lifeguard-type platforms along the beach. There were people stretching as far as the eye could see, all the way down to the water's edge. Fortunately, the weather cooperated perfectly. How everybody assembled in such an orderly fashion is beyond belief, as Nantucket has only a series of two-lane roads, and they are few and far between. But the courtesy, regional pride, and camaraderie on this island are legendary, and everyone was well behaved.

The once-in-a-lifetime event began with an abbreviated cocktail hour, hosted in a tent within earshot of the performing stage. There, the major contributors to the Nantucket Cottage Hospital annual fund raising drive congregated to exchange pleasantries and to enjoy the vast array of cheeses and mouth-watering hors d'oeuvres. I had heard there would be a beach concert going on as we dined. At the appointed time we were escorted to a ringside table of ten. Our group, many of whom we had gone sailing with that afternoon, was front and center.

What unfolded was a twilight candlelight dinner, served to perfection by a series of local volunteers mixed in with the hired guns from a catering service. We began with a chilled seafood platter with salmon, shrimp and lobster, and as we nibbled away, the Boston Pops came to life. The full orchestra of about 100 instruments in total set an elegant tone as we digested our dinner and conversed with members of New England gentry.

Master of Ceremony Katie Couric, standing in for the late Tim Russert, who was a longtime resident of Nantucket and a favorite with audiences of the past because of his charm and his sense of history, kicked off the evening. The wine flowed endlessly as the Pops played their usual toe-tapping John Phillip Sousa music as if it were a premier 4th of July celebration. American flags were flying in every corner of the makeshift amphitheatre, to the delight and patriotic smiles of all those in attendance.

It was a magical evening, with the setting sun, and just enough cloud cover and ocean breeze to add to the comfort level. The ocean waves complemented the momentum of the music as the darkness set in. It was as American as motherhood and apple pie, and then some. Our tables were set somewhat below the sand dunes, so many who sat on the beach were not visible from our vantage point, but you could sense their presence and their vibrations, young and old alike. The crowd in the VIP section, where we were fortunate enough to be seated, is just what you would expect. It included many from the island's WASP community and presumably, most had either attended the top New England colleges and had become quite successful, or had come into large amounts of inheritance with time.

The men wore their standard navy blazers and light-colored slacks, while the women were in full-length brightly colored dresses. As an outsider, I could tell that the tables had been arranged to reflect the pecking order of those who had made the largest donations to the hospital. It was fun to feel part of those who were instrumental in making the event happen.

Transported by the music, I found myself remembering how, during my college days, the Pops, then under the direction of Arthur Fiedler, often played Sunday afternoon concerts in Boston for the masses of college students who appreciated and revered their style. Of course, being one of their greatest fans back then, I still remember the 4ᵗʰ of July 1976, the 200ᵗʰ anniversary of this country's birthday, when I happened to be in Boston and was fortunate enough to hear Maestro Fiedler and the Pops play all the patriotic, eye-watering music to tens upon tens of thousands along the Charles River. Even Queen Elizabeth was there. I savored this fond memory.

People table-hopped during the performance, but most of us stayed put, absorbing the music. Carol and I ran into two couples we knew from Palm Beach who were summer residents of Nantucket; they were beaming with pride about this special evening, which outshines the best functions that we attend during the winter social season in Palm Beach.

The Boston Pops concert was followed by a terrific performance by Joel Gray. Though not a household name, he was the tiny Master of Ceremonies in *Cabaret*, with the German accent. He was larger than life, despite his stature, and Broadway caliber, to say the least. Gray kept the audience captivated for close to an hour, with his lyrics and animated dancing from one end of the stage to the other, accompanied by the Boston Pops. The crowd was riveted.

The finale was breathtaking, with the Boston Pops again in all its glory, and the fireworks shooting off from a barge in Nantucket Sound. After the sensational evening came to an end, we adjourned to the contributors tent for a small dessert party and some after-dinner drinks. The evening raised about $2 million, half of which went directly to the hospital, covering their annual operating shortfall. Having walked through the historic district in the morning and sailed in the afternoon, Carol and I were happy but exhausted, and soon retreated to the White Elephant, sure that we would never forget the experience.

Nantucket is famous for these splashy summer events and its action-packed season. The kickoff is the Daffodil Festival in April, followed by The Nantucket Wine Festival in May, and the internationally known Figawi Race from Hyannis to Nantucket during the same month. June ushers in the Nantucket Film

Festival, and after July 4th, August brings the Boston Pops and the Sandcastle and Sculpture Day, held on Jetties Beach. September brings the Nantucket Island Fair, with hay rides and square dancing. October is the Nantucket Arts Festival, a week-long event where authors, actors, musicians come together. During November Festival of the Wreaths, wreaths are auctioned off for the benefit of the Preservation Society; finally, there is the Christmas Stroll, drawing tens of thousands to see the newly lit Christmas trees, lights, and decorations. Santa Claus is delivered by boat to the wharf area, and many walk the ancient streets ringing bells and singing Christmas carols.

When I visited Nantucket during my college days, it was an odd assortment of culture, people, and structures, somewhat like today's Key West, and non-conformity was the order of the day. Much has changed since those simpler days when Nantucket was seen primarily as an escape from school or from real life, although its sense of history and elegance has been maintained. Change is normal and desirable, but unfortunately, it is no longer feasible to enjoy this magical playground on a shoestring; nowadays, the people who escape to this island had best have a seven-figure income.

SECTION II

THE WORLD IS A BOOK

In my lifetime I have traveled to some eighty countries, and I am always especially intrigued by the other travelers I meet along the way. Some people travel for self-discovery; some because they are fascinated by other cultures; and some want only to get away from the dreariness of home, and to enjoy a rather empty life of luxury. This section features three of my recent trips to upscale tourist locations. Mallorca was a setting steeped in history and tradition, and by experiencing the bullfight and savoring the delicious food, I immersed myself in this rich, unchanging culture. This type of travel brings personal growth and inter-cultural awareness; Henry Miller's statement that "One's destination is never a place but rather a new way of looking at things" comes to mind, as does St. Augustine's claim that "The World is a book, and those who do not travel read only a page." Still, not everyone considers travel in this light. In *Cheeseburger in Paradise*, I comment on the fellow sailors I met in the British Virgin Islands, and I examine their quirks and personalities; I take a look at the various motivations for taking to the sea and for traveling in general.

Yet another chapter describes a re-enactment of a Florida cattle drive in the 1850s. Each of these chapters attempts to capture a moment in our history while simultaneously showing how that moment is viewed today, from the vantage point of the twenty-first century. Much like historical re-enactors, who immerse themselves in the faraway past and make it as real as possible, but whose consciousness is rooted in the here and now, I explore the complex interrelationship between various timeframes, and examine how these ground-breaking moments in our culture continue to shed meaning on the world of today.

MALLORCA, MYSTICAL ISLAND

Mallorca, especially after one leaves behind the capital, Palma, is a charming place with a rich history. To this day it has maintained its tricultural population, consisting of Germans, Brits, and Spanish; each group has its own distinct area of the island. Mallorca has passed through many hands: it was conquered by the Romans, who stayed for over 500 years, only to be followed by hundreds more years under the Moors, and then the Muslims. Next came the British, and then the French; finally the island was handed over to the Spanish in the early 1800s. During Franco's regime, Mallorca was the hub of his fascist government, but after his death in 1975 it opened up and became one of the prime tourist attractions in the world.

Almost the entire island is accessible by a series of roads that either ring the perimeter of the great mountain ranges or that crisscross the wide open plains in the center. On these plains, which are dotted with vineyards and olive trees, there are impressive century-old residences, mostly one-storey, white-washed homes or larger ones made of stone and masonry. These middle-class "farmsteads" are usually surrounded by lush greenery, with the exception of those along the windswept coastlines, which are set far from the road, ensuring privacy.

Small residential hamlets dot the entire landscape, and are tempting wayside stops for one who is traveling around and absorbing the island's natural beauty. I remember stopping often to sample the local wines and cheeses and to acquaint myself with the locals, who brought out water and wine upon my arrival. I found their uncomplicated lifestyle quite different from those I had observed in other parts of the world. Their homes, which have few windows and slightly overhanging roofs that keep the heat out during the warmer times of the year, reflect their agrarian heritage. Inside, the furnishings were far from elaborate. The people, focused on the productivity of their land, enjoyed a laid-back, family-oriented lifestyle, and the attractiveness of their surroundings did not seem to be a top priority.

These islanders were not what we outsiders would consider well-to-do. Sustained by a diet of fresh fish, homegrown vegetables, poultry and numerous wines, they were jovial as only the Spanish can be, cordial and open to conversations with outsiders. Rarely did a day go by that I did not stop and spend some time in these small, delightful hamlets.

Often I would drive slowly down their winding driveways, and they would come out of the fields to greet me. Washing up and offering me warm smiles, they would bring out the refreshments and tell me about the history of their little domains, which were often passed down from generation to generation. Here, everyone had a role or a function, it seemed: the men and boys worked in the fields, while the women and the elderly worked indoors, or in the vineyards. By acting in unison and living simply, they managed to keep things on an even keel.

These people, who owned their small plots and had worked them since time immemorial, were the backbone of Mallorca. When I was ready for a change of pace, from time to time I'd spend an evening in one of the many haciendas. A product of the old feudal system, these were gigantic and grand two- or three-storey residences designed to show off wealth and power in the community. Many had been converted into overnight rental units; some were rented by the evening, and others for longer. But generally, the private apartments of the former owners were made available to the traveling public at fairly modest rates. Many still had heavy old furniture imported from Europe, and impressive artwork collected from all corners of Europe, Africa and parts of India. Most rooms had breathtaking views of the vineyards and the Mediterranean Ocean. Their architectural style reflected the greats of the twentieth century, such as LeCorbusier and Gropius.

These haciendas were delightful places to pass the time. In this rich pastoral setting, there was nothing to rush to or from. In addition, much of the island has been designated a wildlife preserve, thereby offering protection from real estate development and from excessive tourism as well. Even the boat anchorages are quite restricted, at least in terms of access to the steep, sloping land, leaving the coastal waters pristine and picture-perfect. In the outlying areas outside of Palma, not much has been compromised, so those seeking beaches and nightlife usually head for that city.

I arrived in Palma by ferry, and the customs officials looked at me as if I were a breath of fresh air. My arrival fell at the end of the long day, and they knew they would soon be at their wine flasks. They waved me through without fanfare, and their macho attitude towards the others softened; they and their families didn't have much disposable income to spend shopping in Spain, and this led to a feeling of resentment towards their wealthier compadres.

I found that the people of Palma were not as boisterous and exuberant as their counterparts in Greece, which I had just left. Still, they were pleasant and accommodating–just somewhat reserved. These people have a unique and comfortable combination of sophistication and simplicity of which they are proud, a manner that I was to find quite magical. They were not pretentious like the French, but comfortable, like an old worn-out shoe.

The men were bold and sure of themselves and the women the same, but more reserved. They were well endowed, not skinny as a rail, and they held their own. Like the men, they are earthy and attached to the land that is their heritage and their whole life.

Upon my arrival in Palma,I had a day or two to pass until I received some closing documents from my Santa Fe office. So day one, I toured the fort-like city whose walls still reflect the ancient town and create an imperial feeling. Walking around this enclosed part of the old city, you sense that for many generations, the people of Palma have been on the edge of two different worlds. They were part of Franco's military dictatorship; they were not under his thumb, but not totally free, either. Fear and freedom are in equilibrium here, I thought, as I traveled through the countryside.

With a second day to kill, I decided to take a stab at a bullfight in my spare time. Up to that point I had only read about them, especially Hemingway's account of the bulls running at Pamplona. I had great visions of the Festival of San Fermin, with bulls rushing from their pens through the streets of Pamplona, and men and boys scattering in all directions looking for a doorway or crevice to escape the terror of the bulls and the oxen making the historic run into the bull rings; I envisioned thousands of excited people flocking to the parades and fiestas, dancing to the music with botas of wine in hand. But the image was quickly shattered.

The bulls that made the 1000-yard run in two minutes were nowhere to be found. The way Hemingway described it, one did not have to know much about bullfighting, which was largely overshadowed by the pomp and ceremony of the event. But this was certainly not the case in Palma, where there was very little ceremony or excitement. Most of the sparse crowd in attendance were outsiders and like me, didn't have a clue what distinguished a good bullfight from a mediocre one. Nevertheless, it was an interesting experience, one that I have not repeated since.

The Palma bull ring was simple and run-down, as one would expect in a sport that seems to be in its declining phases. The diversity of the music and the costumes were the most captivating aspect. Since I had no way to judge the quality of the bullfights or, for that matter, of the bulls themselves, I enlisted a local tourist guide of sorts who was hovering around my hotel. He tagged along for the price of a ticket, some pocket change for refreshments and a tip at the end of the afternoon.

He was a sight to see, a product of conspicuous consumption in the gastronomy department if there ever was one. His enormous waistline filled in his upper body almost to his chest, and his pants resembled a tent, baggy and blowing in the wind. But he was full of life and laughter. We communicated in broken English and many fast-moving hand gestures for which the Spanish are noted. Fortunately, Luis, as he was called, was able to shed some light on the mechanics of bullfighting.

Here, the bulls were already in captivity, hidden and out of view in the bowels of the stadium. Thousands were in the stadium, expecting a good show, which usually meant a humanitarian killing of the bull, if such a thing exists, and a stellar performance by the team of fighters. Here in the ugly world of bullfighting, the elements seemed stacked against the bulls, although the music that accompanies the men in costume, on foot and on horseback somehow seems to promote a leve playing field. Most of the local spectators anticipated the fight while enjoying their botas of red wine.

It seemed to me that, given the bright-coloured costumes and the exciting music, the whole afternoon's festivities was being played out for the tourists. The sport, I surmised, was initially a throw-back to the old Roman days of the Coliseum, where the masses were entertained by violent gladiators taking on a wide variety of animals and people. It was a diversion designed for the poor but also attended by the aristocracy. I am sure that this so-called diversion was passed down from generation to generation to placate the lower classes, both here and in Rome. I was told that the current aristocrats in Mallorca shun these events, seeing them as a reflection of the brutal days of the Roman Empire, and rightfully so, in my estimation.

As I was to learn from my overweight, almost toothless friend Luis, there are several ways the matador and his supporting cast gains the respect of the crowd. The entire fight can be broken down into five or so venues or equations. Success depends on how many the team does well at, which is measured by style and by force. The final reward is either one or two ears of the fallen bull, which are severed and given to the matador and his cast of characters.

The whole exercise starts with the bull entering the ring to great audience applause; a variety of bands playing loud, captivating music. This is without a doubt the first of the venues, and the crowd gets to size up the stature and stamina of the bull before the cast of characters and their horses enter the picture. It seemed to me that this is the bull's crowing moment of glory, if there is such a thing.

The bull comes to a temporary standstill and the crowd goes berzurk. My guess is that the bull is either out of his element, or just plain disoriented. However, it's like the old three-ring circus of days gone by, where the animals are on display and judged by the audience for their beauty and capability before any thing else happens. In all the confusion, the bull looks quite majestic and in charge. His demeanor changes when the horses and their riders appear on the scene, and the crowd's attention shifts to them.

Those of the lower classes who fill most of the non-tourist portion of the stadium let their imaginations run wild. They live vicariously, thinking of themselves as potential heroes; even though most are well past the age of partaking in such an event, they see themselves as surrogate matadors, sharing in the glory of the daring profession. They are much like our youngsters who watch their hero in the warm-up circle at baseball games. For a few moments, their imaginations fueled by red wine, they see themselves in the ring with the bull as they talk excitedly among themselves, telling the others how they would proceed with the fight, had they the chance to take on the now-circulating beast, and how they would best bring him to a quick demise. This agenda is, of course, shattered when the real matador enters the ring and is greeted by much celebration.

When those wearing colored garments on the edges of the ring begin moving, the crowd becomes silent; the hunt begins to unfold. Occasionally the bull catches the horse and rider, his horns falling on the padded covers draping down from the saddle, making it look like a piercing blow, which it is not. However, this elevates the crowd's cheering and surely must give some encouragement to the bull and his survival techniques. They play this cat and mouse game for a few minutes to the crowd's delight, with music and wine flowing in all directions. The playing field seems level, even in favor of the fierce and majestic animal, who seems to be in a class of his own.

Then the next phase unfolds, in almost total silence. You could hear a pin drop in the arena. The horsemen are now armed with a pair of banderillas, long, pointed weapons that are thrust into the back of the bull's neck, either to sap his strength or to sever some of the muscles he uses to turn his head. Upon their insertion, the crowd goes ballistic once again, and this excitement goes on non-stop until another horseman places two additional banderillas alongside of the first two. Of course, by now the playing field is no longer level. The bull loses much of his majesty in the eyes of those watching. After all, they are here to watch him die, and now the process has begun in earnest.

The horsemen are judged by their execution of this important act that brings the bull down a peg or two. If the fight is a stunning success, which it was not the day I was there, the horsemen, I'm told, get one of the two severed ears. By now, most of the locals have come to the realization that man has conquered beast, and it is only a question of how long until the end comes.

The next stage begins when the matador enters the ring, and usually parks himself center-stage, often with his exposed back to the bull, to show off his glamorous costume and his astounding level of courage. The crowd stands at reverent attention for the killer, who shifts his position towards the awaiting bull. You would think that the King of Spain had entered the ring, given all the respect that is given to these time-honored, privileged characters.

Luis, now a bit under the influence of the grog, told me that even the best matadors only fight a handful of bulls each year. He added that the young, inexperienced matadors often have to pay to enter the ring, to cover the cost of acquiring the bulls, who are later slaughtered and sold in the local meat markets for much less than they are worth live on the hoof.

The bull and the matador, and to a lesser degree his supporting staff, do a series of passes at each other, the bull charging at the cape in what seems to be a life-threatening way, until his range of motion is restricted by the banderillas. One learns that the colors of the cape are what really infuriate him. After a dozen or so passes, both the bull and the crowd seem to go somewhat flat, and almost seem to lose interest in the whole exercise. But the suspense builds again when the bull suddenly takes a passive stance, for whatever reason; the crowd can now sense that the end is near. Intuitively, the spectators know that the loss of blood and agility as well as a sense of discouragement have taken their toll. They wait for the end in hushed silence.

The final phase starts when the matador is handed a sword, which he conceals in his cape. Now the audience's attention focuses on how clean the kill will be. Both the killer and the soon-to-be killed face each other, knowing what comes next. The bull must come to realize that he was placed there strictly for the entertainment of those in the stadium, and his initial salutations were nothing more than a cruel hoax, in his estimation.

Next, the matador stands erect, with both feet together like a wooden soldier. He is just a stone's throw from the bull's bowed and defeated head. When the matador senses that the bull has been sapped of his energy, and is unable to raise his head and charge one last time, he lunges for the dormant head, but in fact lands on the bull's shoulder and firmly plants the sword in the lower end of the neck, severing the animal's life.

The jubilant crowd stands to show their respect even if the piercing sword does not kill the bull instantly, which rarely happens. They wave their white handkerchiefs. The bull stumbles for a while and then drops into a lifeless heap; the carcass is then paraded and around the ring, dragged behind a tractor.

Prior to his being pulled from the ring, the ceremonial severing of an ear takes place. Apparently, the only honor ever given to a fallen bull to mark his heroism is the fact that he leaves the combat zone with both ears–not much of an ending, in my estimation. If he is truly a less-than-honorable combatant, he loses his tail to the matador as well.

The matador and horsemen parade around the stadium after the fight to get their kudos, measured by the types of missiles that take to the air. Flowers are tossed in the ring for praise, and empty wine bottles for scorn. Again, those in the crowd are fantasizing, imagining being the subject of such adulation. The young and old alike seem truly in awe of those who seemingly risk their lives for the entertainment of others, and this is what keeps them coming back for more.

I watched three fights, which generated moderate calls of protest, and some of outright contempt, from the crowd. When I had seen enough, I left with Luis, and we proceeded to wet our whistles at a local bar, which as it turned out was quite entertaining. The inebriated patrons reenacted the matador's entire performance to the cheers of those who had been unable to get off their bar stools. It seemed to me that in the final analysis, only the photographers knew which bull and which matador had performed the best, since they provided the winners' photos for the next day's newspaper.

After my office documents arrived by FEDEX, I rented a small German car and took to the hills, making the trip around the island in a counter-clockwise direction. The coved beaches on the island are not only numerous and secluded, but outstandingly beautiful. My beach exploration often involved taking my bed roll and sleeping under the stars to the sounds of waves crashing against the rocky shore, whose grey sand seemed to be an extension of the surrounding mountains.

When I tired of the outdoors, there was always a small-scale resort located in a distant ravine or perched on a hilltop with a terrific view of the Mediterranean side of the Sierra De Tramuntana mountain range along the southeast shore of Mallorca. The scenic, finger-like roads and ridges, branching off the loop roads on the island, were magical. Occasionally I would come upon a small village such as Portocristo, Cala Millor, or my favorite, Cala Ratjada, on the northeastern tip of the island.

In most of the mountainous areas, there were jaw-dropping caves to explore, their exteriors carved out of limestone by the early inhabitants who used them as shelter from the pirates. The massive interior caverns were sculpted by nature. Some of the carvings have religious significance, and many are quite massive and have shades of reds and browns. Often they are illuminated by man-made colored lights, and have lakes inside; from time to time you can find a local entrepreneur with a small boat and a musical instrument who will entertain you for hours on end if you have the wherewithal and the inclination. The magical music reverberates off the canyon walls as the boat glides through the cave.

You can hear the dripping of the water that seeps into the caves from the damp ground above to the icicle-like limestone ceilings. There are hundreds of caves on the island, but only a few provide tours. Some of those that were carved out naturally are often the height of a five-storey building; most are accessible through carved-out steps and winding walkways, with artificial lights to facilitate the trip. In a way I felt like *Alice in Wonderland* as I traversed the bottoms of these huge and mysterious caverns.

Not much in the line of crops or greenery was found along the shoreline, which was laced with boulders and shrubs. Every so often I would come over a hill and find a small village perched overlooking the water. Usually the small villages were dotted with a couple of windmills. Today they are mostly decorative, but in the olden days they must have been used to pull the ground water up from the limestone caverns below.

Most of the small buildings in these villages that are not occupied by the locals have been converted into small bed and breakfast operations or shops catering to the tourists. I found that without exception, all of these villages have a small bar or two, offering local wine and companionship. In the British section of the island there was no shortage of gin. It was the same with the German and French enclaves, where herbal liquors and lobster stew were also served.

Travelers who explore the outskirts of Palma as I did tend to honor the customs and heritage of the islanders who have been there for generations. Likewise, much of the residential second- home development on the island is in keeping with the long-standing traditions of the population. Palma feels a bit like an artist's community, and reminded me of Santa Fe, where I lived for over a decade.

For a few days I settled in to a unique series of buildings that was a former hacienda, later turned into a monastery, and was now a resort. Obviously, the original owner had had a glamorous lifestyle, before the Spanish initiated land reforms. The grand hacienda was located just off the perimeter road, and a short pleasant walk from a spectacular view of the Mediterranean. It was very similar to the converted monastery I stayed at in Santorini, which I wrote about in *Jewel of the Aegean*, except it had massive grounds with a vineyard and olive trees.

I arrived in Mallorca in late spring, and it seemed that the whole area was alive and in bloom; the orchards and vineyards were just starting to come into their own. The harvest was still months away. It was the perfect time to take long bicycle rides through the small country roads around the property.

The peasant workers, with their wide-brimmed hats, would look up and smile as I rode by, often having only a few stained teeth to show off their greeting. They were thin as rails, and generally tall. They took great pride in their work, which did not require any formal training, but demanded great stamina and dedication, and reflected their heritage. Occasionally I would spot an owl taking it all in, or a few local birds circling the skies, looking for fallen grapes in the vineyard, or picking off fruit from the trees in the abundant groves.

The main chateau was beyond belief, and with a bit of imagination one could visualize the grand lifestyles of the former owners. The large kitchens and dining areas, the sitting and music rooms, were majestic and spacious. The outside areas were not set up for entertaining, though there were several small verandas overlooking the vineyard, where the original occupants occasionally entertained friends over a meal, I was told.

My somewhat limited budget dictated that I occupy what one might now be classified as a youth hostel in other parts of Europe. The large former bedrooms now accommodated half a dozen or so bunk beds for those who traveled modestly. The communal bathrooms were located on the floor below, in areas that I surmised were the former living quarters of those who had worked the fields long ago.

I did get a view of the original owner's living quarters, whose furniture, paintings, light fixtures and wall coverings were strictly old school. The current owners, aristocratic Spaniards, were gracious transplants who enjoyed a glass of wine at the end of the day with the guests. Also, they dined in the old Spanish tradition, late in the evening, and kindly invited me and a few of the others to join them in the main dining room one evening for a late supper.

The room, the size of a football field, had very dark walls and a low ceiling with lit chandeliers. Pewter serving dishes, vintage china and silverware, brass candlesticks and numerous wine bottles filled the room. It was like something straight out of a museum, or like a room in Versailles.

Our host and his wife, standing to greet us, gave a brief description of the oil paintings on one wall. They depicted members of his family, whose jackets were decorated with numerous military medals. Like other members of his family, they had posed for hours on end so that their descendants could one day appreciate their contributions to humanity, if any.

On the other wall were the supposedly aristocratic members of the family, with the titles of duke, marquis, count and baron. Since I have been fooled over the years by people who have recently accumulated great wealth and status and displayed a similar array of oil portraits, which they in fact bought at estate auctions, I found it quite humorous to see this array of ancestors, though I never questioned them about it.

We were all seated around a large wooden table on wooden chairs, except for our hosts, who were at the far end of the table, which made conversation difficult. Our host was an intelligent man of means, a Prince Phillip look-alike, but with obviously far less standing in the world. Nevertheless, he treated us to an enjoyable evening.

Even though military portraits dominated the walls, it occurred to me that in other parts of the island, there were few signs of former occupations, such as that of General Franco. I don't recall seeing statues of fallen military heroes, except in places like Palmo, which had been conquered and lost several times. Between the courses of our meal, much wine flowed; the entree was a delicious roast pig. There was never a shortage of conversation. The host's generosity was complemented by his docile wife's beauty and her well-rehearsed accounts of the island's culture. The evening seemed to flow on for hours, and was well worth the price of admission.

The host and I seemed to bond while discussing world architecture, a part of which he was preserving here. He took great interest in my background in the real estate development field, and especially the Frank Lloyd Wright Pottery House that I built in Santa Fe in the mid-1980s. He was impressed when I told him it had been featured in *Architectural Digest,* which he knew to be one of the top architectural magazines in the world. He shared my view that when you put great time and effort into a residential project, often the commercial value of the finished product comes second to the pride you feel in your accomplishment.

This exquisite meal concluded sometime after 10:00, and we were all sated by the lively conversations we had enjoyed all evening. Rarely in one's travels does one have such a chance to enjoy the splendors of the past. The host couple had a few small children whom they home-schooled. Over dessert, the women of the household talked about their frequent trips to Barcelona and Madrid, where the shopping and the museums were top-notch; when they visited the city, they also made sure to visit their close friends and relatives, who were very dear to them.

Halfway through the dinner, though, the conversation turned, rather awkwardly, to the topic of the so-called "ugly American." I don't think their comments, which remained very diplomatic, were pointed in my direction, but it was abundantly clear that they were disdainful of Americans in general. Of course, on some level they were quite justified in their comments. They put forth the usual barbs and complaints–that our TV and movies were broadcast worldwide, that we had little knowledge or understanding of other cultures, our lack of history, our conspicuous consumption and overindulgent lifestyles, our indifference to learning foreign languages, our divorce rates, and children born out of wedlock, and so forth. Some of the comments were surely tongue-in-cheek, since I would bet the farm that the man of the house had a mistress, but fortunately this part of the conversation was short-lived, and did not seem aimed in my direction.

Interestingly enough, those who reside outside of Palma don't seem attached to the water, except for those who fish for a living. Those in Palma and on the nearby beaches on the southern end of the island are also dependent on the water, since there are many yacht harbors. In places like Calle Major, where high-rise buildings are abundant along the sandy beaches and vendors sell everything that people are willing to pay for, water is again what draws the tourists. Some of the rocky shorelines up island are ideal for those with a small dingy, who can make their way to shore from their yachts; the seclusion of these protected coves is unparalleled in most other parts of the world. Many of the locals I came across were quite weatherbeaten and wrinkled, a sign that Elizabeth Arden had not yet reached this remote part of the world.

Next I was off to the relatively flat open plains that are found in the interior portions of the island, along the northernmost coastline, whose plains are often nestled on the flatter slopes of the mountains that ring the interior. The villages are the way one would expect, with terraced homes built to afford a view of the flatlands--probably for security reasons. The narrow stone stairways provide access to the fertile fields below, and to the numerous cafes and open marketplaces. During the warmer parts of the day, there are few signs of humanity, except for a few shopkeepers standing guard at their doorways, hoping a small amount of business will find its way to their cash registers.

Often I would start the day with a cup of coffee in the town plaza, people-watching and taking note of the city's remarkable architecture. But by high noon, those serving the refreshments would move the chairs into the shade or inside of their establishments, preparing for the noontime meal, which would be followed by an afternoon siesta.

The whole ambiance of Mallorca lends itself to picnics and relaxed leisure activities. With ideal weather and a soft, cool ocean breeze, it's a place that soothes the senses. At the height of the day's heat, people take refuge under the shade from the groves. This imposed relaxation is a great way to just put on the brakes, as the mood dictates, and reflect on who you are, where you are headed, and why you are here. I have never fully understood why people do not take part more often in such secluded picnics; nowhere is it easier to satisfy your hunger and your spiritual needs, and to be in harmony with nature.. Here, as I sat on the jutting rocks, I was grateful to have been given many opportunities to travel to new places and to relax and enjoy life. I was reminded of the 46-foot Morgan I owned in the Carribean that sunk with Hurricane Hugo. Often I would sit on her bow, listening to the waves crash over the sides of her hull at anchor. The tranquility was so special, and my visit to Mallorca reminded me of those hazy days filled with rest and simplicity.

The abundance of delicious food and fine wine made my stay even more divine. Grilled fish, smoked meat, local cheeses and a bottle of white wine were daily pleasures. Even if the bread was days old and hard, it didn't matter, since the setting was so perfect. Going on an open-air picnic is one of the most civilized things a human being can do for himself, especially if he is with good company, but even if he is alone, as I often was. Sharing the scraps with the birds that normally found their pickings in the olive trees was great entertainment. How many people, I wondered, have never taken the time to spontaneously set up shop on some desolate mountaintop overlooking a large body of water, just letting the hours drift by? It is a most enjoyable way to satisfy your physical and spiritual needs.

Just filling one's lungs with the salt air flowing over the abundant orchards is enough to rekindle the spirit. Often, I did so in close proximity to the cattle that roamed the areas, penned in but not overly restricted. Somehow, these domesticated animals that were destined for slaughter seemed to have an almost perfect life, even if it was short-lived. I found myself dwelling a bit on the topic of reincarnation as I watched their carefree contentment. It seemed to me that if one could spend a great part of one's existence under these conditions, the finality of life would not be too hard to take.

Next I took a small diversionary road through a flat, marshy stretch known as Parc Natural De S'Albufera, an environmentally protected area where one could park and walk the well-marked trails, which were on the way to the great monastery, Monestir De Lluc. The wildlife was truly at home here, and the many species of birds numbered in the hundreds. The elegant herons were my favorites; many tourists and a few locals were picnicking along the dirt roads with binoculars and exotic bird guides, hoping to glimpse something special. In general, they were Europeans, since North Americans don't seem to value this kind of passtime as much as some of the older, more grounded cultures. Many of these visitors were on day trips, and had traveled here on bicycles from their overnight lodgings.

These protected areas are quite special, since they have all the ingredients for those who love to be in the moment, or in my case, to be alone and at peace with the birds that nest there. The freedom of movement that birds have is something that fascinates me, and I often wonder what kind of creature comforts they enjoy at the end of the day, when the sun sets. The Spoonbill is one of the species that favors these areas; apparently they migrate here from parts of southern Europe, their natural habitat having fallen to the wrecking ball. At first it is hard to spot their nests, but a German couple pointed out to me that all you have to do is look below the limbs of the trees and see the skeletal remains of the fish that those providing for the young chicks drop from the nests.

Once I knew the secret, I was amazed by the number of nests I could find. Most were empty, since the young birds had comfortably left their nests in this most protected of environments. You could walk around for a hour and find literally hundreds of nests, some quite large, the size of half a basketball; they were made mostly of interwoven tree twigs from the orchards. The German couple told me that often, birds come from dozens of countries to nest in these protected preserves, since they are only marginally drained for agricultural purposes, and so the mosquitos and other insects are in ample supply for the young chicks after they leave their nests.

Ducks were also prevalent, and I suppose some form of migrating geese generally stop here for a while. The larger nesting birds are also located here in the abundant forests that are just over the mountain edges on the northwest, leeward side of the mountain range, which provides ample shade and sun for the toddlers' physical and spiritual nourishment.

Even the vultures looked majestic in this environment. I think they are fascinating, despite their undeserved reputation for picking on the defenseless and on rotting corpses. Most people see them in a very negative light, but I view them as somewhat special. In my estimation, the way their digestive systems have been conditioned to do away with rotting flesh that we find obtrusive can be viewed as recycling personified.

There is a great colony of falcons from around the world here. The preserves, mostly located on the north end of the island, are known far and wide for their ideal breeding climate. It is a naturalist's dream to spend time here, where the balance of nature is held in check: birds, wild rabbits, squirrels, you name it, they all live in perfect harmony. There is no apparent starvation, no abusive pesticides, and no human intrusion. There is such equilibrium that, according to the German birdwatchers, the vultures are a declining population. The remarkable balance that has been achieved here was a nice thing to carry with me when I left the sanctuary.

At the end of that day, I found myself at a most unique momentary, a massive series of structures that were originally built in the mid-1600s, and added onto over several hundreds of years. In recent history, it was a place for those of the faith to be trained and schooled, as well as a retreat for the huge number of civilian pilgrims who flocked there. In past days, the momentary was known as the spiritual center of Mallorca, but currently it was more of a stark museum to the past: much of it was closed up, and hidden from human eyes.

It is hard not to think of the thousands of people who lived and toiled there over the centuries, even though much of the primitive furniture and household and field equipment has since been removed. For instance, I took a short tour through the kitchen, where you could visualize dozens upon dozens of cooks at any given time, as well as those who fed and rounded up the livestock, slaughtered the chickens and stoked the fires that cooked it all. Countless numbers must have washed the vegetables and fruits and the dinnerware afterwards, and scrubbed the floors. Then there were those who prayed or acted as scribes or religious instructors, not to mention those who sang and played musical instruments. Thousand must also have done the planting and the harvesting, and there must have been people whose job was to bury those who passed on. Then there were the leaders, those who made decisions for the people who followed their orders. It must have been quite an experience for those who dished out the discipline to ward off enemies, like Franco's fascist army, and to preserve and protect the unique lifestyle that had reigned here for so long.

And many came here on a pilgrimage, some wanting to face up to reality and others trying to shy away from it. It must have been like a giant university, with so many disciplines and opportunities for learning that evolved over the centuries. Today, the stone and red tile buildings where prayer and instruction once took place had been transformed into an extensive giftshop, or shut down for good.

No account of Mallorca is complete without a look at the seaside fishing villages, underwater grottos, and quaint coastal hamlets on the northwest side of the island. They remind one of the artists' communities of Europe in days gone by. Here, the traditions and customs of the old families are still firmly set in centuries-old stone.

Occasionally I would pass by a group of fishermen in the harborm either at anchor or at dockside tending to their nets. Nestled between a few foreign luxury yachts, they would often sell part of the day's catch to the cooking crews of their wealthier neighbours. Sometimes the yachts' crew just carried on a friendly conversation with the fishermen. Both had relaxed, leisurely lives and could afford to share some pleasantries at the end of the day.

Late in the afternoon, it was customary to patronize the small sidewalk cafes, where the movable tables, it seems, were set up literally on the streets, to accommodate all of those who wished to be part of the afternoon scene. As the evening progressed, those with parked cars, which were available for hire, were asked to move their vehicles so that more tables with their white linen tablecloths clothes could be added for the festivities. The growing number of tables added somehow to the excitement as everyone prepared for the evening's entertainment.

As the wine flowed and the sun set, the small streetlights would come on in the tiny winding streets. These lights are not terribly noticeable, but they brilliantly illuminated the dramatic, massive stone buildings that were found along the waters edge. All of this romanticism, with the salt water and the raw fish smells in the background, was absolutely captivating. The dreaminess of the evening was highlighted by the odor of the food being cooked just inside, the most desired dish being the famed lobster stew; everyone who comes to Mallorca is enchanted by the fresh fish, which is the best in the world.

Needless to say, it is the perfect opportunity for people-watching. People of all shapes, sizes and colors from all corners of the world are here to see and to be seen. Some are glamorous and sleek; others look as if they've spent too much time over the decades living the good life and indulging themselves at every turn.

And, when the dawn comes, the very same places open for coffee and sweets for breakfast. They are ready to accommodate the small groups of tourists before they take off for the day's sightseeing, which can include anything from exploring around the abandoned stone watch towers, whose altitudes provide an excellent view, to stopping ni at the dive shops and inquiring about some underwater adventure, such as snorkeling, in the numerous grottos along the coast line. All over the island, you see those enticing indented limestone rock formations, which look blue from the reflections off of the water.

Then there are the fish and vegetable markets that are patronized by the locals and the inquisitive tourists who are preparing for their outings and picnics on the bluffs that overlook these magnificent seaside fishing villages. Another great way to fully appreciate this thrilling landscape is to rent a horse, and ride to the highest mountain peaks, and then canter down to a secluded beach, savouring every bit of this once-in-a-lifetime experience.

I found it highly enjoyable merely to walk down the streets, and wander across the plazas, admiring the statues of mermaids and other creatures that seem quite disconnected from modern-day life. I puzzled about the various topics and figures that had been made into statues; I find myself wondering if these beings were part of the area's folklore, and had been important figures in Spanish legends and stories. Many of the statues had an aura of fantasy or magic, and it was extremely rare to see statues of military figures, left over from prior conquests. In this tranquil setting, the images were uplifting ones that startled the imagination. I found myself wondering why anyone in this part of the world, in this idyllic setting, would ever take up arms against another. The presence of citizens from dozens and dozens of countries in this area added to my impression of Mallorca as an enchanting place of peace, beauty, and mutual understanding.

I walked by many of the little arcades, which provide great relief from the heat. They are mostly Moorish in their facades, reflecting the original merchants who settled here, as well as in other parts of southern Europe.

There are dozens of these quaint fishing villages along the north and western edges of the island. One area I found quite attractive was Port de Soller, and its land-locked counterpart, Soller. Soller is a quaint little town nestled in a valley surrounded by mountains. The two cities are connected by a train or trolley called Red Arrow, which also travels further down to the capital city of Palma. I skipped the ride, but later found out it offered a breathtaking view of the island and the mountain ranges. The trolley gives one a great view of the port and the beaches, not to mention the town itself, and its interesting historic buildings.

I checked into my hotel, which was a paradore, the result of a unique program the Spanish government set up to convert older homes into small hotels. The government finances and manages the buildings for a few years, and sells them off once they become profitable. After checking in, making myself at home, and becoming familiar with my surroundings, I went for a stroll. I went past a few churches and a small cemetery surrounded by trees that were at least two hundred years old; I walked through old plazas with their fountains and endless statues, all surrounded by local old-timers, sitting on benches and having endless conversations, or feeding the numerous birds in the square. Before returning to the hotel, I stopped at a small tavern nearby for a nightcap.

It was a most unusual place. A television set was in the corner, and many were gathered around it, apparently watching a Spanish soap opera or a sitcom. The bar patrons were absolutely transfixed by the story. The women on the screen were yelling at each other; the men were shaking their fists and attempting to change the subject. No one was eating in the main part of the restaurant, with its countless wooden tables. Instead, everyone who was there was riveted to the television, enjoying a drink and making loud comments to one another about the story unfolding on the screen.

Later, I was to learn that television sets were very scarce in this little town. Only a few wealthy people owned them, so what I had witnessed was a popular form of communal entertainment. Not having much of an interest in television myself, and sensing that they found my presence a bit of an interruption, I quickly relocated to the small bar. I spent a short time by myself, until the owner's wife came over. We struck up a conversation with a combination of broken English and expressive hand signals.

She was quite large and jovial, as over-stuffed people can sometimes be; obviously, she was a by-product of her delicious cooking at the family restaurant. The husband, small, wiry, and subservient, was the type of man you would expect to find working in the fields. He had a ruddy complexion and a healthy look to him. He was perched in a chair on the other side of the room, dividing his eye contact between the television and our conversation.

You knew immediately who was in charge. As the sun started to set, she asked if I would like to see some of their family photographs and possibly join them for dinner in their private residence. Then she signaled to her husband and daughter to attend to those drinking around the television.

What transpired was magical.

We moved our wine glasses to a more private area outdoors, with little terraces were all around us; on these small plateaus, they harvested their limited wine selection. We sat among the lemon and orange trees with a few olive trees in the distance. Scattered in between were beds of rose bushes, potted flowers, and hedges of peonies–an abundance of flowers that stretched as far as the eye could see. It was like a brilliantly conducted orchestra that was designed to enchant the nostrils, and together the blooms produced one of the most beautiful aromas imaginable. The tinkling sound of water in the small fountains dotted with lily-pads went nicely with the sweet and pungent aroma. The wine we drank was right from their vineyard, and in the back room of their residence I could smell the flavor of roasted almonds, which they would be serving with dinner.

In the distance were footpaths to the fields and a small number of outbuildings where equipment, produce and grain was stored. These footpaths, I am sure, have never been touched by the tire of a motorized vehicle. There were a few stray dogs, but they kept to themselves; some goats grazing in the distance added to the bucolic setting.

Before too long, we got deep into conversation about the beauty of the place. The husband joined us grudgingly, perhaps out of curiosity, but certainly not out of affection for her. Interestingly enough, she never once mentioned his name, and always called him "husband," as if he were some old doormat that had worn out with time. I began calling him "husband" as well, for lack of a better way to address him. Her name she gave me at the bar; it was quite complicated and slipped away as the evening wore on. We did settle on Carlos for mine. The rest of the patrons and the assorted family members stayed in relative obscurity for the balance of the evening.

We moved into the private residence an hour or so, when we were ready to begin our meal, just as the sun began to set and the sky turned orangey-red over the foothills in the distance. A beautiful silence had set in, even though I was aware that in only a few short hours, it would be the start of a new day, and breakfast would have to be provided for the patrons. What a wonderful cycle existed here, I thought, with each day ending, so gently, only to give rise to the breaking of tomorrow, which was bound to be equally beautiful and serene.

As we passed through the Moorish wooden doorway, the grandchildren stood respectfully off to the side. After the owner's wife took me on a brief tour of the public areas of the home, which excluded the kitchen, she introduced me to her grandchildren. They had received their dinner earlier, I was told, and were now there to serve us and clean up. From time to time you could see one of them peek around the corner to catch a few words, or to catch a glimpse of me. It was rare for the family to have a foreigner for dinner, especially a writer from America, unknown to them, who was far from being internationally known.

We dined under a small chandelier overhead, certainly not the type you would find at Versailles. There were a few candles positioned on the sideboard tables, where the grandchildren set the warming dishes. We drank and talked animatedly about their productive vineyard. This family was old-school to say the least, not terribly wealthy or successful by western standards, but obviously part of the power structure of this community, and had been so for many generations.

"Husband" spoke no English and I had only rudimentary Spanish, so when he wanted to enter the conversation it was for a very short time. She would stare him down until he dropped his thoughts, and she would then carry on. I suspect this type of dialogue went on when others were also at the table. She was in charge, and he was content to work the fields, and to be fed and served wine by his grandchildren.

We had four separate courses of fresh fish, all announced in Spanish, and all served with a different vegetable, most of which, I assume, came from their garden. She bartered for the fish for her table and restaurant with products from her vineyard: the thirsty fisherman dropped fish on her doorstep in exchange for a few glasses of wine at the bar, she said. My guess is that the fishermen filled their bellies with alcohol, and then fabricated a story when they got home to their wives that the fishing wasn't too good that day. I got that impression from the good old boys' club sitting around the television. Clearly they went to the bar more often than they admitted, to themselves or to their families.

Everything, with the exception of the fish, was home-produced. The boiled eggs, with some great seasoning from the chicken coop, the eggplant and olives from the garden, the endless variety of greens, the stew with some of the fish mixed in–everything was delectable. The cheeses, possibly an issue from the goats in the distance, the onions and garlic, the fruit, the breads, everything she offered me was perfection itself. I would be as big as the side of a barn if I stayed there for a few months, just like the gracious lady who was my hostess. I guess husband was lucky to be able to work it all off during the day.

And so the evening progressed. I saw endless albums of photographs, special menus from the past, and wine labels from the vintage years that they and their customers had found extra special. We uncorked one bottle after another as the pictorial history unfolded. When I left, there was not a dry mouth at the table. As I walked back to the hotel, past the carts the vendors had abandoned until morning, I thought to myself how magical it was to have been part of this special place.

The following morning, I took a short drive to Jardines de Alfabis, an area where the Kings of Mallorca had once lived. Then I drove back to Palma, in all its glory and sophistication. I took my last looks at its great restaurants and art galleries, its magnificent harbor with mega-yachts from all over the world. Others will write about Palma, as it is a very special place. Most of my time in Mallorca was spent in the untouched, unspoiled areas, and it was downright magical.

CHEESEBURGER IN PARADISE

To really understand the mystique and the fascination of sailing, it is a good idea to consider the different types of people who fall in love with this unique pastime. Usually, they are adventurers who seek wide open spaces and unimpeded independence. The endless, majestic sea seems to be the magnet that attracts people like myself; the waves go on as far as the eye can see, meeting no boundaries, and recreate themselves in a new way, equally as exciting and challenging.

Some men spend their lives chasing rainbows, or experiencing life vicariously. The sailor, however, truly lives, thriving on every moment and every shift in the wind. Some suggest that this solitary lifestyle reflects the sailor's inability to deal with reality. Those of us who sail are, of course, thankful that such misconceptions exist; otherwise, our paradise might soon become overcrowded.

With that quick overture out of the way, it is now time to categorize those who find the great oceans so appealing and mesmerizing. Those who do tend to be obsessive when it comes to caring for—and paying to maintain—their varnished teak vessels, their expensive mechanical equipment, their sparkling chrome accents, their sails and ground tackle. Outsiders have likened sailing to standing in a cold shower and tearing up hundred-dollar bills, which in fact is not much of a stretch of the imagination.

In the course of my sailing adventures, I have encountered all kinds of characters. In a light-hearted way, I find that I can conveniently pigeonhole them into four distinct categories: the *thoroughbred yachtsman*, the *competitive racer*, the *sophisticated cruiser*, and the *free-spirit sailor*.

It is another breed altogether who owns power boats; I admit that I myself once had such a vessel, a 60-foot, mahogany-planked motor yacht of 1927 vintage, which I chartered for the America's Cup Races in San Diego. Elegant and sleek, it had special historical significance, having formerly been owned by Howard Hughes. Apart from enjoying that beautiful yacht, which I chartered for some eight years, I have never had the slightest desire to sit on a fan tail and smell the diesel discharges. In any event, those who take to this form of recreation have a different set of rules and budgets when it comes to fulfilling their fantasies, which I will leave to others to unravel.

The thoroughbred yachtsman dons his blue blazer for cocktails at any hour of the day or night. His caloric intake, be it liquid or solid, is served on silver platters by a crew that is not on a first-name basis with him. His yacht is fully crewed, spit-shined and mobile, and can be re-located to any port of call in the world that he desires. He has a cast of dozens beside those who reside aboard, who support his insatiable habit of conspicuous indulgence and consumption. It is a vast network that includes those who put the latest toys into his pipeline, manage a wide variety of social contacts that stem from his yacht club memberships, or arrange and maintain the vehicles that provide access to his floating world, such as the helicopters that land on the fan tail. These toys are designed to show his neighbors, be they floating or land-based, that he is a man of means, highly accomplished and wealthy. We all know the type, so any further explanation serves no purpose at this juncture.

The competitive racer is also a unique breed unto himself, and falls into a class similar to the thoroughbred yachtsman, except that he has first-hand knowledge of the massive inventory of winches, bags of sails, sophisticated rigging, ground tackle and the elaborate electronic navigational devices scattered all over his yacht. He, unlike the thoroughbred yachtsman, knows trivial facts like, for instance, how the shape and length of his hull combined with the configuration and the square footage of the sails determines the maximum speed of his toy.

He knows, and generally ignores, the cost of every improvement that will advance his standing among those he competes with, and continues to drain his checkbook in order to add half a knot to his toy's speed. Like many sailors, he tears up his hundred-dollar bills, even though he knows that his finely tuned racing machine might well be obsolete before the next race appears on the radar screen.

The thoroughbred yachtsman usually adorns the decks and cabins with attractive ladies, somewhat his junior, including women who pose as crew. Sometimes trophy wives are the order of the day as well, since they can help to showcase his ample success in the commercial world. The competitive racer, on the other hand, tends to pass up an occasional economic opportunity in the business world for the thrill of chasing the wind—and might even divorce his wife or send his squeeze packing if she gets in the way of his heart's desire.

The first two categories are not found in large numbers in the British Virgin Islands, where I recently enjoyed a week of sailing. They tend to stick to the rarefied atmosphere of the sailing world. So, it falls on the last two categories to define why water-loving people are drawn to the BVI, one of the most unique sailing paradises in the world.

The sophisticated cruiser is found at the helm, or once in a while in the engine room, or at the rigging, when events dictate that his expertise is required. More often than not, at day's end, he is tied up to a rented mooring close to the action on shore, and can recite, verbatim, the featured drinks and entrees of the numerous bars and restaurants clustered around the popular anchorages nearby. His sometimes oversized girth is often quite visible on some sandy beach, especially at nap-time; he preserves his energy for the upcoming "over the yard arm" cocktail hour, which he seldom misses. Generally self-sufficient, he needs no one to serve or pamper him, although that does not mean that he lives without his share of creature comforts.

He does not relish the idea of owning custom-designed yachts, which are not only expensive but have little resale value down the road. Instead, he opts for the molded fiberglass models, with hulls that are simple and time-tested and require little maintenance. He accepts whatever the manufactures put forward without much resistance, and in time makes minor modifications. Unlike the Racer, he likes the idea that his engine is a stock diesel; all he has to do is fine-tune a few things once in a while to get the much-needed satisfaction he expects from his toy.

He is traditionally a member of the upper-middle class, rather than one who has had to claw his way through their ranks to the top. He thrives on the ambition and the status symbols that go with this station in life. The Internet and high-speed computers allow him to sail to the places he desires without having to take time-consuming, irrelevant courses, in, say, celestial navigation. His dingy is expensive, clean and sleek, not ostentatious but a cut above the others, since his arrival or departure from the restaurants and bars must be conducted with a certain degree of style. After all, when he has just told, or is just about to tell, the onshore inhabitants all about his string of successful ventures, he can't be seen in an inferior light, or in a dinghy that is not of the highest quality. Of course, he needs an auto-pilot, so he can tell friends how simple the overnight passage was, and how he sipped Chardonnay as the moon and stars passed quietly overhead, and then slept below in total bliss.

He is generally a family man, or has close circle of friends or associates. Often he and his wife are both professionals, which tends to limit his water dreams, and thus he charters, not owns, the boat he is currently enjoying. He is one of the many men who have made this country great, and he realistically knows that he will soon have to return to work; once there, almost immediately he begins to plan the next trip, which is usually much the same as the last one. His relatively fixed time schedule provides little, if any, variation from the norm. Therefore, unlike the free-spirit sailor, he usually charts the entire voyage and anchorages long before leaving the dock.

The free spirit sailor is in a category of his own. Although I have repeatedly been exposed to the other types while sailing for several decades, the free-spirit sailors are the ones I can more easily relate to. For this was a lifestyle I myself embraced in my late teenage years, when I raced iceboats on the frozen lakes just west of Milwaukee with my high school friends. However, these were ordinary, relatively inexpensive toys, sailed under harsh and punishing conditions, needless to say for short durations. Not counting the ongoing maintenance costs, rarely were the stakes any higher than having to buy the first round of beer at the bar closest to the finish line.

In my estimation, the free spirit can not be pigeonholed, like the three others groups. Typically self-employed, he is oblivious to the concept of working 9 to 5. To outsiders, he has no professional or marketable ambitions, and yet nor does he seek charity or handouts, except for a drink or two or an occasional meal when the nautical company is right. He certainly feels no need to draw on the expertise of others when conditions are rough or equipment heads south.

He is comfortable with the idea that he has the capacity to deal with whatever comes along, a skill that comes in handy on the vast, sometimes troublesome oceans he traverses. Confident but very aware of the ocean's might and her changing moods, he is cautious, and always facing the wind, trying to get in tune with it.

You will seldom find his boat at the docks that charge an evening fee by the running foot, even though he may occasionally resort to them, if only to impress on a few well-endowed females the fact that his boat was too large for any of the available slips. He is at ease just on the edges of the other three groups, since for most, sailing is an adventure to be shared by all, regardless of one's pocketbook or status in life.

His personal freedom cannot be measured in terms of the almighty greenback. The free spirit decided against this long ago, a decision that becomes more irreversible and permanent with each passing year. His legacy will be measured terms of the adventures and the quality time he has enjoyed, rather than by the judgments of mainstream people; he cares very little about the length or readership of his down-the-road obituary.

These are the guys who don't count on year-end bonuses, stock options or expense accounts that go unmonitored by the corporate bean counters. More likely than not, this type sails on until becoming destitute, and when the day of financial reckoning comes, he grudgingly takes on menial jobs, not always associated with the sea, in order to prolong his dream, at least to the next horizon of freedom. Unlike the others, the free spirit has no fixed schedule and no need for Maalox; his chemical imbalance is often a result of liver deterioration caused by having too much free time, or too much time in association with those who often end up looking at the empty end of a whisky bottle.

They eventually reach a point of no return, and the ever-changing world of commerce becomes a mystery to them. The younger generation marches forward, developing skills not easily learned at North 18 degrees, 26 minutes, West 64 degrees 44 minutes. When that point of no return finally arrives, sometimes a personal fantasy or a deep-seated denial sets in. The free spirit consoles himself with the knowledge that the next batch of beautiful people and experiences is just beyond the next horizon, and that all is well.

In a way they are much like the land gypsies of old Europe, the Roma, whom I wrote about after visiting Granada, Spain, in my piece entitled *Forever Wild*. Both groups accept life and its twists and turns on their own terms, and don't care that mainstream society often looks the other way at their completely unstructured lifestyle. They rely on their charming personalities and their ability to captivate others with their music, storytelling or tales of over-the-horizon to get what they want. They are not parasites in the true sense of the word, but non-conformists whose vision for themselves is categorized by others as putting a square peg in a round hole. The free spirit thinks that eventually, his charm and wit will find him a younger female with whom he will sail off into the sunset; of course, her inexhaustible trust funds will be a cushion that takes them to any port of call of their choosing. It's an appealing dream, but one, as they find out in the long run, that seldom materializes.

So, with that brief introduction to the different types of sailors, let me tell you about my latest sailing adventure in the British Virgin Islands (BVI).

Our crew of seven sailed from the docks in Tortola three days after Christmas 2005, leaving from the massive Moorings charter operation. We had provisioned and received briefings on how to handle our yacht the evening before. After dodging a few channel marker buoys on the way out, we finally got the chance to inhale the fresh air and look at the sunny out-islands in the distance.

The BVI is a place where the free-spirit sailor and the cruiser mentality merge. In this environment that, bar none, is one of the most fabulous recreational sailing waters of the world, both the experienced sailor and the novice have the opportunity to traverse thirty or so islands that effectively shield them from harm's way. Besides the spiritual experience associated with sailing, many are drawn here because they can move around with relatively uncomplicated, high-tech global satellite systems of navigation, thus indicating to the inexperienced, within a hundred feet or so, where they are in relation to their projected destination.

Although real dangers always exist on the sea, those sailing in the BVI feel quite secure, and can relax and enjoy the consistently warm, dry weather and the fabulous, ever-changing water, which shifts from midnight blue to turquoise as one moves from the coral reefs into shallow, sandy water. These hues seem specially coordinated with the sky, which is by turns sunny and cloud-covered, or occasionally flooded with moonlight, on evenings when the heavens open up their magnificent theater to those who simply want to stargaze and forget about the civilized world, and the umbilical cords, like family responsibilities or business connections that tie us to reality.

And if that is not enough of a diversion, every once in a while one can drop anchor and set foot on shore, tip-toeing through the soft, sugar-sand beaches, as we did late one morning at The Baths, a snorkeling haven on a relatively uninhabited island. Anchorages are available, though not overnight ones, since the beach area is relatively unprotected from tides and winds.

After the experience of diving in and around the caves, my mind turned to a book I read several years ago, *The Barefoot Mailman*, which tells the story of those who delivered the mail in South Florida before roads were constructed between Palm Beach and Miami. I was able to block out all the people who had accumulated near the dive site, and imagine what it was like for the mailmen, walking the beaches day in and day out and earning a reasonable living before the development came.

The landscape in the BVI is unusual, in that most of the island formations resulted from volcanic activity; the black residue was ground into white powder by the action of the waves over millions of years. Some of the islands are covered with a green blanket, mostly low to the ground, and capped by a never-ending series of white clouds that eventually turn to gray, producing the necessary fresh water that the islanders depend on.

Others islands are dry and windswept, almost desert-like in nature, which seems odd since they are totally surrounded by ocean. Many are populated with cactus and other dry, small forms of foliage. The nearby coral reefs are loaded with colorful tropical fish. The trade winds are predictable from the northeast, averaging about 15 knots, which allows one to traverse the islands without using one's power plant. The temperatures, equally predictable, are in the mid to high 70s with the humidity in the 60 % range, providing a great deal of moisture to the skin that offsets the dryness associated with the direct sun.

Our voyage was a family affair, a way to celebrate the new year with my younger brother, John, most of his family, and my sometimes-traveling companion, Judy. For the occasion, he rented a 47- foot sailing catamaran, designed and built in South Africa. Drawing only slightly more than four feet, and being 24 feet in width, it contained four sleeping compartments, each with a shower and toilet, plus an elevated cabin housing an ample kitchen and indoor and outdoor dining facilities. The larger classes of sailing catamarans have recently taken over the charter fleet in these islands since they are not only spacious, but ride smoothly, especially into the wind. The structure is such that the boat seldom heels or tips like the traditional monohull, providing a unique, safe, and comfortable experience on the water.

To boot, they are equipped with a generator and are fully air-conditioned, which makes sleeping a joy when one is anchored in a small cove where the cooling winds and ventilation are minimal. There was also a first-rate stereo system, with speakers below and on deck, enabling us to pass the daylight and evening hours listening to steel drum or calypso music, some of which was gathered in past trips John and his family made to the islands. For them it has become a favorite family vacation that gets repeated over and over again with only slight variations.

What makes sailing so special here is the fact that many of the British Virgins run horizontally close to each other, extending east to west and forming an almost perfect pocket through which one can sail without ever having to take on the unprotected waters of the Atlantic Ocean or the Caribbean Sea. This inside body of water, known as the Sir Francis Drake Channel, offers the creature comforts associated with relatively flat seas, combined with the feeling that one is indeed on an ocean crossing of some sort. Being tucked into this unique land mass, about 40 miles long and 10 miles across, offers the best of both worlds: blue water, somewhat flat ocean sailing, and the ability to island-hop at the drop of a hat.

The BVI have a diverse history. Occupied over the years by the Spanish, Dutch, French, and Danish, they were finally sold to the British. Originally they were the stopping-off point for the swashbuckling pirates like Blackbeard, who would attack the Spanish galleons returning to the mother country laden with gold. This lifestyle and mentality influenced Robert Louis Stevenson to write *Treasure Island*. In those days, many of the cities with deep harbors were packed with bars and houses of ill repute, and served as an outlet in which pirates unloaded their ill-gotten booty in exchange for the pleasures of the flesh.

Today, the same pirate mentality exists. But those same harbors have been deepened to accommodate massive cruse ships packed with thousands of tourists. They, too, are also seeking booty, and make the most of the islands' duty-free status; the credit card has replaced the sword, and shopping is one of the main rituals of the land experience. I, for instance, purchased a one-liter bottle of Johnnie Walker Red for $11 dollars, about half of what it would cost in the States, and was struck by how silly it was for our society to levy such great "sin taxes" against us.

It can be about as ugly a sight as one can imagine when these cruise ships unload their overweight, over-aged, pear-shaped, wrinkled, hunched over characters on land. They descend the gangplanks like bees leaving a hive and, plastic in hand, seek the queen bee of bargains. As if sucked up by a huge vacuum cleaner, the masses are propelled towards the taxis waiting nearby, which take them to the shopping areas. Tiny, sleepy towns are instantly transformed into major centers of "trinket" commerce. For a brief time, the harbor is turned upside down: gone are the sweet smells of ocean breeze. Instead, dilapidated cars whose owners have ignored the environmental protection laws for years trail fumes behind them, rushing tourists towards the next shopping area.

The local strays, the dogs and chickens, duck for cover as they, for a short period of time, must give up the right of way to those with a different agenda. This free-for-all must remind those watching from the sidelines of a smaller version of Black Friday in the States, the notorious day after Thanksgiving where shoppers practically slit each other's throats on their way to the booty, just like the pirates of old did here.

I found the cabbies just as rude and pushy here as they are in New York. Respect for past traditions and heritage turns to indifference and flies out of their windows as foreign credit cards arrive en masse. I would guess that the shelves in the stores are most likely emptied in short order, only to be restocked by more Made in

China goods before the next morning's onslaught; I never entered to find out.

We met and conversed with two of these crazed shoppers on one of the ferries that interconnect many of the islands. Like many, they were still working off last evening's hangover, recharging themselves by power shopping and occasionally having a bit of the hair of the dog to nurse themselves back to reasonable health. The contagious "shop til you drop" mentality seemed to run aground after several rum concoctions, paving the way for an afternoon nap, after which they were ready to start the degenerative process all over again.

Who benefits most from this commercialization? The local blacks have shifted their livelihood from the sugar and cotton plantations of old to tourism, but still look as poor as church mice, reflecting the seasonal, temporary nature of the tourist influx. They seem trapped with a glass ceiling over their heads, unable to move upward, especially as the tourist industry grows; they rarely own the tourist facilities and venues, and instead are offered menial service jobs.

Since almost everything here is imported, the locals are at the mercy of merchants who cater to the wealthy. But on some of the more remote islands, like Jost Van Dyke, the locals seem to benefit directly from the fruits of their labor. When the plantations dwindled, the European owners moved on to bigger and better things, leaving the land as well as its perceived ownership to those who had worked it and been enslaved on it. However, as the larger islands with deep ports and pristine beaches caught on with the sailing crowd, those with birthright found that they did not have the tiger by the tail: they had no legitimate title to the land, which was quickly becoming a valuable holding of multinational corporations and well-heeled individuals.

Nevertheless, the true sailing crowd bypasses the commercial areas described in the dozens of tourist books that constantly rate the islands' hot spots. Still, on our first day out, we ventured to one of these trendy hangouts, Cane Garden Bay, on the northwest end of

Tortola. We tied up to a mooring early in the afternoon and enjoyed some trusty Jamaican Red Stripe Beer, famous among the sailing community as a "docking drink." We then spent the latter part of the day snorkeling, snacking and cocktailing, either on the protected back deck or on the sunny trampoline on the fore deck, and anticipating the big fling we would have the following evening, New Year's Eve, at Foxy's.

It was a delightful evening. As the sun set, we watched the trade winds bend the coconut palms as we replenished our rum or tequila-based drinks, mixed in a rented blender. When the mood changed, we switched to the various wines we had purchased the day before on Tortola. Along the way, we grazed on hors d'oeuvres as we listened to the faint sound of the waves breaking over the reef.

After sunset we went ashore for dinner, and ended up at a beach bar, Quito's Gazebo, whose steel drum music kept the atmosphere lively. We had several tapes of Quito, obtained in prior visits, and had listened to them on the way over. His Caribbean music was spectacular, and we danced all night, all the while enjoying the islands' trademark drink, the painkiller: two parts rum, one part coconut, orange and pineapple juice, with nutmeg on top. Quito, famous throughout the islands as a songwriter and entertainer, has a way of creating music whose beat gets right into the rhythms of your circulatory system as the evening goes on.

The following morning we were awakened by the smell of freshly brewed coffee, and a soft, sweet-smelling wind that told us it was time to move on in search of Foxy's Tamarind Bar. An hour later we found ourselves looking for a mooring at one of the two protected locations at Jost Van Dyke, a small island named after a Dutch pirate. We tied up at Small Harbor in the late morning and found it to be a gem of a place.

Main Harbor and its commercial district, if one can call it that, was a short distance away, and had none of the big-name resorts, restaurants, or shopping areas so prevalent at the other popular stopping-off points. Just six bars, a boarding house with five rooms, and a bunch of dogs and chickens that seemed unaffected by all the activity. In fact, the entire commercial district, completely unspoiled, is only a quarter of a mile long and 50 feet wide, and looks like something out of a Chamber of Commerce advertisement.

The whole strip consists of fun-filled bars along the one-lane road that goes through the district, parallel to the white sugar-sand beaches dotted with sunbathers. The cars seem old and unreliable, and the few local water craft lining the beach are in great disrepair as well. Many are no longer seaworthy a result of neglect or obsolescence; one explanation for this sad phenomenon is that years ago, the Japanese stripped the waters of the once-abundant fish that either migrated or were indigenous to the area.

We were told that boat-building, as it pertained to small fishing vessels, was once a way of life here. Builders using hand-me-down techniques and tools would cut down and shape wood taken from the island's forests, which they had soaked in salt water to cure it from cracking. In the old days, we heard, great celebrations would take place when a new boat was launched; today, this legacy is barely remembered, as one looks at the derelict boats that were yesterday's dreams.

The laidback nature of the island is seen in the carefree way people meander about, mingling with the large population of stray chickens and dogs. There's no such thing as a purebred dog on Jost, and even the humans seem to be part and parcel of other eras. We pass a small cemetery, sandwiched between two small huts, with several large concrete caskets protruding above ground. One doesn't ask why, but presumes that the caskets are either a sign of affluence, or designed to weather a high tide that might very well wash all the other remaining parts of the inhabitants out to sea. Life goes on here without much hardship. The islanders go about their business as they have done for generations, performing menial tasks and errands with a smile attached to their faces.

Jost Van Dyke is world famous with the sailing crowd, not so much for its anchorages or snorkeling, but for a local saloon,

Foxy's Tamarind Bar, a watering hole that has grown in a haphazard fashion over the years into a major institution patronized by those who follow the wind. With time it has taken on an identity of its own, even though it is nothing more than a series of buildings with sand floors and tattered corrugated metal canopies. It's the perfect backdrop for those, that serves as a backdrop for those who want to partake of the local grog and listen to Foxy play his guitar and tell stories of his adventures.

About as unique as they come, Foxy could easily pass for a homeless man in any of our large urban areas. His last name is Callwood, and his family has been there since the days of slavery. He is typical West Indian; he wears his hair in dreads and seems to have not a drop of Caucasian blood in his veins. Many, including himself, refer to him as the West Indies "Renaissance Man," and the title has some merit, given the influence he has on the island, its inhabitants and the environment, which he strives to protect.

He is an institution within the sailing community, and almost anybody who considers himself a blue-water sailor eventually finds his way to Foxy's on New Year's Eve. This year, some two thousand people had made the pilgrimage. The beach and the piers along the waterfront managed to handle the overflow. Most people arrive as the night proceeds, drifting in and out of this open-air "theater of the absurd," as a non-sailor might call it. The upper floor offers a pricey lobster dinner, but most patronize the abundant barbeque stands on the beach. But one's appetite is not the main reason to be here: people come so that they can say they have been to Foxy's on New Year's Eve.

The majority arrive by dinghy, though we came by taxi. Most anchor out in the three harbors on the southern side of the island. When the obvious anchorages are taken, the boats raft up to each other, adding to the party scene and all but eliminating any element of privacy, especially in Main Harbor. As the bewitching hour arrives, hundreds upon hundreds of dinghies are pulled up onto the beaches; the next wave of arrivals must raft up to those on shore, in the open water, making it a bit challenging when it's time to go home. You often have to step from one dinghy to another until you reach your own craft. If this isn't complicated enough, most of the dinghies are from the few recognized charter fleets, and are almost identical. And, as more and more landing craft arrive, the configuration of where one's boat should be changes, with the new arrivals and shifting currents. So, after the festivities are over, finding one's ride home becomes problematic at best, and is further complicated by the evening's worth of rum-based concoctions,

Foxy is notorious for several things. He bills himself as the laziest man in the world, and if you look at his somewhat sagging physique and demeanor, you will understand why. He is shaped somewhat like a balloon that has lost some of its air and shrunk down some. He sports a head and face full of unkempt hair and has very few teeth, though he smiles constantly. A funny but unsophisticated storyteller, a third-world philosopher, a peerless stand-up comedian, he is a living legend among the yachting community.

Rumor has it that he reads *The New York Times* daily and through its content, concocts his stories about the ultimate fate of humanity. And all this nonsense, of course, he sets to music. He takes a witty, current-affairs approach to storytelling, and adds in his mesmerizing musical beat. Foxy is also known as one of the sponsors of Jost's Wooden Boat Regatta, which has been going on for twenty years, and attracts vintage yachts and their skippers from around the world.

Over the years he has built the largest waterfront "sandbox" saloon in the Caribbean, not to mention the adjoining T-shirt store that is a virtual gold mine, since no one can leave Foxy's without a cap, postcard or T-shirt that commemorates the experience. I, like the rest of his newly found disciples, stood in line for my one-size-fits-all shirt, likely made by political prisoners from China for a fraction of what he gets for them. Just ahead in the queue was a German man and his Asian wife, who managed to run up over $400 on their credit card.

Foxy has built up a lucrative enterprise here, and it's a real departure from the other 150 or so inhabitants of the island, who don't seem to share his entrepreneurial spirit. Most owe their existence, in large part, to the drawing power of Foxy's saloon. The locals, said to be the friendliest people in the Caribbean, not only idolize the man, but take great pride in their mostly-native-owned island.

Foxy usually sits on his perch overlooking the front part of the bar, guitar in hand and sipping a Tennant's Stout. He spins tales and smiles to all who parade past, and his tip jar always seems full. His style of music defies definition. Here is a man who clearly did not graduate from Juliard; as a matter of fact, he has no sense of rhythm or even continuity as his repertoire unfolds. No advance preparation is evident as he just rambles on about whatever comes into his mind, his West Indian accent as difficult to understand as his music.

The whole party scene takes on a life of its own, especially on New Year' Eve, and Foxy's arrival in the early afternoon gets the ball rolling. I exchanged a few pleasantries over a dreadful Margarita as Foxy babbled on, accompanied by a few occasional guitar chords when he wanted to emphasize a point, or make the crowd laugh a bit. This guy could clean up his act a bit, and could certainly take a few lessons from Jimmy Buffett, the other great Caribbean entertainer whose song *Cheeseburger In Paradise* is so famous. Foxy told a long, rather tedious story about how he had traveled the world in search of a wife. As he tells it, he was God's gift to women, and he methodically eliminated women from various countries around the globe. The party began at 11:00 am and continued, for some, until sunrise the following morning.

Because of the sheer numbers of those present, most of us were eliminated from the pricy seats assigned to those who wanted to be ringside. I for one passed when I saw the meat that was to be served that evening sitting in plastic containers in the hot sun for part of the afternoon, waiting for the cooks to arrive. But regardless of whether one was on the inside looking out, or on the outside looking in, the merriment was as good as it gets. The starlit evening and the second-rate fireworks ushering in the new year were well worth the trip.

Foxy's was not without its antics that night. As the evening wore on, a certain corner of the saloon was taken over by those who felt the need to lubricate the tables with beer, enabling them, with a running start, to slide across the surface on their stomachs. As they got more and more proficient at this pastime, they simply added more tables to the event. Our Homeland Security could not have orchestrated a safer activity, even though the island's police force consisted of a single man in uniform, and an unintimidating one at that.

I assume that Foxy's does not jump like this all the time. We were told that usually there are about twenty boats anchored off the island, with a dozen or so people coming ashore to frequent the five other bars along the sandy strip. On the off days, Foxy stays home, and only comes in when a cash-paying customer sits down at the bar. At these times, he mysteriously appears at his perch and the show goes on. Otherwise, things can be quiet, with only locals patronizing his place. On New Year's Eve alone, it is the place to be, and to be seen by the upscale yachting community; believe me, they were all accounted for and standing at attention for the big event.

Foxy's offbeat and incoherent style is what makes him so loveable, at least to his fans. His funny demeanor and lack of appreciable talent is part of the attraction; somehow he makes everyone in the audience, after a few minutes, think that they, too, have a shot at becoming a musical star. Foxy also bills himself as the funniest man on the islands. I would vote for him being one of the laziest, but whatever you want to say about Foxy, he always turns the tensions and turmoil of life into good and happy stories.

I was told that he often talks about his dog, who generally lies under a table here. The conversation goes something like this. "Can anybody tell me what type of dog this is?" After a few people take a guess, he says, "You're all wrong—he's a pure 'island dog,'" and of course people wonder what type of breed that is. Foxy goes on to explain that there are "three characteristics of an island dog... the dog is black, lies around on his ass all day, and doesn't know who his father is." It sounds a bit silly, but that is typical Foxy. After a few drinks, it becomes hilarious, I was told. In any other setting in the civilized world, Foxy would be playing for pocket change on the streets of New York. But here, he is king of the hill.

A few of the non-sailing crowd have darkened his doorstep. The likes of James Mitchener, Burt Langcaster and John Travolta are featured in pictures on the walls, but mostly he is a "sailor's man" who loves life and refuses to grow up, and finds plenty of company in the sailing community.

The island of Jost Van Dyke is a joy to behold. Not only are the people friendly and accommodating but the fact that the westernized form of commercialization has not set in is refreshing. According to a local guide book, there are only 18 students in the entire school system, suggesting that the islanders are not exactly marching towards the world of high technology with lightning speed. For most inhabitants, the island provides for their basic needs, and in return they treat visitors with respect. This is something that doesn't happen in some other parts of the Caribbean, especially in the American Virgin Islands. Unlike the other islands that prey on the tourist dollar, here the warmth of the people is not motivated by wringing the last few dollars out of one's credit card. The have an unhurried friendlessness that adds a sense of sincerity to the whole island.

The locals are tremendously proud of their heritage. They made the transition away from agriculture in the mid to late 1800s when the last of the plantations, owned by Quakers, fell on hard times. In many instances the land was left to the local black slaves who had previously worked on the land, and they supplemented their income by fishing. It is said that during the Quaker period they tasted the bitterness of not controlling their own destiny, so when the transition came, they took hold of things and have not relinquished them since. Each subsequent generation has refused to sell their real estate holdings to the highest bidder. However, the island is not without its problems. We attempted to fill our onboard water tanks and were informed that the water plant had been down for a week, and no date for reopening had been targetted.

We found a mooring on New Year's Eve at Little Harbor, a place some five miles away from Great Harbor, where Foxy's is located, that hasn't changed much in the last half century. We partied at a small bar/restaurant owned by Cynthia and her mother. Cynthia Harris, as black as the ace of spades, is a true delight. She is a very effective salesperson for her restaurant, a bit on the pushy side when she doesn't get her own way, but nevertheless fun to be around. They have owned Harris' Place for the last thirty years, so we sat through more than our share of interesting island stories as we dined in preparation for being at Foxy's at the appointed time for the New Year's Eve celebration

During the meal, the seven of us who had made the trip did the traditional T-shirt signing, using one of my shirts that everybody felt had seen better days. The theme of the inscription centered around the University of California football team, where my nephew, Johnnie, played center linebacker. His wife did the honors in constructing a theme based on the fun that the entire family had over the years watching the Cal games. The rest of us wrote something silly on it. It was passed around several times, and a new idea emerged with each subsequent glass of wine.

After leaving a wide assortment of "dead solders"—red and white wine bottles—on the far end of the table, we folded up our masterpiece and signed off on the shirt as the "inebriated crew of the *Queenie,*" and took off to Foxy's to hang it with the thousands of others that have accumulated there over the last thirty years. Following the tradition, we stapled it to the rafters on the ceiling for posterity's sake.

The trip by taxi to Foxy's was an experience in itself. Taxis here are glorified pickup trucks with a three seat box inserted into the truck bed, designed to accommodate nine or ten passengers in relative comfort. The drivers are all macho, to say the least, and were desperately needing to show off their high-speed driving talents on this, the last day of the year. NASCAR drivers could have taken a few pointers from the way they cut in and out of traffic, somehow missing other passing automobiles on a road that was a lane and a half at best.

Cynthia arranged our ride with a friend who owned a taxi company. As it turned out, this single road to Great Harbor had once been a goat path, and was widened and paved as Foxy's became better known. Since the road was extremely narrow and there were virtually no road shoulders, one vehicle had to pull over to the side to enable another one to pass. Had anyone gone off the road, it would have been a straight shot down to the Atlantic Ocean.

Somehow, those who navigate these roads must have an implied understanding of the right of way accorded each other, just as boaters do. In any event it was a harrowing experience, to say the least. In the end, the whole evening was special and memorable, shared with thousands of relatively sophisticated people in a markedly unsophisticated place. It was not the booze-guzzling, woman-chasing crowd that you might imagine would gather here, even though some people of that ilk were present. Overall, the visitors were a polite, inebriated, happy-go-lucky bunch who enjoyed the sailing lifestyle.

After ushering in the new year in style, we splintered off in different ways. John and Chris, his wife, and their son and daughter-in-law chose to enjoy some chilled wine and the solitude of Cynthia's front deck. Judy and I watched the clock turn on Foxy's dinghy dock, watching the masses of humanity, in different sizes and shapes, participating in this multinational free-for-all. Karissa, John and Chris' oldest, being part of the younger generation, sought and found those of her ilk at the party scene, and occasionally crossed paths with me and Judy as the evening wore on. The bottom line is that Foxy has created a multi-generational, multicultural experience that should be taken in at least once in a lifetime by those who worship sailing.

As the sun rose on the first day of the new year, we counted our ranks in preparation for casting off, only to discover that Karissa was nowhere to be found. We delayed our departure from Jost to seek out our lost crew member, who conveniently waved to us from Cynthia's saloon about the time we were finishing our second cup of coffee. We dispatched the dinghy to fetch her and learned that Cynthia, also, was a short-term casualty of the night before, and was folded into a pretzel-like position and sprawled over two chairs in the main salon of her dining room, which looked as if Hurricane Katrina had just hit.

With Karissa now in tow, we decided not to further delay our departure by going to wish Cynthia a belated happy new year. So, we left her to her apparent bliss, and cut loose our mooring lines in anticipation of a difficult beat into the weather that would take us to the island of Virgin Gorda, and the Bitter End Yacht Club, where we found a slip with all the creature comforts. We used the "iron jennies," or the diesels, as the sailors call them, the entire distance, about five hours, and once secure at dockside, we were again ready for the festivities, which now included a complementary reception at the yacht club.

On the way up, we encountered 15-mile-per-hour headwinds and three to five-foot waves most of the way. The noise of the waves slapping against the fiberglass hull had the ladies aboard a bit nervous, but these charter vessels are designed to withstand great punishment. Some of us took extended naps on the way up, in anticipation of further partying. The one inconvenience of the trip was the fact the hatches in the forward cabins had not been secured, so the mattresses were soaked throughout, causing some discomfort that evening.

We passed several out-islands with uninspiring names like Great Dog, Cockroach, and Beef and Mosquito Island. Needless to say, they fell into the current to our stern without much fanfare as we motored toward Bitter End.

As much as Jost was a "free spirit" type of island, Virgin Gorda is a cruiser's haven. As you approach, you can just imagine the eyes of the luxury hotel owners and the restauranteurs lighting up when they see you. It's a place of pina colladas, margaritas, and steel drums, and we partook of all of these. To the true sailor, balance is necessary between the solitude of the great oceans and the madness of the shore activities, and Bitter End well understood the sailors' need for entertainment and socializing.

Bitter End and Peter Island are what the upscale sailing community craves and finds in the BVI. Manicured grounds, pristine beaches and fresh-water swimming pools abound; there are beach massages and other pampering treatments, as well as an assortment of upscale gift shops which the ladies always make their first priority as the men make the dinner reservations, pay the mooring fees, and check on the bowl game TV schedules, all the time sampling the local Bloody Marys or rum-based specialty drinks. People from all over the world flock to places like this. Many Europeans, especially Germans, are found at the cocktail tables and bars at Bitter End. At times their accents seem as heavy as their bar tabs. But here there are no shattered dreams of what cruising is all about; it's the closest you can get to the freedom of movement that sailing represents. It's an environment where fantasy and reality truly merge, a place of sheer relaxation that is as carefree as it gets.

The complementary cocktail party featured fabulous hors d'oeuvres by the Bitter End Yacht Club, as well as rum concoctions and steel drum music. It was non-stop fun; many were awarded "repeater" T-shirts, indicating that they had been here in the past. This broke down social barriers and made the introductions easier. I met an interesting man named Guggenheim, which I wrongly assumed was from the New York museum family. I started rambling on about Frank Lloyd Wright, who designed that museum in the 40s, stressing my association with Wright's architectural group when I purchased his unbuilt plans, which permitted me to construct his only adobe designed house in Santa Fe in the mid-1980s. Midway through my pitch, he informed me that he was not of the famous Guggenheim clan, but that he owned twelve remote parking lot locations connected to some of the major airports in the U.S. Nevertheless, we had a grand talk, mostly about sailing the islands, and then parted company for dinner.

The BVI attracts some of the most interesting characters in the world, and even though many come here to escape, some are anything but low-key. Take, for instance, Richard Branson, of Virgin Airlines fame. His private island, Necker, is within eyesight of Bitter End, and can be rented by you and 25 of your closest friends for a modest $42,000 per evening. I must say, it looked great from a distance.

As if Branson's pad was not enough, at dockside, our modest 47' toy *Queenie* was sandwiched in between two mega-yachts, worth well over $10 million a piece. Crew members attended to the every need of the thoroughbred yachtsman and their guests. Constantly in movement, they served drinks and meals, polished the hull and rearranged the water toys for easy access, always keeping just out of the owners' line of vision. Whatever other pampering they got, we were not privy to, as often this closed world is not unveiled to outsiders. But we lived the "Life of Riley" anyway, even though we fixed our own cocktails, cleaned up the cabins and carried the morning trash out to the end of the dock.

Next came Day 5 of 7. We backed out of the slip and slithered by the big boys on both sides, on the way to Cooper Island. Once outside of the harbor at Bitter End, we anxiously dodged the killer reefs that the Virgin Gorda Islands are so well known for; fortunately, they are well marked, and detectable with our navigational equipment. Most sat on the front deck and sunned themselves as John and I monitored the jib during the down wind reach and kept a steady eye on the G.P.S. tracking system. We ran the diesels steady at about 2000 RPM so we could hasten our arrival at an intermediate stop at the Baths.

On that leg, the first downwind one, we found the wind conditions were not the only things we had to contend with: the currents, less obvious to the untrained eye, altered our course substantially. As it turns out, the narrow channel that separates the string of horizontal islands accelerates the currents as they rebound off the opposing shorelines. Combine that with the ever- shifting northeast winds tunneling through the land masses along the route, and you find a challenge not found in any inland, fresh-water sailing.

These irregularities are normally quite easy to correct, with all the sophisticated navigational equipment installed on these charter vessels, so we never faced a life-threatening situation. Generally, my nephew Johnnie worked the ground tackle, winches, anchor and mooring lines, and John and I traded off at the helm of our catamaran. The ladies did light housekeeping and fixed lunches, which often consisted of a tuna melt on an English muffin.

Given the safety of these protected waters, many "bare-boat charter," which means they cruise the islands without a licensed, professional captain. These sailors are largely inexperienced, but have convinced themselves that they can manage on their own, and wish to avoid any intrusion on their freedom and solitude. There is an old saying on the high seas that applies to independent charter captains: If one senses friction on shore, it will multiply at sea. Many of the charter captains are natives of the islands and have developed attitude problems towards those who come from environments where things are so plentiful. Envy often becomes the licensed captain's own worst enemy, something I have seen over the years in my charter experiences both here, in the Leeward Islands, and in the Windwards, south of here.

As an example, I had the misfortune of hiring a captain on a 46-foot Morgan sailing vessel that my brother John and I owned and leased to the Moorings Charter Group for five years in the early 1980s. It was located in St. Lucia, where wide open, rough, sailing is the order of the day, and demands a captain, unlike here. In those waters a mistake could be life-threatening, and a captain was a must. We used a Jamaican captain, but this turned out to be an unpleasant experience; any form of compromise in terms of our sailing activities was not an option, at least in his mind.

I have never taken one on since. Even late at night, the captain insisted on taking the dinghy ashore. He would go into the foothills and participate in strange island music that we could hear from the

anchorage. We were later told that they were practicing some form
of Voodoo. In any event, often the two cultures don't mix. I and
many others just hope that these types, and they are quite abundant
in the islands, keep their footings on dry land.

On the way to the anchorage at Cooper Island, we stopped for an
hour of snorkeling at the Baths, where giant granite boulders offer
underwater caves unlike any other in the Caribbean. Scientists say
that this uniqueness is a result of the last Ice Age. In any event, the
Baths, while difficult to enjoy for long events of time because it is
so crowded, is a remarkable place to snorkel.

Cooper Island, a natural stopping-off place for those heading to
Peter Island, was our next destination, and it was our last evening
aboard. Time on Cooper seems to stand still. The gulls soared
overhead as we snorkeled below, watching a turtle feed off the sea
grass. On shore, we talked with a woman at the dive shop who had
found two baby turtles, less than a day old, which somehow had
become disoriented after they hatched, and had gone inland rather
than heading out to sea with the others. She showed us these tiny,
helpless creatures, which she planned to take to the island's marine
conservation station.

Cooper, a newly developed mooring area, is controlled by one
family with a small hotel and a not-too-fancy restaurant and beach
bar. Here, fresh food is hard to come by, except fish; most items,
shipped in from the U.S. or Mexico, have to be imported by the
ferry boats that ply the islands. The owners installed 40 mooring
balls, which usually filled up before sunset, so we arrived in time
to get one close to shore. Moorings are a necessity there, since the
currents and winds shift often and can drag an anchor off its
setting.

We spent the next day at Peter Island, a short hour-and-a-half sail
from Cooper. This stopping-off point it is typical of what money
can buy. The island was purchased forty years ago by the two
brothers who started Amway, and they have kept it relatively
uninhabited since then, except for their exclusive hotel and both of
their personal residences. Prior to that, it was owned by the

Brandenburgers, the German slave-trading family. It is "pamperville" personified, with massages on the beach, stunning grounds, and a staff that seems at times to outnumber the guests. We were fortunate enough to rent one of the three mega-yachts slips, which normally had to be booked months in advance.

Peter Island is what romantics only dream about. Brightly colored bougainvilleas and the sweet smell of orange blossoms combine with the clean-smelling ocean breeze, and the protected white beaches, the finest in the island chain. The starlit or moon-filled evenings, the delectable gourmet food, the overwhelming luxury make this a picture-perfect, idyllic place.

And, if that wasn't enough for a lifetime, we watched the football game of the decade in the open- air enclosure, on a big screen. It was the late-evening televised Rose Bowl, where Texas beat U.S.C., the favorite, in the last few seconds. I for one am captivated by college football, being from Florida, where the three top teams are always in contention for the top twenty in the nation. I can't say the same for professional football, of which I haven't watched a single came in the last decade.

Our week was virtually perfect. The people on board were totally compatible, happy to grant others their own space. Everyone learned to take a good book onto the front deck, to enjoy a nap below, or to swim to shore for a little quiet time on the beach—to keep enough distance from the others so that tensions didn't mount, and conversations remained fresh and interesting.

The Moorings had provided us with a vessel in top condition, so we had no mechanical problems and no clogged toilets or faulty equipment to speak of. We had some difficulty with the radio, but otherwise all was smooth as silk during our week on the water. A week is about the ideal time for such an excursion—any less and you don't get the flavor of the experience, as it takes a few days to unwind from whatever you left behind. Any more, and you have to be committed to that way of life, and not in a rush to return to something else.

It takes a special group of people to enjoy themselves in such close quarters. I learned this when I owned and chartered *The Blue Moon*, a vintage 1927 60-foot motor yacht once owned by Howard Hughes, in southern California for many years. Although I rarely captained the yacht when we were under charter, for insurance purposes, the whole experience was demanding on both the crew and those chartering, to say the least. It doesn't take friction long to develop under the wrong set of circumstances—yet we never had an inkling of it during our week in the BVI.

Soon we were on our way back to reality. After a short early morning trip to the Moorings dock, where we unloaded, they inventoried all that was left on board. Next, off to the foul-smelling ferry ride back to the grungy, traffic-congested city of Charlotte Amalie, in the American Virgins. Then we were accosted, at least mentally, by a group of Homeland Security drones, whose IQs were about the size of my waistline. God help us if they, as a group, were left alone to keep us out of harm's way.

And then the trip back to Fort Laudable on Spirit Airlines, crowded by a woman and two young children in the adjoining seats; prior to take-off, she was yapping to some unknown person on her cell phone, most likely expressing her dissatisfaction with her life and venting her frustrations, putting me face to face with just the thing we had escaped only the week before.

So, back to the land of milk and honey, where most people wander mindlessly through their occupations and their meaningless household chores. Think of all the nondescript hours, which lead to days, and overflow into months and years, and decades—think of being trapped in this world where people have lost their souls and personalities. I, for one, am thankful that I can sometimes escape this cast of characters and this society that has become depersonalized by institutions, corrupted by the almighty dollar, and devoid of moral integrity. However, for those of us who love and need the freedom and solitude associated with the oceans, these barriers to happiness are only minor inconveniences, tolerable in small doses. We are fully aware that before long, it will be time to return once again to the tranquility and the enjoyment that this special lifestyle offers us.

THE CRACKER BOYS:

A RE-ENACTMENT OF A FLORIDA CATTLE DRIVE DURING THE CIVIL WAR DAYS

My immediate family and I have always had nostalgic feelings about southeast Florida. Back in the late 40s and early 50s, when we as children attended school down here to escape the horrible Wisconsin winters, things were not as sophisticated as they seem today. Back then, trinket and citrus shops, open-air cocktail lounges, and ma and pa motels dotted the landscape from Miami to Jacksonville; roadside stands, which sold anything from baby alligators to coconuts, were run by folks who had come here to eke out a living and enjoy the wonderful climate.

There was not much equality among the populous at that time—affirmative action was not even a term in the dictionary yet. The well-to-do had their magnificent ocean-front mansions and all the toys that went with them, and those less fortunate, or of a different color or heritage, existed nearby, ever-respectful. Some, like those who fled to the Everglades at the end of the nineteenth century, sought only to survive, and to make the best of whatever cards they had been dealt.

I remember from my youth the beauty of the manicured lawns and the elegant black-tie events that were so much a part of the Palm Beach scene where my maternal grandparents had purchased an old "beach house" structure in 1936. It was not exactly on the beach, but we still got a taste of the finer things that southeast Florida could offer. Even in those early days, it was a rough-and-tumble place despite the surrounding affluence, and the Black people, who mostly lived on the edge of the Everglades, far from the glamour of the beach, had to sit at the back of the bus when they came to work, and drink from separate water fountains.

Florida's early settlement history had involved many people who had been considered "undesirable." Some had fled Georgia, the Carolinas and adjoining states during and after the Civil War. Uprooted by the horrors of war, and too exhausted to deal with their burnt homesteads, their stolen possessions, and the destruction wreaked by both the Union and the Confederate soldiers, they moved on and began new lives.

And, as we know from the history books, the reconstruction period was often even more difficult for the true southerners than the war itself had been: after Lee surrendered, they became slaves to an uncivilized, lawless system. It was a sad conclusion to a messy, unnecessary war whose issues could have been solved through negotiation and by compensating plantation owners for the loss of their so-called chattel, their slaves.

Some, in desperation, simply packed up after losing everything at gunpoint or threat of arrest and fled to the northern part of Florida, settling in the coastal areas. Before long, the undesirable elements of the Union occupation followed them there, and as usual, the spoils seemed to go to the victors. To get away from the looting and the persecution, the downtrodden escaped further into the Everglades, a wilderness with thick areas and swamps teeming with dangerous, life-threatening wildlife. Much of this I learned from an old rancher named Doc, who explained that in the early years, there was no law of the land out there, nor did anyone own the land we now know as the Everglades. The cattle grazing there were free for the taking.

This, then, is a story about the groups that settled the vast inland parts of central Florida and survived the harshness of that land through sheer Yankee ingenuity, often forming strong alliances with the indigenous population and runaway Black slaves. It is a story told through the eyes of Doc, a fifth-generation old-timer who loved to tell of those who made it and those who did not; of those who had no solid roots, no permanent home, and often ended up buried in shallow graves along the trails they traversed, and of those who miraculously managed to establish new, improved lives for themselves and their descendants. Doc was exceptional in his ability to recount what his ancestors had gone through. The early settlers, their stomachs often rumbling with hunger, faced hardship with great determination, and expected the next generation to settle down in a more permanent way and to become more knowledgeable about this strange environment.

The story unfolded for me when I had the opportunity to do a six-day horseback ride across the state in what was known as a re-enactment of the famous cattle drives that took place during the Civil War period (late 1850s and early 1860s). I participated along with 230 others associated with the Florida Cracker Trail Association. Florida played a prominent role during the Civil War, shipping abundant cattle north by water; Florida cattle was one of the main life-support systems of the Confederate soldiers, until the Union naval forces succeeded in their blockade of the southern harbors.

Florida's history is marred with violence. Prior to the Civil War, there were the three notorious Seminole Indian Wars, where the Union troops drove the Indians from their coastal homesteads into the Everglades. The last battle, on the Manatee River near Doc's family ranch, was the final spike in the Indians' soul, and had started with a dispute over the soldiers taking over a banana plantation.

My adventure focuses on the cattle industry, which was not well organized at the time. Wild cattle were there for the taking, readily available to those wanting to become land barons in this no-man's land. Undomesticated cattle were brought into captivity, branded, and claimed as personal property—not an easy task given the nature of the beast and the roughness of the terrain. Enterprising men and women became wealthy overnight by hiring men to round up and brand the wild critters and take them on long, arduous cattle drives, either to the Gulf or the Atlantic Ocean ports, for distribution to Cuba or up north to feed the Confederate soldiers.

Few realize that Florida was a major cattle area at the time, rivaling even Texas. There were thousands of cattle to be driven across the land, an attractive target for those who chose instead to rustle the cattle of others. As Doc mentioned, these rustlers were often found hanging from a tree branch, gutted with a knife like the cattle, as a warning to others. The interior of the state was a wild place with some 20 million acres of land that we now call the Everglades. This land had been given to the state of Florida by the federal government with the idea that it would be parceled out to homesteaders, but as with so many other land grant programs, like the Spanish Land Grants in the southwest, it was abused by those in power, who used the lands for political and economic gain.

Initially, the railroad barons received large tracks of land in exchange for laying down the rails using semi-slave labor, and cutting their way through the thick underbrush of palmetto trees and other swampland that most considered useless. Next came the citrus and sugar plantations, many of which are still subsidized by federal crop price-protection plans. Today, about half of the 20 million acres has been "developed" in some way, either into residential areas, strip malls, or golf courses or for agriculture and ranching.

Commercial development has had a detrimental effect on the fresh water supply for those living in southeast Florida, due to the contamination of pesticides and nutrients that are added to the soil, and to the slow intrusion of salt water into the drinking supply as fresh- water pools are depleted. This, combined with the deforestation that is a direct result of all the development, is taking a major toll on the environment. According to Doc, the entire coast of south Florida was once full of hardwood trees, like the once-treasured cypress. Few remain today, since they were cut down for houses or commercial development, for the building of the railroads, or just to drain the swamps. Back in those early days when my grandparents came here to winter, they'd joke that the land was sold "by the quart," since much of it was underwater and had to be drained before development could occur. The state even imposed a real estate tax (50 cents per acre) to set up a fund to eventually drain the Everglades for development.

As my grandfather told it, land was traded sight unseen on the streets of West Palm Beach. Contracts were marked up daily, some by obscene amounts, and buyers, who were required to make a small downpayment, were told that a large profit could be made just by "flipping" the contracts. It was just like the modern-day real estate market, though back then, there were no fences and no surveyed land. With the endless stretches of swampland, the countless Cyprus trees, and grazing land that went on as far as the eye could see, what you got was the luck of the draw.

It is hard to imagine myself being on the borderline of these two distinctive worlds, back then and today. In the contemporary setting, with all the glamour, the air-conditioning that was unheard of when we lived here in the 50s, the unbelievable number of multi-million dollar yachts, aircraft and homes that dot the landscape, and the miles and miles of retirement villages, you are struck by the sheer diversity of the people, and by the state-of-the-art communications and entertainment found here today. It is hard to imagine what the place was like 150 years ago.

Back then, the area had largely been left to the Indians, ranchers, and trappers, and to a lesser degree to the escaped Black slaves. What would it have been like, I've often wondered, to live on that frontier, making your living skinning alligators and cow hides, or selling smoked deer meat? Or skinning coons, possums and rabbits in the hope of eking out an existence? Spending time on the trails with Doc fuelled my imagination and brought history to life.

The river boats on the Kissimmee River came long before the railroads. Many of the early settlers, according to Doc, homesteaded in shacks along that wide river that empties into Lake Okeechobee, once one of the largest fresh-water lakes in America—that is, until the Army Corps of Engineers got their hands on the entire system. For many, this majestic body of water was the only source of contact with the outside world, providing mail and communications, building materials, and essential goods.

I have often wondered what it would have been like to travel only a few miles a day and be thoroughly exhausted and defeated by the elements—the rain, the heat, the swamps with their menacing critters. The early settlers who had cleared the land and fenced in the cattle ranches were a hardy lot; the women and children often cooked and lived in covered wagons as the men went off in search of homesteads. At night families would gather around campfires close to the wagons and listen to the cries of the wolves and coyotes, who would often attack the horses and domestic animals. It was these people, said Doc, who organized the first large cattle drives of the period.

For months on end, those who participated the cattle drives were unable to hide from the elements. They had no doors to close, no roof over their heads, and they became captives in their hostile environment as they waited for the cattle to fatten up. It was nothing like today, with our high-tech feedlots and refrigerated slaughterhouses. Nor could the frontiersmen defend themselves against the rustlers, who would slaughter the ranch hands and drovers in a heartbeat to get the lucrative herds that were being taken to market. The settlers were also easy prey after the drives, with their wagons full of gold coins. As we rode along the trails, Doc pointed out the many shallow graves of those who had perished during the drives.

This was the twentieth year, and possibly the final one, that a group of men and women would be re-enacting the cattle drives, riding from Sarasota in the west to Ft. Pierce in the east. Even though they had quite a following, it was becoming increasingly difficult to get the permits they now required from the Department of Homeland Security. I came into contact with the trail boss, a delightful woman named Sam Harper, who lives on the edge of the Everglades and is part Wisconsin Indian from generations past (in fact, her great- great- great-grandfather was the founder of the city of Milwaukee). She thought that including me, an adventure travel writer, in the venture might help to preserve this piece of history.

The Cracker Trail Easement has been compromised by the various counties it traverses, which have made concessions to developers to create residential and commercial projects to increase their tax base. Much of the easement that the Cracker Trail Association was granted must now follow the state road system, although the original idea was to preserve the old way of life in undeveloped land for future generations.

The people who settled around here, mostly men, were known as Cracker Boys, while their counterparts in the west of the United States took on the name cowboy. The name was derived from the rawhide whips they carried, and it was common knowledge that they could take the head of a rattlesnake off at 20 feet, according to Doc. They'd crack their whips while attempting to control the wild swamp cows that they rounded up for branding. And when there were enough of them, they fattened them up with the grasses found in the open plains and moved them slowly to the coastal markets for sale. The most famous market, Punta Rassa, was south of Fort Meyers, and sent cattle over to Cuba.

Usually during the colder winter months, the cattle were shepherded by "drovers," men who rode on the edges of the herd to keep them in the intended direction. Sometimes they got off track because of an unexpected stampede, a torrential rainstorm, a lack of knowledge of the marked trails, or the drowning of cattle in a flooded swamp. Or the wild wolves and coyotes, or the renegade Indians and cattle rustlers, would manage to scatter the herds. According to Doc, the drovers would often arrive at the Gulf of Mexico with no town or trading center in sight, and have to guess which way to go to get to market.

I had assumed that my having been an experienced rider in my earlier days would stand me in good stead. I had spent endless hours riding in the open mountain ranges around Santa Fe, without a saddle, using a homemade bridle with no bit. Now, twenty years later, I had to face up to the sad realization that I could not just pick up where I had left off. My second mistake was to make a week-long commitment to ride a horse you have never been on before. Of course, you can't really interview a horse in advance, over the phone or the Internet; the chemistry has to be there, and in this case, it was not. As I learned an hour into the trip, the horse was out to test me. He also had some inherent flaws, from an abusive prior owner, no doubt, that I was not willing to overcome or even tolerate. Needless to say, our temperaments were not well aligned.

I had asked Sam for a compatible horse, and had actually gone to her ranch to see the mount first hand. Everything looked copasetic, but then I learned that my mare had been put in the same enclosed corral as a recently neutered stud who mauled her. I had to find a substitute mount at the last minute, and this was not an easy task. Fortunately, my cousin Annette from Milwaukee, who had decided to make the trip as well, did some searching on the Internet and found a delightful family south of Sarasota, whose hobby was to adopt unwanted and abused horses and nurse them back to health. They brought six of their horses to the trail, along with the necessary tack equipment. I took one of them, and was happy to give the horse a chance to go on a long ride and to spend time with other healthier horses.

I had picked up Annette at the Sarasota Airport, with all her camping and riding gear, before we all congregated at the Kibler Ranch late Saturday afternoon for the first evening's festivities and a briefing on the week's events. The 50-acre ranch was covered with pickup trucks, horse vans, and tethered horses, making it hard to drive my antiquated black Lincoln town car to our campsite. After some frustration, I managed to set up my borrowed tent near the trailer of Suzanne and Paul, the owners of my borrowed horse. We all proceeded to the evening meal and the campfire briefing, not knowing that the temperature would drop to the high 20s that night, and rain to boot.

After bracing myself for the upcoming adventure with my trusty, time-tested, personally engraved flask of scotch, Annette and I joined those at the campfire for introductions and small talk. We were pleased to find a few hardy souls who had made the trail ride before—including three from West Palm Beach whom I still keep in touch with. Being regulars, they went on about how much they enjoyed the cattle drive re-enactments, and somehow I got an incomplete or distorted picture of what lay ahead.

That night, in a hopelessly romantic moment, I left my tent open on the top so I could see the stars, since it looked clear, but at daybreak I awoke to find myself freezing cold, and wrapped in wet, cold blankets.

This was nothing compared to the agony that lay ahead.

By 6:00 am we were grooming and saddling the horses so we could break camp and be on the road by 8:00.am. I soon learned that it was more to my liking to skip breakfast and stay in my tent until the sun rose; somehow, stumbling around in the dark on the wet, cold grass in my bare feet just wasn't my idea of living. I was in the minority, and most of the others would greet each other enthusiastically as they went out to see to their tethered horses, coffee cup in hand. The exception were the children, who were permitted to sleep in. I said to myself, what a treat to not have to grow up too fast, and followed suit for the balance of the week.

Day one was a disaster....and then I met Doc.

I kept thinking to myself, how did I get into this? How could I have undertaken this project with so little advance planning and actual knowledge of the requirements of the trip? Most of the problems lay with the horse and the equipment. As it turned out, my "substitute" horse had a serious attitude problem. Also, I had failed to tell the owner that years back I had had a hip replacement, and unbeknownst to me she had brought me the biggest horse in her stable, 16 hands tall. Mounting and dismounting was a serious problem, given my limited range of motion.

Carl, as he was known, had been a racehorse and was conditioned to be near the inside rail, which in this case meant the highway. So I spent a fair amount of time attempting to keep him off the asphalt that first day. If there was any racehorse spirit left in him, I never found it: I had to kick him constantly in order to keep up with the others. Needless to say, my groin muscles were a mess after the first morning, so I cut a switch from a nearby branch and used it to bring him into submission. Fortunately, I had programmed about

18 hours of music into my iPod. By mid-afternoon I thought the bright side of the trip would finally surface.

But somehow, in the early afternoon, the cinch on my saddle broke, and I and the saddle ended up under Carl's belly. He was not inclined to move much, so he stood there just like a statue in a park dumb as a doornail. My injuries were limited to a bruised shoulder and a black and blue wrist—and then there was my bruised ego. I had to ask one of the hands to re-saddle my mount and help me re-board. By nightfall at the campfire, everybody on the trip had heard about my experience, and many came up to express their sympathy, which I could have done without. But the best part was making the acquaintance of Doc, who would soothe my bruised ego the following day.

Feeling not too anxious to board Carl again the next day, I decided to give my shoulder and wrist a rest and hooked up with two salty old cowboys, about my age, though their skin was so blistered from the sun that it could have been mistaken for alligator hide. Derrick had brought his "covered wagon" down from Tennessee for the ride, pulling it behind his pickup. It was not a true replica, being equipped with hydraulic brakes and comfortable seats taken from an automobile, but I was glad to get into it. Doc was the other passenger in the chariot, and he and Derrick each owned one of the mules, which they tried to give away to each other as the ride progressed. The mules were attached to the wagon with a fancy rigging system designed to make the two mules pull the wagon's weight equally, which never really happened, and was the subject of much conversation between the boys. The way they went on, you would have thought that these less-than thoroughbreds had won the Kentucky Derby in their earlier days. The three of us talked and laughed about it all day.

Robert "Doc" King was quite a character, a retired eye surgeon with a degree from Harvard. An old-time rancher at heart, his family was one of the first to settle in Bradenton, a suburb of Sarasota. Despite his sophistication, he had never lost his southern drawl. A virtual encyclopedia about the history of cattle ranching in south Florida, he especially liked talking about the drives. He had never been able to participate in them, since his schooling and his medical practice had filled most of his days when he was a young man. Derrick, on the other hand, hailed from Tennessee and was a successful chicken farmer and feedlot operator who apparently fattened 60,000 chickens every 60 days and sold the whole lot to Purdue Farms.

Doc and Derrick both had a great love affair with their mules, Peanut and Jimmy, and carried on an ongoing conversation with them. Their only function was to pull the wagon at a steady speed of 4 mph, setting the pace for the hundreds of horses that followed. The boys debated endlessly about which mule was pulling the most weight. Then the topic changed to which one was the best at driving the wagon, though there was not much to judge the driver's ability by, at the rapid clip of 5 mph. Whenever things heated up to the boiling point, they would laugh and change the subject. They had been friends for years, but this was their first time on the Cracker Trail Ride. Like old horse traders, they were negotiating the sale of their mules and the wagon for the entire trip and finally concluded some kind of an arrangement on the final afternoon, at an undisclosed price, at least to me, which probably reflected the fact that they didn't want to bother sending the mules and wagon back to Tennessee.

I had never seen two grown men be so fascinated with two such stupid critters, but on and on they went, sometimes chatting with the mules about their families and their lives, as if it were easier to communicate with the humans through this medium. One said his wife was stubborn like a mule; other comments were not worth repeating, mostly dealing with their posteriors, mules, I learned, were a cross between a donkey and a walking horse; they need much less water than a horse and provide a smoother ride. Much of the west was explored using mule-driven covered wagons. Mules, Doc said, rarely fetch over $100 today, but farmers often buy them and let them loose among the cattle to function as a security system: they are tough fighters that can kick a wild dog or coyote to pieces. In a way, they seem to have replaced the Cracker Boys of old, who used to camp out with the cattle at night, rifles at the ready to shoot whatever varmints would materialize.

After my somewhat trying first day on Carl, we had camped for the first night on a 14,000 acre ranch owned by Duck Smith and his wife, both fifth- or sixth-generation ranchers with almost 4,000 cattle grazing on their land. Being of the old school, Duck hosted a wonderful barbeque on our second evening, followed by an informative speech, near the campfire, by a university historian who knew the complete history of the Cracker people and their cattle drives. The interior of the ranch house was magical—the ranch house with its wood floors, throw rugs and mounted animals of every conceivable species, the numerous large warm fireplaces that were a welcome presence as the chill of the approaching evening came along. The meals were what one would expect, grits and bacon and eggs for breakfast and ample portions of meat and potatoes for dinner.

Mr. Duck, as many respectfully referred to him, was a colorful, generous man whose wife had inherited several ranches in the vicinity. The next day we rode across one of them, the Bar Crescent S Ranch, in Doc's wagon; we traveled about 14 miles that day, with Duck often at our side, without reaching the end of the ranch. A man right out of GQ magazine, Duck was trim and well groomed, with not a wrinkle to be found on his clothing, and he was a delightful conversationalist. In retrospect, I wish I had asked him how he got his nickname, but he was so dignified that I would have felt awkward doing so. He had a remarkable memory for names, and knew mine after only one introduction; he said he had learned this skill from his father, a politician.

That evening we camped on Duck's property near the Kissimmee River. Doc told stories of those who had lived along its banks, fishing to keep alive, skinning animals, and selling hides for 25 cents a piece to gain access to gold coins that they would spend after canoeing downriver to a variety of trading posts. The alligators got $2 back in those days, but many lost a finger or limb trying to bring them into submission. The Cracker Boys would also sell their fresh meat and fish, at a premium, to the tradesmen and tourists on the paddlewheel boats. These cumbersome vessels would slow down just long enough to transact business. Sometimes they'd get stuck in the shallow water and it would take days or weeks to free the boats. Doc said the Cracker Boys would supply the passengers with fresh deer and alligator meat while they were lodged on the sandbars.

By the time Doc had finished with his tales, you could just imagine these little shacks spread a mile or so apart with their life-sustaining gardens and domestic animals, cattle and pigs, all penned in for survival. He said it was all they had in this hand-to-mouth existence; people lived off the land, fishing in the river and hunting deer and bear. Doc's ancestors used to talk about the rainy or monsoon season, which took place in the fall. Many of the settlers' homes were built on stilts, and when the torrential rains came, everything that couldn't be stored in the small houses was lost to the flooding. There was little trust among the river dwellers back then; Doc said they'd shoot first, if a suspicious character came around, and ask questions later.

That second day on the trail, still on the Smith Ranch, Doc, Darrell and I talked non-stop. Doc had an answer for almost everything that we came across, and often pointed out things that only a trained eye could observe. Being on the Smith Ranch was a great way to get a feel for what the land and the lifestyle were all about during the Civil War period. We rode over open pastures that stretched as far as the eye could see, with the horizon broken only by tall pine trees and shoulder-high palmettos, which looked eerie in the early morning, before the fog had lifted. Rarely can one block out civilization for such an extended period of time as we did that day.

Every once in a while we would drive over a pasture where the wild hogs had dug up the ground in search of grubs, which they thrive on when it gets dry and the other prey animals go into hiding. They shred wire fences and leave big holes or trenches in the landscape, which caused our wagon to bounce from side to side. The holes were so large that one could not steer the wagons around them with out losing the momentum of the riders behind us. Boars are ugly, hostile creatures and when they are angered, their sharp tusks can cut a human or a horse to ribbons in short order. Unfortunately, Doc told us, wild hogs have taken over some of the better ranching and farming terrain, so they are hunted down by the ranchers. However, they cannot be shot on private property, and so they continue to grow in number.

As we rode that week, I watched as farmhands burned sections of the various ranches we crossed in order to get rid of the "wire grass," as Doc called it. About a third of the land is burned each winter when the grass becomes so tough with age that the cows can't eat it. When calves are born in the fall, new grass has grown for them to eat. They are sold when they are about a year old, and 300 pounds, whereas in the Civil War period, the Cracker Boys would move them very slowly, and the calves weighed around 600 pounds when they arrived at the loading docks. Today, the mother cows' ears are tagged to show that they are fertile; the barren ones are sent off to the feedlots.

Much of Doc's rich understanding of cattle ranching came from his mother's family, which hailed from Georgia. During the War of 1812, his family constructed ocean-going wooden boats with which the U.S. Government took on the Spanish. However, they were never paid, and they went bankrupt. They left Georgia with a covered wagon, some tools, and a sack of flour, said Doc. First they moved to the middle of Florida, and then in 1842 they moved on to Bradenton, which was no more than a small dot on the map.

As they soon learned, it was not safe to travel or homestead along the coastline, especially on the Atlantic side, where reconstruction solders and corrupt court administrators were laying in wait, hoping to deprive them of their possessions and their dignity. As a result, many, like Doc's family, chose to slug it out in the interior part of Florida now known as the Everglades, where there was really nothing worth fighting over. Doc said he had often wondered how the settlers communicated with the Indians. The poor, displaced settlers, the Indians, and the runaway Blacks were all motivated by the fear of being killed or assaulted by greedy, rough-and-tumble characters who were out to steal their land and their belongings.

Doc's family, like many other early Florida settlers, stopped from time to time to build homesteads. But often, hard-core Union soldiers, who hated the southerners and wanted to punish them for their lack of allegiance, would take over or burn homesteads in the north of the state. Most Floridians wanted nothing to do with the war, and that was the main reason they had fled the Old South. Only when the railroads opened up the south part of Florida to the tourists and to enable the export of cattle and citrus did the area become recognized by the rest of the nation. Today, the area around Bradenton and Sarasota has become one of the most attractive places in the world.

In the 1930s Doc's parents started a tomato business on 160 acres of homesteaded land. They also rounded up stray cattle and grazed them on thousands of acres that were there for the taking. According to Doc, ranchers had a hard time when the fever tick came; transmitted by cattle imported from Texas, it took a great toll on many of the herds in south Florida. True to form, the government, in its infinite wisdom, decreed that all cows be bathed in arsenic once a week to get rid of the disease, or they would be shot on sight. The Texan cows were rounded up and shipped back home. They were sold for $10 each, and the dead ones fetched just one dollar for their hides. This epidemic was followed by the arrival of the screw worm, which lived, like maggots, on the cattle's flesh and burrowed into their skin.

Around the time of the fever tick, ranchers were forced to fence in their herds to meet governmental inspection dictates, and the whole landscape of Florida changed forever. Open ranges were no longer viable, and the politicians and businessmen divided up these lands. Ranchers were able to obtain deeds for this unproductive middle land at bargain-basement prices. Many of the acquisition funds came from those who had participated in the lucrative cattle drives before the arrival of the railroads. Citrus followed next, said Doc; groves were deeded for a pittance to those from the north who were not drawn to the ranching lifestyle. The gold that fell from the trees took over, and the land took on great value for those who worked the orchards. The citrus industry was greatly enhanced by the advent of refrigeration, which arrived around the time when I was a youngster in Florida.

Doc's ancestors struggled in the years before the pasture lands were fenced in and turned into orange groves, because the cattle would graze off the young trees and kill them. Only those with money could afford full-grown trees, which were shipped in from booming places like Miami, Fort Lauderdale, and West Palm Beach. When the deeded land became the letter of the law, range wars often followed. Those with the deeds wanted nothing to do with those who would cross their pastures and consume their grass on their way to the markets. The days of the open ranges were now ancient history.

It was only a question of time before the big time money moved in from the north, and that seemed to coincide with the arrival of the railroads and their well-funded owners, who were given vast amounts of land in exchange for grading and laying down the tracks. The wealthy newcomers tended to wear fancy, splashy clothes, whereas the cattlemen, if they had one at all, would wear a suit only to their wedding and their funeral, according to Doc. The wealthy railroad barons often denied the ranchers access to the trains, unless they were using the railroads to ship their cattle, according to Doc. It was not uncommon for cattle to simply be run over by the trains: the "cattle catchers," triangular-shaped metal devices on the front of the engines, pushed them to the side and killed them.

One could easily visualize from our ride through the Smith Ranch how difficult it would be to round up the wild cattle. They scattered immediately at any sign of humans, even a few hundred yards away, and dashed off into the thick palmetto bushes. In the old days, it meant dogs cross-bred with wolves would corner them and flush them out corner and flush them out, and would also keep predators at bay. Having to corral one wayward cow at a time and fishing them out of the palmetto trees was exhausting and painstaking work. Stampeding was another challenge that the Cracker Boys had to deal with, Doc explained. Apparently, it didn't take much to set these wild cows on a rampage. Once the cows started moving en masse, the Cracker Boys, who generally rode on the edges of the herd, could get seriously injured. And then there was the threat of the mosquitoes and locusts, who often took over entire herds as they were moving around marsh lands. Often they were so abundant that would get stuck in the cattle's throats and noses and sometimes suffocate them. Occasionally, the cows' eyes even popped out, since their lungs were so full of the critters. Millions of mosquitoes could hatch, under ideal conditions, in a matter of four or five days in the marshy areas after big rainstorm, making the cattle's survival almost impossible. People in those days did not understand the life cycle of mosquitoes or locusts and heir herds were sometimes wiped out because of sheer ignorance.

Every once in a while, being the lead wagon, we would flush up a group of egrets, which would scatter in all directions. Unlike the other birds which you could hear in the distance, they remained stationary, camouflaged in the dense wooded areas. Most were perched in the high pines and thick palmetto bushes. The egrets, who moved in great numbers, are truly magnificent to watch, beautifully white, elegant and slim as they take to the air. They are the most graceful creatures on this planet that I know of, more elegant even than the pink flamingos in Africa, which before this trip were the ultimate, to my way of thinking.

Occasionally we would cross a small stream. It was winter, the dry season, and it was easy to portage, especially with the drainage culverts now in place. During the days of the big cattle drives, Doc said that often the cattle that came to the streams for water got stuck in the mud, or refused to move from the sandy bottoms, which cooled their hoofs; many would drown. Life-threatening conditions were not uncommon during the fall months, when the hurricanes came. The mosquitoes could also be quite problematic in the monsoon weather.

As we wove our way through the pine forests and plateaus filled with thick, intimidating vegetation that seemed to take over everything, the mules needed a lot of coaxing to make all the sharp turns that were required to get around the trees and shrubbery. Derrick, who drove that day, would give a friendly poke to the mules' posteriors with a sawed-off broom handle, but his verbal commands usually fell on deaf ears. It was delightful going through the pastures that day and seeing the trees, which had not been manicured in decades upon decades, and whose low branches were covered with Spanish moss from the tops to the ground. The sunlight would occasionally peak through the grey hanging moss, a beautiful scene to behold; we crossed small streams, and the tinkling sound of running water filled our ears and the tantalizing smell of orange blossoms hung in the air. These were the trails of the 1850s, perfectly intact, except for the pasture areas, which were now fenced in. Of course, the cattle of today were high-grade, prize-winning beasts rather than the emaciated creatures that used to run wild in these same fields.

Doc explained that when the railroads came, the big cattle drives changed. The remaining ranchers built holding pens to keep the cattle in place along the rail beds as they waited for their trip to the marketplaces. Before the railroads, the cattle were moved by the cross-bred dogs, the Spanish-bred cracker horses which moved easily forward, sideways, and in reverse, and the hardy Cracker Boys, their whips flashing in the air.

In the early days, many of the poor, mostly Blacks and Indians, worked the turpentine trees for the white settlers, cutting notches in the bark and installing metal or wooden funnels to catch the sap, which they sold to be made into turpentine in refineries up north. When the railroads came, many of the trees were cut down and made into ties along the road bed, and the turpentine men went to work for the railroads, where the money was much more plentiful and convertible to a more liquid form.

Many of the dislocated Indians and Blacks lived together in small villages, mostly for protection from federal agents or bounty hunters who were paid by the federal government to capture them. Treated like wild animals, the Blacks were caught and auctioned off to those who wanted them deported for one reason or another. The slaves had a bounty on their heads for running away from the plantations, and the government wanted the Indians deported to reserves in places like Oklahoma, Doc explained.

Generations back, Doc's family did not move cattle herds to market for profit, but instead had domesticated cattle. Nevertheless, Doc had some wild stories about the great cattle drives across Florida, and he shared them in spades. Often these annual cattle drives moved thousands of cows, who fetched $10-$15 dollars apiece if they arrived at the cattle stations healthy and fat. The cattle were so valuable that they were paid for with some form of gold, and not the worthless Confederacy currency that many had been stiffed with over the years. The gold came from Cuba, Doc surmised, and certainly not from the Union side. The Cracker Boys that were part of the drives were the envy of south Florida and indeed the South in general, since they had hard currency to bargain with, unlike their counterparts who traded in paper that you could plaster the bathroom walls with.

Several years ago I spent the better part of two weeks in Cuba, and I could see how a century and a half ago, Cuba played an important role in the development of the early Florida cattle and sugar industries. Even today, the Havana skyline consists mostly of impressive sixteenth-century European-style homes; back then it was called the Paris of the West, and the wealthy class, consisting of sugar and tobacco plantation owners and rum distillers, ran the island with alacrity.

The descendants of many of these well-to-do characters settled in Florida after Castro's takeover, and were certainly in a position to purchase any imported goods, at premium prices, with hard currency. At one point in time, much of the Cuban cigar trade was located in Key West and Tampa. During the Civil War days, Cuba was a thriving and exciting place to be, especially Havana, long before Florida came on the radar scope of civilized people in the northern part of this hemisphere.

Doc told me that in the early days, it was a common practice to have someone clear the land of the palmetto and pine trees and drain the swamps in exchange for having the use of it for three to five years, at which time it reverted back to the owners. Many of the large ranches of today were accumulated in this fashion. But after the railroads arrived and opened things up, homesteading simply no longer worked. The free grazing land started falling into the hands of those with money, who acquired land deeds. When the land fell under legal ownership, the homesteaders simply picked up their stakes and moved on.

The arrival of the railway was not the only threat. Doc's family and others in the area lost a lot of citrus when the fruit fly invaded south Florida. The disease, spread by birds, wiped out grove after grove. Oftentimes the government contributed to the spreading of the disease by driving their trucks, which had fruit flies on them, into uninfested groves. When the groves were condemned, many just cut the root stock from the dying trees and moved on to other locations in sheer desperation.

As we rode through another ranch a day or two later, we were in citrus country. Doc explained the economics of agriculture before the turn of the century and how it has changed today. For instance, wild bees were found everywhere in south Florida, and today, because of climate change and pesticides, wild bees are virtually extinct. Now they bring in bees by the cartons on large semi-trucks to pollinate the orange trees, as bees are no longer raised to produce honey in Florida. They are simply too valuable to be used for honey anymore.

The smell of the citrus trees, especially the orange trees, is an aphrodisiac as one rides along. That unique scent makes you think you must be in the Garden of Eden. You know what it's like when you slice into an orange? The smell of the cut peel is magnificent, but in the groves here, the aroma flows for miles on end.

One day we stopped at a cattle station that had been in continuous use since the days of the Civil War. Pens sat next to the loading ramps for the trucks that still picked up the waiting cattle, but on a much lesser scale. It was exciting to see the large numbers of cattle there, with their distinctive smell of manure and their loud noises protesting their captivity. If you closed your eyes and blocked out the contemporary setting, you got a feel for what it might have been like in the old days.

Doc and I got into a rather windy conversation about what the small upstart towns must have looked like at the end of these massive cattle drives, before the arrival of the railroads. Towns like Punta Rassa, just south of where Doc was raised, and Fort Meyers, where their main attraction was the shipment of cattle to Cuba, were all business. Cattle buyers were there waiting with Spanish gold coins to scoop up the herds and ship them off, at large profits to both those who brought the herds and the middlemen. According to Doc, these towns were somewhat akin to those that sprung up during the gold mine days in the west, especially in California. The men, especially the drovers, would go off on spending sprees, while those of a more responsible nature would go to the merchandise stores and stock up on supplies, or to the blacksmith shop and the livery stables to reshoe their horses and fix their wagons for the return trip. Doc had heard that the drovers tended to be emaciated, unwashed, and unshaven for years at a time. Gaunt and undernourished, they often headed straight to the saloon to wet their whistles and maybe buy a few jugs of rum to put in their saddle bags for the trip home, wherever that might be.

On a typical ranch, Doc said, there would be the owner and his immediate family and the steady ranch hands, augmented by the drovers, who would move the cattle from the ranch to the loading pens, often taking weeks or months. They would be fed along the way but not generally paid until the cattle were sold; the money was then divided up using some predetermined formula, as the drovers were not the most dependable of the lot. Often on the long, hot trips they would buy cattle from other ranchers, adding them to the herd. When the cattle were grazing for days in one location, the drovers would go off and round up a few wild cows, brand them, and add them to the herd. Their reimbursement at the end of the drive depended on how many were lost or perished on the way. They were paid in Spanish gold "Doubloons," Doc said, a term that is now obsolete.

There could be literally thousands of wild cows scattered along the trail as the men moved their cattle to market, and it was not uncommon to double or even triple the size of the herd on the way.

The men on the drive literally lived off the wild, sleeping under a poncho when it rained. The food, much of it canned, was bland but filling. Often they would be pestered by rattlesnakes, who sought them out for warmth and sometimes spent the night in the boots the men had removed. Drovers usually got only a few hours of sleep, as they took turns keeping the wolves and coyotes away from the herd. They were mostly renegades, with no families, who were picked up by the boot straps for the drives, and then fell back into their old ways until the next drive came along. Cattle driving was not an easy life, even for those who owned the herds.

I could see where these guys were coming from, as often I would collapse in my tent after the day's ride, long before sunset, from sheer dehydration and exposure to the sun. I did recover after a few hours with a drink or two of scotch and a slow walk to where the catered food was located. It was a real effort on most days. Rarely did I stay up late, even though those who organized the trail ride had planned extensive evening activities, such as rodeo-style barrel races. I was surprised at the recuperative powers of the body after an evening's rest. I'd go to bed thinking I would never be able to get up again, but at daybreak I'd feel fresh and restored.

Once we had passed through the seemingly untouched Smith Ranch, the balance of the trip was dull as dishwater. We had to put up with a wide variety of humanity most of the way, the mini-ranchettes with all their silly suburban toys, the commercial developments, endless franchise operations that have spring up over the years in and around the Cracker Trail Easement, as well as the traffic congestion associated with the tourist industry. The evenings, however, were fun. Most of the participants were NASCAR-loving, beer-drinking, blue-collar people who loved the outdoors and enjoyed connecting with others. There was never a shortage of conversation on and off the trail; everybody was interested in each other and their lifestyles, and that made the difficult times during the day worthwhile, even though most of us would not come in contact with each other again, except for the hard-line repeaters.

One thing that struck my attention was the way the riders interacted with their horses. There was a certain body language that took place between horse and rider. Those I met on the ride and at the campfires at night were attempting to bridge the gap between the human and animal worlds. They longed to have an intimate relationship with their horse, similar to what they shared with the cats and dogs that shared their homes. A certain fear among the two parties needs to be put aside: horses have historically been treated harshly, especially those who were trained for war (1.5 million were used and 1/3 died in the First World War) and for heavy labor. And humans must be wary around horses, who are massive and often temperamental. One man I met, Allan from West Palm Beach, was purchasing wild mustangs from the government round-up program at auction and breaking them in a rather harsh way, to my thinking. He'd bind their front and rear legs together and lower their heads until they came into submission, often for days at a time. He commented that to reduce the danger of being thrown, the rider should whip the horse between the ears—a method that is apparently used quite frequently in horse training..

It seems that a horse's first ride is the most memorable and scary thing it will ever go through, something they are trained to do for the most productive part of their life. One woman had an interesting alternative theory, that if you lead a wild horse to water and let it swim, you could mount it in short order and become its companion—it's sort of like water birthing, she suggested. The water also provided a softer cushion if the rider was to be thrown off. The Indians of the southwest, apparently, used this technique with great success. Eye contact seems to be the trick as well, once there is some degree of comfort with the horse. Since they are flight animals to begin with, adding fear to their lives only means that they might turn their back on you, she said. She spoke from experience, and suggested that while most men like confrontation with animals to a degree, women, like horses, are inherently fearful, like when they walk the streets at night without an escort.

Many use just words, not complete sentences, when talking to their horses, and do it slowly, and also use their hands as a way of communicating. In other words, talk to a horse like you would to a dog, to get to the innermost emotional parts of their body. Don't jump on with a whip and spurs and expect the animal to be a sympathetic companion.

That's what I did with Carl, out of total frustration. My second mount, Lady, was different kettle of fish, and we became one almost from the time I mounted her. She rode like a dream until the last three or so miles on the final day. When we stopped for a water break, she politely went down on her two front knees, and started to turn over slowly on her right side, permitting me to dismount in safety. She simply had exhausted all her strength, and politely let me know it. Her owner said that when she was acquired, she was all skin and bones, and had put on 200 pounds since, but apparently the extended trip was too much for her to handle. She was the only horse to totally give out, but some chose not to ride the whole trip. In years past several horses have died, I was told. After she was cooled off with water and unsaddled, a truck came and picked her up for the last few miles. All was not lost—I jumped in the lead wagon with Doc and Derrill for the final journey of the trip, only to find out that they had sold the wagon and the mules.

SECTION III

ICONIC MOMENTS FROM THE PAST

The interplay between the past and the present is always fascinating and complex. Over the last few centuries, there have been many keystone moments that continue to resonate and have meaning in the present-day world. The chapters in this section take a closer look at a few of these iconic moments in our history. One sketch tells the story of the American Indian in the West, who was tragically annihilated, via the Trail of Tears, after the Civil War. Another, by presenting research that includes in-depth interviews, tells about the drama and the repercussions of dropping the atomic bomb on Japan.

The final chapter takes a look at West Virginia's Greenbrier Resort, which despite being temporarily threatened by the paranoia of the Cold War era, continues to be a place of dignity and grace, a destination that reminds us of our rich heritage and the unchanging values that are at the foundation of our country.

"LITTLE BOY": 48 SECONDS THAT CHANGED THE WORLD

For over a decade I lived in the shadows of a modest but secretive city—though it would more accurately be called an enclave of people than a functional city—that arguably has had a greater impact on the world than any other place or gathering of humanity. Los Alamos, New Mexico, with its grey, military-style Quonset huts, was nothing like Santa Fe, whose charm, beauty, and tri-cultural richness made it a dynamic, thrilling city. But with its world-renowned laboratory, the birthplace of the atomic bomb was, and remains today, a place unto itself, utterly unique. Nestled high in the mountains, it boasts the country's most educated population, with over 62% of adults having a Baccalaureate or higher.

From time to time, I had occasion to pass through Los Alamos when my real estate development business took me there; I developed several residential subdivisions that serviced the local market. Until recently, I had no idea of the significance that it played on the world stage about the time I was born.

I guess one could classify this city as a large university campus, a think tank *extraordinaire* that was home to more than 5000 scientific inhabitants in the mid-1940s. Located at the base of what was one of the major volcanic eruptions millions of years ago, this sky city, it seemed, had Nobel Prize winners walking down any given street. But of course, in those days, scientists didn't roam around freely. Everything was off limits: mail was screened, phone calls were tapped, and newborn babies were often fingerprinted as well.

In a way, these inhabitants were truly the "war gods" that changed the world forever, charting a new course of history for an upstart nation that would not be denied its place in history. Some who have written books on the subject have compared Los Alamos's inhabitants to the gods on Mount Olympus whom the Greeks worshipped and from which they drew their military prowess.

Turning an old, mostly abandoned boys' camp into the planet's ultimate think tank was an experiment of dubious virtue, not to mention the fact that it was the most costly venture in the history of the world up to that point. It was an experiment so shrouded in secrecy that the second highest elected official in this country, the Vice-President of the United States, was not privy to its existence.

In July 1945 the whole multi-year exercise was reaching completion; a metal tower had been placed in the middle of an ancient, barren strip of Apache land. Here, a single bomb was to be detonated. The exact nature of its destructive power was anybody's guess, including the top brass at Los Alamos. Reliable estimates ranged from complete failure to setting off a chain reaction in the atmosphere that could destroy much of the landscape and inhabitants of the southwest. Here, at the White Sands Missile Range, a hundred miles south of Los Alamos, was the do-or-die aspect of the atomic bomb program. For years men had constructed concrete bunkers containing a wide variety of scientific instruments; many were created just for this experiment, which involved installing over 500 miles of telephone cables to monitor this one test, which could be measured in a billionth of a split second. The far-reaching concept involved going back to the very essence of creation, splitting and harnessing the smallest thing known to mankind and the Creator, the atom.

There it sat, on top of this lonely tower, a device weighing four tons that had the potential to change the nature of the world and rewrite its history books. The tower site was named Ground Zero, a name that had many ramifications, regardless of whether it was a success or a failure, and that has recently been resurrected after the Twin Tower tragedy in New York City.

The strange series of events that followed was left in the hands of a political, non-scientific and non-military individual who had only learned of its existence a few months earlier, and who was now half a world away from the test site, in Berlin, Germany, negotiating the end of the European conflict known as WWll. At stake was a power play, partly real and partly contrived, regarding the division of the spoils of war. Surrounding Truman were two of the most powerful men in the world, Churchill and Stalin, daunting figures who overpowered the diminutive former railroad worker and haberdasher. This new kid on the block would move up the ladder to become the top dog in the world of politics if the Pandora's Box he was about to open in New Mexico worked.

Many saw it as his bargaining chip to end conflict in the Pacific Theater, while others viewed it as his ace of spades in negotiating with the power-hungry Stalin, who was bent on world domination, just like the man they had recently defeated, Hitler. As it turned out, the Russians were not only aware of the development of the atomic bomb, but they had actually planted spies at the Manhattan Project, as it was known in Los Alamos, who were relaying information to Soviet scientists right up to the end.

Over the preceding three years, the Allied losses of life in the Pacific Theater were enormous as they moved from one Japanese island to the next on their way to the mainland. Around the time that the atomic bomb was dropped, the Americans were losing 5,000 men a week. Surrender was not in the Japanese vocabulary, since death in battle was the greatest honor a man could receive from his country. On the island of Okinawa alone, 12,000 soldiers were lost, and thousands of kamikaze pilots sent their planes into the sides of our naval fleet, adding further to the death toll. A massive attack on the southern end of the Island of Japan would involve more than 3/4 of a million men, and it was estimated by General George Marshall that 30,000 of them would lose their lives in the first thirty days. By some estimates, as many as a million men would perish if the war went on to its final completion. Not a pretty picture, especially if there was an alternative.

But that was about to change, or was it?

The whole scheme revolved around a metal product not found in nature, or any other place for that matter, that had to be created by this talented team. No such thing had existed previously, and it was left to the scientists at Los Alamos to assemble the complicated pieces of the puzzle. This unknown metal was named "Plutonium," after Pluto, the god of the underworld. The core concept revolved around Einstein's equation focussing on the relationship between energy and matter. It was Einstein who wrote a letter to President Franklin Roosevelt in order to get the Manhattan Project off the ground. He convinced the powers that be that the Germans were developing their own atomic weaponry, which they would not hesitate in the least to use.

Einstein figured that matter could be converted into energy, and that 99.8 % of all matter in the universe was contained in the atom. The concept was to split it, converting it into energy that could accomplish powerful things, both destructive and otherwise, that were up to that point unknown to mankind. Of course, no one, including the Los Alamos scientists, could predict the enormous destructive power of this process until it was tested. Some even thought it might set off a chain reaction that could destroy the entire world by setting fire to or torching the atmosphere, blocking for extended periods of time the elements, including sunlight, that are so necessary for human existence. One of the reasons Los Alamos was chosen was its remote location in the event that an accidental explosion did take place. Damage to the civilian population would be minimal.

The detonation process is quite complicated, and beyond discussion here, but the actual explosive device used at Hiroshima was about the size of a tennis ball. The idea here was quite simple, though of course the execution and delivery were quite complicated. A piece of doughnut-shaped enriched uranium 235 was placed in a machine, and then another piece of uranium was dropped through the hole in the doughnut. For a minute second, the additional uranium dropping through the hole would achieve what was known as "critical mass," and the explosion would take place. Up to that time they had only worked with "sub-critical mass," so the chain reaction could not be measured, or even accurately predicted.

To complicate things further, the fixed location at the Trinity site had to be overcome, as the weapon to be used over Japan had to be armed, dropped and detonated at the proper height by an airplane, at the exact location to be determined by the military, in order to be effective. Here, the idea, according to Parsons, the man who would eventually arm the bomb on the way to Hiroshima, was nothing more than "a good old gun, a five-inch cannon with a six foot long barrel" located just on the other side of the bomb bay doors. After the bomb left the plane, a piece of uranium 235 about the size of a soup can would be fired down the barrel when it reached the proper elevation, triggered by a altimeter device, into a second piece of uranium fixed to the muzzle.

An experienced team of pilots and navigators had been picked for the delivery, and had been training for endless months for just such a mission. Everything took shape simultaneously: on the same day that the Ground Zero explosion was taking place, the two components for the Japanese bombs were sailing under the Golden Gate Bridge on the *USS Indianapolis*, headed for Tinian Island, the biggest Air Force base in the world, located 1500 miles south of Japan.

If the scientists were able to validate their theories, and the military managed to deliver such a weapon, it would change the nature of warfare forever. The weapon packed a 50-million-degree temperature punch at its core, ten thousand times hotter than the sun's surface, with devastating shock waves moving at thousands of miles per hour, all accompanied by a deadly radioactive cloud that would climb at a rate of over a mile a minute up to 40,000 feet. Only one member of the military delivery team scheduled for Hiroshima was present at Ground Zero that day, in a B-29 observation plane. He too would be in Tinian within 48 hours to brief the rest of the 509 Air Squadron, the group that was assigned the task of delivering Little Boy, the name given to the first atomic bomb, which was to be made out of uranium. The stage was now set, with the achievement of positive results at Trinity, on the

White Sands Missile Range. The next explosion was only three
weeks away. The real McCoy was on its way to pay dirt over
Hiroshima.

The effort, time, talent and expenditures that went into the program
are legendary. The years spent at Los Alamos; the ten months of
training on the Salt Flats for the 509 Air Squadron in Utah
focusing on target practice for the eventual drop; dropping dummy
bombs from 30,000 feet to designated places marked in the desert
floor. In conjunction with the release of the dummy bombs, they
practiced high altitude steep turns, often rotating the big planes to
literally stand on their wing tips to gain speed before going into a
dive earthward, all with the idea of eventually putting enough
distance between them and the drop zone, thus clearing themselves
of the anticipated life-threatening shock waves from the explosion.

After Utah, it was on to Tinian for more practice. Tinian was a
massive Allied air base where some 260 B-29s were located, all
flying daily missions to Japan. It was a beehive of activity, with
engines roaring about one minute apart, carrying their incendiary
bombs which, for instance, on one single night, March 9, killed
over 100,000 people in Tokyo alone. Over a four-month period,
these B-29s almost totally destroyed fifty other Japanese cities, as
their planes traversed back and forth 24-7 over what was known as
the Hirohito Highway.

The 509th was a special group located on the fringes of that base,
and they never partook in the bombing missions over Japan. The
group, with their fourteen B-29s, was special, and the planes were
highly recognizable, with black arrows painted on their tails. The
elite of the air wing, the 509th were given the best accommodations
and showers; fresh food and whiskey were flown in for them, and
they enjoyed their own private movie theater. Within a few days
after their arrival, the island was buzzing about their special
mission. How come they had the best and flew every day, only to
drop bombs that never detonated, often sending them to fixed spots
over the ocean? To boot, these bombs had a funny pear shape to
them. The 509th were on a special mission, and only one man on
the team, their commander Colonel Paul Warfield Tibbits, knew

why they were there, although many had connected the dots, especially after the Trinity explosion. One of these was their navigator, Dutch Van Kirk, who over a period of time filled me in by phone on what happened in the final days leading up to the Hiroshima drop, and the after-effects of this historic event.

My interest was piqued by a recent *Time Magazine* story related to the 60th anniversary of Hiroshima, and the lofty goals of the Manhattan Project. It all sounded like ancient history, but I decided to take a deeper look at what really transpired when the first atomic bomb was dropped in Japan. I well know that the history books are often slanted towards the victors; it is the winners who get all the glory, while the losers get the shame. The information provided to the historians usually comes from the conquerors, with one of their motivations being to make war look glamourous so that they can preserve their military numbers and budgets during peacetime.

I started by Googling General Tibbits, the commander of the 509th and pilot of the *Enola Gay*, which dropped the first atomic bomb. After I dialed the telephone number I had found, his granddaughter answered; I seemed to have reached a kind of family museum and gift shop where autographed photos and other memorabilia, including autographed copies of Tibbits's biography, were offered to the public. General Tibbits was in his waning years in Cleveland Ohio, and I asked his granddaughter if I might fly up and have an audience with him for a few hours. She replied that he was in his early 90s, and with the exception of going out for lunch daily, he was a man who preferred to be by himself. Additionally, she said, due to his flying experiences and his love of firing guns, he had been stone deaf for years and was unable to communicate with others.

She did, however, steer me towards some of the articles the general had written in years past, explaining the entire operation from soup to nuts; some of these, I have incorporated into this piece. She suggested I contact then-Major Theodore "Dutch" Van Kirk, the navigator of the airplane on its historic mission of August 6, 1946. The airplane, I learned, had been named *Enola Gay* after

Tibbits's mother. As I was to learn, Major Van Kirk is the last surviving member, besides Tibbits, of the first plane to deliver the atomic bomb. I immediately thought to myself that it would be a great treat to get the full story first-hand, from one of the key players on that eventful day.

So, after another round with Google, I dialed up Van Kirk at his home in Stone Mountain, Georgia, and found a delightful guy on the other end of the phone. He was totally articulate and full of enthusiasm, beyond my wildest imaginings of what man in his early 80s could be like. As it turned out, the widow of the other key figure on the flight, Bombardier Tom Ferebee—a dashing, poker-playing lady-killer, according to some—was staying with the Van Kirks when I arrived. Apparently, all of those involved in the historic flight have kept in close contact over the years. Van Kirk said that until recently, he had been in touch with Tibbits, who had taken a turn for the worse this last July; Van Kirk recognized that he was, in effect, the last one left, and that it would fall upon him to pass on the legacy of the 509th.

So here is how the story goes, at least as I visualize it, with parts taken from some of the 509th's public documents, and many of the holes filled in with Major Dutch Van Kirk's anecdotes.

On July 15, 1945, the day of the Ground Zero explosion at Trinity, they knew then that they had a winner. Those on the carefully assembled flight teams of the 509th were informed that the time had come for them to step up to the plate. Still to be determined, though, was the ability to arm and deliver the atomic bomb, as well as the measure of its destructive forces, should the destructive military nature of the bomb prove to be viable. Due to time constraints, Colonial Tibbits and the military members of his crew could not attend the Trinity Blast; they were on Tinian, making the final preparations for the bombing run. It was only a matter of weeks, now that the results were confirmed, that they would be under the microscope of the world for their historic flight, according to Van Kirk. Soon the entire civilized world would get its first glimpse of the most destructive weapon designed by mankind. It was up to a handful of men from the 509th to deliver the payload.

At the time, only a few had heard this devastating weapon referred to by the atomic bomb, the name by which we now commonly refer to it. Some who were present at the drop, like the rear tail gunner aboard *Enola Gay*, the only one to see the actual explosion as the plane was headed away from the drop zone, said it was like witnessing the birth of the universe. It was like the moment of creation where the Lord said "let there be light," he said.

The team that was to deliver the payload had been chosen for they ability to work together under demanding combat conditions. Ferebee, the bombardier, and Van Kirk, the navigator, had served under now-General Tibbits, then a Colonel, in North Africa and Europe. Tibbits was by and large the most experienced B-29 pilot in the Air Force, often flying fifteen hours a day, six days a week. According to Van Kirk, he himself had participated in 58 missions as a young navigator, when he was only 24 years old, and Ferebee had 60 under his belt, all of which were at or over 20,000 feet, but none higher that 30,000, the level for the Hiroshima drop.

They were a close group back then, and remain so today, although Tibbits, because of his advanced age, has dropped out of continuous contact; Van Kirk remains in close personal touch with Ferebee's widow. These three men had together faced some of the toughest fighting of WW11, especially in the North Sea arena, where many pilots and their crews did not make it past ten bombing missions. They were survivors, a close and dedicated team that did not make mistakes, and, equally important, they knew how to keep a secret.

According to the history books, the existence of the atomic bomb was a secret known to very few. Given the nature of the project, I asked Van Kirk what he knew of the whole exercise. Officially, the 509th was supposed to be without knowledge of the payload; however, "if you could not guess we were dropping the atomic bomb, you were pretty stupid," Van Kirk told me. "If you talked about it you were even stupider," he added. The brain power was consolidated on Tinian. "Scientists running around, physicists, well-known guys on national magazine covers were there." Van Kirk went on to say that "I was aware of the Trinity site drop, and didn't have to be too smart to put two and two together."

It remains questionable how much of the details of the destructive forces attached to the bomb were common knowledge around Los Alamos, and especially among the three top people on the team, Tibbits, Van Kirk, and Ferebee, none of whom were present at the Trinity site explosion. Probably very little was known of the vast destructive nature of the weapon, especially the aftershock of the radiation. But they were aware of the significance of the weapon, according to Van Kirk, and of how it could save tens, even hundreds of thousands of lives. The priorities were established in their top-secret code name "silverplate," which granted them access to creature comforts not available to the other fliers on Tinian, as well as their unique back-up, in terms of logistics and equipment. The 509th, top dogs in the Air Force, they could not tell a soul what they knew of the mission. As an example, often they were sent fresh fish from New Orleans and fresh fruit from Florida in special military transports, luxuries unheard of during these trying times in the Pacific theater.

Most of the conventional bombing raids over Japan and the Japanese-controlled islands involved dropping a series of bombs at lower altitudes. This simply did not work when it came to the atom bomb, as the crew had to release "Little Boy" from 30,000 feet in order to give them time to turn away from the drop zone and dive to achieve a speed not inherent in the aircraft at cruising levels, all with the idea that they had to get out of the way of the destructive shock waves that would follow the detonation. That was quite a feat, according to Van Kirk, who says modestly that it was all in a day's work. It was quite an accomplishment when you consider the accuracy needed to be effective, especially in those days prior to satellite navigation.

Today, most commercial airliners fly at that altitude and at speeds far above the capabilities of that time, but back in those days military and civilian planes were not designed to fly at those lofty elevations. It is hard to imagine how a pilot could drop a bomb from 30,000 feet and be within a few hundred yards of the target. Back then, destiny—the success or failure of the drop—was still in the hands of humans, whereas today, such an event would be controlled by high-tech forces.

The 509th were there to prove their salt. For months on end they practiced and improved on the accuracy of their drops using dummy bombs. They also focused on putting their aircraft, the B-29s, into a 60-degree diving turn to exit the area as quickly as possible in less than a minute, hoping to build the speed of the aircraft to 350 miles per hour in order to accomplish this feat. This went way beyond the capability for which the B-29 was designed, Van Kirk told me. If they were off by a few degrees, the plane and its wings could potentially disintegrate, but this didn't cross the minds of those aboard that final day. They had rehearsed the exit strategy to perfection.

The basic survival concept, not confirmed by experience but only an educated guess, was that in order for the airplane to stay intact, the crew had to get out ahead of the supersonic wave generated by the explosion, and then ride these lesser waves, which were non-destructive to the aircraft. According to Van Kirk, at "in their first meeting with the Los Alamos scientists, they indicated that it would be appropriate if we were nine miles away when the bomb exploded." He asked, 'what do you mean, you 'think'"? The guy then answered, "We don't know; some people are saying 50 miles, some say 5, but our best calculations are that you need to be 9 miles away." Many history books say 5 miles was the magic number, but in retrospect they would have been wrong according to those who evaluated the ramifications of the explosion The time allotted for putting a safe distance between the plane after release and the explosion was "approximately 48 seconds," according to Van Kirk—not much of a window, when you are dealing with the unknown.

Parsons, the only crew member to witness the Trinity explosion, said that the estimated impact of the shock waves was a sophisticated guess, but the suggestion was that it would take approximately two thousand fully loaded B-29s to deliver the same payload, obviously something that could never happen all at once. Many of the crew sat in shock after the detonation, trying to absorb it all, Van Kirk recalled. At no time was any mention made of the radiation aspect of the bomb, both to the crew and to those who would suffer below. The wild card, needless to say, was that the bomb had never been dropped from an airplane before, and from a height in excess of that found at the tower at Trinity; as it turned out, the crew was 12 miles away from the drop zone when the bomb ignited, far enough to survive intact.

And so the tension, the practice runs, the questionable weight at takeoff, the level of fuel needed for the round trip, and the unknown aspect of survival of the shock waves went on and on until August 4, 1945, when the moment finally arrived. The weather patterns were perfect for dropping the "Pumpkin," as it was called by the crew members. Van Kirk noted that "the uranium bomb was not much different in shape than a normal bomb, but of course much larger." He estimated it to be "about ten feet long and about 36 inches in diameter." The size of the bomb's encasement was "so large as to contain the firing or the triggering mechanism of the explosion"; its size was required to generate momentum for the explosion, he explained.

Such a tremendous amount of energy was required to keep "the shot focused on the detonation zone that the bomb had to have a massive structure, to self-contain the potential matter and energy that would be released upon detonation," Van Kirk explained, even though the explosive device, as mentioned earlier, was only about the size of a tennis ball. The second bomb, consisting of plutonium, not uranium, that was dropped on Nagasaki was "larger around the middle and looked like a giant egg, with a great tail fin," according to Van Kirk. It was nicknamed the Fat Boy.

But I am getting a bit ahead of myself.

Seven B-29s would fly the first mission, with Hiroshima being the prime target. Weather scouts had been assigned to each of the three potential target cities. Nagasaki was the back-up drop zone in the event that weather conditions called for an alternative to Hiroshima. Three scouts would fly one hour in advance of *Enola Gay* and radio back the conditions at each area. As it turned out, Hiroshima was selected about halfway through the six-hour, 1500-mile flight to Japan. Two other B-29s would follow *Enola Gay* to record the event and a third would be stationed at Guam, along the way, in the event that the other aircraft were having mechanical problems.

Since the bomb had to be dropped visually over the target site, cloud cover was one of the major factors in picking Hiroshima. Ferebee, the bombardier, and the navigator Van Kirk took over the plane's direction on the last five miles of the flight, since they had to make the final call and adjustments for wind conditions and the bomb's trajectory as it fell, prior to releasing Little Boy. No mistakes would be permitted; there was little tolerance in terms of the drop zone, since they only had two atomic bombs in the arsenal in Tinian, according to Van Kirk. If they were to make a statement to the world, and impress upon the Japanese that the game was over, it had to be done right the first time. A failure would surely have caused a significant delay in the second bomb, possibly forcing the Allied forces to start the amphibious landing on the mainland of Japan until assurances were received that the bomb would create the necessary effect.

August 4th— the moment arrived

At the afternoon briefing, the crews were to be shown a film of the Trinity blast, giving them some idea of the magnitude of the explosion and the shock waves associated with it. The celluloid film became entangled in the sprockets of the projector, causing the showing of the film to be aborted. It wasn't a good start. Parsons, the only one who witnessed the Trinity test, stopped the projector and told them verbally what to expect, which of course was only a fragment of what was in store for them over the drop zone.

August 5th— the bomb is dropped.

There was time for a last trial run over the nearby ocean, where a dummy bomb was dropped to ensure that the fusing system worked. It was supposed to have emitted a slight puff of smoke as it went through 1,850 feet, but the bomb plunged smokeless into the ocean. Tomorrow was the real thing and this last test was a failure. Some of the crew were beginning to wonder if tomorrow's "real McCoy" over Hiroshima would be a dud as well.

At 3:00 p.m. the team installed the console with twenty-four wires that would monitor the bomb's health status in flight. The system was designed to check the batteries for electrical shorts, and to spotting any malfunction in the barometric pressure device needed to activate the firing of the bomb. At 3:30 p.m. the scientists and security people moved the bomb onto a trolley, with the whole enterprise still draped in secrecy. Some likened it to a military funeral cortege, as it traveled half a mile down the asphalt runway to the *Enola Gay*. It was hoisted up into the bomb bay and the fifteen-foot doors closed ten hours before takeoff. Bomb # L-11, one of two that could be armed, was ready to go. Prior to that it had sat in its air-conditioned room for those first four days in August, inert and waiting to be shipped to the drop zones when weather conditions permitted.

At midnight, Paul Tibbits addressed the twenty-six airmen who would be flying in the fleet with him to Japan. At 1:15 a truck picked up the crew and delivered them to the *Enola Gay* and the other waiting support aircraft.

A few days before takeoff, it was determined that the bomb had to be activated in flight and not prior to takeoff in the safety of a hanger on the base. The powers that be let it be known that a crash landing on takeoff at Tinian with an "armed" atomic bomb was not acceptable. The base was too strategic to either be destroyed or put out of temporary commission if the flight had to be aborted. Activation of the bomb required that several fuses had to be put into place to set off the detonation process. Among those were "a time fuse, a barometric fuse, and a radar proximity fuse that had to be installed once airborne," Van Kirk explained. "A few days before the flight we tested the radar proximity fuse and it did not work...It made us feel real good," he said. But such is life!

We were only nervous about "two things," said Van Kirk: "getting the plane and the bomb off the runway, and putting enough distance between the plane and the 'lethal' shock waves after it exploded." The possibility of a crash was always there. "The plane was 7,000 pounds over the designed weight and many of the conventional B-29s could not pull 'full' power on takeoff anyway, and often some would crash on the end of the runway on Tinian. It was common knowledge that the 20th Air Force wing lost more B-29s at the end of the runway at Tinian than were lost over Japan." The plane weighed 150,000 pounds (65 tons) with 7000 gallons of fuel, and of course the 5-ton atomic bomb and the twelve men aboard added to speculation about a potential crash.

According to Van Kirk, the second problem, getting away from the shockwaves, involved major improvisations to the fleet of the 509th, now stripped down B-29s. "The conventional B-29s could not get up high enough, and could not get enough speed to survive the blast. They took about 6,000 pounds off the bomb-carrying airplanes. All the guns and turrets and much of the radio equipment were removed so it would work"

Before boarding the truck to drive to the *Enola Gay*, whose name was painted on the fuselage just hours before takeoff, Van Kirk recalls that he, Tibbits, and Ferebee "worked out the final details of the fight plan," including the lower altitudes they would fly at on their way points en route to conserve fuel." In those days fuel efficiency was marginal at the higher elevations, unlike today, when aircraft are propelled by higher-powered engines. The three reviewed the communication passwords needed to communicate with the three advance weather observing planes, and the speeds at which they would enter and move through the drop zone for both the primary and the two alternative target cities.

As the hours closed in before daybreak, the three hammered out loose ends and final details. The hours and minutes passed slowly as they moved towards the takeoff time of 0245. The weather would determine which site was to be attacked: Hiroshima, Nagasaki, or Kokura. There were different things to consider for each site, such as the cloud clover, and the true versus calibrated wind speeds necessary to find the target. The plan was to fly low to Iwo Jima at about 5000 feet above sea level to save fuel, and then up to 31,000 feet, or six miles, as they approached the mainland of Japan, according to Van Kirk. Two other B-29s would be in the tail of *Enola Gay* for purposes of photography and monitoring the radiation and shock waves after the blast.

Shortly before takeoff, the silence of the secret Manhattan Project was lifted: the project went public. It was too much for the Washington brass to keep under wraps. Flashbulbs went off, and movie cameras and audio recorders were everywhere. These twelve men were destined to be heroes, and America's pride and prestige were on the line. The Air Force even decided to record the crew's in-flight conversations for posterity. So, the stage was finally set.

Van Kirk explained that, for all intents and purposes, the "Japanese were defeated" before the drop, a viewpoint that did not come out at the news conference. One of the reasons that the *Enola Gay* met virtually no resistance from Japanese aircraft, artillery fire or radar jamming was that "there was no Jap resistance; 85% of its industrial capacity was burned down, overseas the navy had been ruined, and the air force as well. It was the nature of the Japanese never to surrender." Van Kirk went on to say that "Their home-based land armies as well had been virtually destroyed, except the land armies overseas in China."

At 0220 Tibbits said to the newsmen. "Okay, fellows, cut those lights. We've gotta be going." And then said to his men, "let's go to work."

And at 0245 the engines on *Enola Gay* started to move, with an 8,800 horsepower capacity designed to achieve a takeoff speed of 123 miles per hour. The propellers turned at fifty revolutions per second as the overloaded plane fought to get off the ground. As they approached the end of the runway, the co-pilot Lewis said to

Tibbits, "She's too heavy! Pull her off—now!" as he moved his hands in an effort to control the wheel. Tibbits replied, "No, leave it alone," ignoring his advice as the plane lifted off just a hundred feet from the end of the runway into the blackness of the surrounding sea.

The next hurdle to overcome was arming or activating the devices on the bomb that would automatically trigger the explosion at 1850 feet. Previously, attempts to activate the bomb were in air-conditioned, well-lit hangers. Now the task had to be accomplished in an environment where the plane was vibrating enormously, the temperature was extremely hot, and the work space around the bomb was quite limited. To complicate matters, there was no natural or artificial light.

At 0315, Parsons said he was ready to crawl back into the bomb bay and activate Little Boy. There were 11 items on the checklist, and each one was radioed back to the flight deck as it was completed. It was hot and dark. Parsons's assistant, Jeppson, followed Parsons with a flashlight, handing him tools whenever he needed them. The two men squatted inside the bomb bay with their backs almost touching the hatch facing the tail end of the bomb.

By 0310 the gunpowder was being inserted, and at 0320 the two men crawled back out of the bomb bay. The arming mission was accomplished. They needed one additional fine-tuning of the mechanism about an hour before the target was reached, but that was secondary to what they had done in the last 20 minutes. But the plane had lost radio contact with Tinian, so they were on their own as far as the outside world was concerned. This probably would have served them well, had they been unsuccessful in their mission.

They all stared blankly into the night, Van Kirk recalls. The sky was clear and the stars were just hanging there, with the pitch black ocean just below. Back in those days, they used Loran, a non-sophisticated navigation system compared to our current satellite-based network. The system focused on two land points, along with the moveable third leg of the triangle, the *Enola Gay.*

As they moved through the night, the crew took turns having cat naps, said Van Kirk. A few stayed awake to look for enemy aircraft, which were non-existent. The Japanese routinely let single or small groups of airplanes pass by without challenging them, especially at high altitudes, since they generally put them in the category of reconnaissance planes. Most of the conventional bombing runs over Japan were at a fraction of the heights at which the *Enola Gay* moved.

The drop zone over Hiroshima was determined by Bombardier Ferebee. It was as an easily recognized area where several rivers intersected near the Port of Ujina, and it was decided that a bridge of recognizable quality was to be the target. The mechanical devices of the nuclear explosion were programmed to start the split-second detonation process at 1850 feet above the target, the height that would cause the greatest initial and subsequent damage, according to those at Los Alamos. A series of events would take place once Little Boy was released, all based on monitoring the barometric pressure switch designed to close and activate the detonation process as the bomb went through 7000 feet above sea level. Traveling at more than 700 miles per hour, the bomb would explode just 48 seconds after clearing the plane.

And then, reality set in.

At 8:05 a.m., Van Kirk announced "10 minutes to AP," just as the crew was monitoring the Japanese fighter control frequency, where there was still no indication of activity. Parsons took his position at the bomb console, where all lights remained green. Without a hitch, Van Kirk had delivered the *Enola Gay* to the exact height, at the predetermined speed, and to the point for the final bomb run. It was 8:12.

Hiroshima was naked as a jaybird, making no effort to defend herself, not even sounding the warning alarms on the ground for people to move to the shelters. The Japanese simply dismissed the B-29s as reconnaissance planes moving effortless through the skies at 325 miles per hour, or about 5 miles per minute. Now the black-and-white, two-dimensional charts that Van Kirk and others had studied lit up in the morning sunlight in color. The real thing, a mirror image of what they had envisioned so many times, was now there in three dimensions. Their target bridge, now 16 miles away, just a short three-minute run into the wind.

Now it was up to the bombardier to calculate the wind and drift for the last time. Bombardier Tom Ferebee, hunched over his M-9B Norden bombsight, had the final say. For 6 ½ hours he had little to do but wait for these final three minutes. Nobody had time to worry about whether the plane's wings would buckle or the windows would be blown out because of the two aftershocks, causing certain death to all aboard. This was the heart and soul of this special mission, and they thought of little else on the final run to the target.

In a way, their bombsight was as advanced as any piece of equipment the Air Force had in its arsenal. It was so sophisticated that after the conventional B-29 bombing runs to Japan, they were all removed and placed in safe-keeping so that the enemy could not discover their make-up and composition.

At 0913 bombardier Feebee announced to Tibbits that he had the bridge on his scope ten miles away. Ninety seconds prior to the drop, Tibbits freed his hands of the wheel, and Ferebee took control, adjusting the plane's movement, all the while with the target bridge in his cross hairs. Then the Bombay doors opened and at exactly 0915:17, the switch was thrown and Little Boy was on her way. At first it seemed to be suspended in mid-air, the bombardier recalled, but then it wobbled a little and picked up speed, eventually heading to where it was supposed to.

Enola Gay shot up several feet as the weight of the bomb was released, at which time Tibbits disengaged the autopilot and took over the yoke, putting the B-29 into a diving right-hand turn of 155 degrees. Now the bomber was virtually standing on its wingtip, and the increased gravitational forces kept the men pinned to their seats. Hiroshima below swung like a kaleidoscope with all its magnificent colors, and every rivet, it seemed, was about to pop as the B-29 attempted to outrun the first wave of devastating shock waves from the blast. Behind *Enola Gay*, another B-29, the *Great Artiste*, dropped a series of gages in an attempt to record the nature of the blast, and went into a similar dive but to the left. As the *Enola Gay* came to the completion of its death-defying turn, it was about five miles from the drop zone, and speeding away at 350 miles per hour.

Van Kirk describes pushing the envelope. "Tibbits told the other pilots, during the lead-up training exercises, to make the turn so tight that your tail starts to stall; then you know you have turned enough. It was quite a maneuver at that altitude." Needless to say, the practice paid off.

With thirty-eight seconds left, Little Boy was dropping through the atmosphere with its eight spring-wound clocks counting down toward the fusing relay. All this destructive power was aimed at a city of high density, with 25,000 people per square mile. Little Boy went through the magic number, 7000 feet, and the firing device went into the final stage of the fusing relay. In a few seconds the firing device moved across the arming plugs toward the breach primers, detonating the cordite charges and propelling the uranium 235 projectile down the gun's six-foot barrel towards the uranium target. The projectile hit the target at the "speed of sound," sending billions upon billions of splitting neutrons in every direction and releasing tremendous amounts of energy in an ever-widening chain reaction.

Those on the ground didn't have a clue what was happening; there was no trace of the bomb's impending arrival, since it was moving faster than the speed of sound, in complete silence. At 5,000 feet the barometric switch tripped. At 1903 feet the crashing sound came, the last that over a hundred thousand people ever heard. The bomb exploded about 200 meters off the above-ground cross hairs of the Aioa Bridge site.

Before anyone on the ground realized, in the first billionth of a second, the temperature at the burst point reached 50 million degrees centigrade. The blast literally carbonized a large portion of the population below. Within one kilometer of the hypocenter, all was lost; even the steel structures lignified, all in the first 3 seconds. Of the 320,000 inhabitants of the city, it is estimated that over 80,000, of whom about a third were military, died in those first three seconds. And then the nuclear aspects of the weapon took over, releasing gamma rays and neutrons from the bomb's chain reaction and eventually destroying the structure of tissues found in the human body. Tens of thousands would die a few days afterwards, or some years down the road.

Van Kirk never saw the destruction on the ground at Hiroshima, and only witnessed the scene from the air. But he did visit Nagasaki, and he estimated that "at Hiroshima there was complete devastation within a four-square-mile area, two miles by two miles." There was lesser damage to life and property when the inhabitants were further from the drop zone. According to Van Kirk, there were three causes of death: "shock waves, heat and then radiation. I might say that the scientists in those days grossly underestimated the areas that would be affected by radiation."

After the first split second, next came the shockwave, moving away from the hypocenter initially at 7,200 miles per hour, or 10,000 feet per second, and then slowing down to around the speed of sound. This unforgiving wall of high pressure demolished everything: buildings, schools, and factories, not to mention people. It moved at an alarming speed of 7 tons per square meter, destroying 62,000 of the 90,000 buildings in the city, and killing at least another 50,000 people. The shockwaves sucked out most of the air behind them, leaving a low pressure system that literally sucked the insides out of people.

The ring of destruction moved forward. The city was surrounded on three sides by mountainous terrain that corralled the damage. The destruction moved into the rice fields on the edge of town, flattening homes and their occupants in the process. All it took was two pounds of fissionable uranium 235 to flatten the entire city. Some 30 minutes after the release of the bomb, Hiroshima literally no longer existed. Some 140,000 would perish, and thirteen square miles were reduced to rubble. Almost 90% of the hospitals were

inoperative, and the majority of the telephone services were
trashed, as were the radio stations.

Most doctors, firemen and police were simply liquefied. Water,
electric and sewer lines were destroyed, so those who survived
lived in a world that could no longer function. Even those who
made the initial cut, those who wanted to escape the destruction,
could not: most of the bridges leading out of the city were
destroyed, as were the water carriers that normally moved people
in more peaceful times.

In this devastated city, there were thousands of breaks in the water
lines, and the city's sewer pumping stations became dysfunctional,
resulting in a lack of drinking water. The intense heat created such
a thirst among the survivors that when the rain came down after
the cooling of the mushroom cloud, they drank it, seeing it as a
blessing from above, only to learn later that the water was highly
radioactive and would cause great death and sickness. Many
simply did themselves in, or asked others to do it for them. The
heat and lack of oxygen in the air was unbearable. Many simply
lost consciousness, and perished in time from their untreated
injuries.

The only man to observe the true force of the bomb, and the
formation of the mushroom cloud, was tail-gunner Bob Caron,
who watched things unfold through his welders' goggles from the
rear turret. Eleven miles away from the drop zone, the light from
the explosion caught up with the crew. Tom Ferebee, his back to
the mushroom cloud, said it "felt like an enormous flashbulb going
off." An ethereal glow formed over the cockpit and its instruments.
Tibbits could taste the brilliance: "it tasted like lead," he recalled.
Every part of the plane took on a bright radiance. Nobody spoke
for a while until Caron "announced that the shock waves were
about to hit them," according to the crew's recollections. The first
wave hit the B-29, tossing it up like a feather; later it was
calculated that the force measured fifteen kilotons, the equivalent
of 15,000 tons of high explosives.

Caron, the first witness to the atomic bomb's shock wave, later described the approaching shock waves, one from the blast and another also from the blast, reflecting off the ground and much less stressful. He said it looked as if "the ring around some distant planet had detached itself and was coming up toward us." He went on to say that "the air was so compressed it seemed to take on a physical form."

Van Kirk recounted that the shock wave felt like "a burst of flack under the wing, just like in Europe," and he assumed they were under enemy fire. He was corrected by the tail gunner Caron, who said it was not flack but a shock wave. Caron then announced that a second wave was about to hit. According to Van Kirk's recollection of the incident, it was like "a pebble in still water, with waves emulating outward." The wave was very visible because of the compact nature of the air.

The second and last shock wave came and went without as much fanfare. Van Kirk said that at Nagasaki there were "three such shock waves, since it was a larger bomb." And then *Enola Gay* was in the clear, climbing to a respectable altitude and circling Hiroshima to determine the nature and extent of the damage. In the distance was the mushroom cloud, a mile wide. Caron remembers still seeing the bright red ball of destruction, with every imaginable color in it, from the tail gunner's spot, some 350 miles away. It could have been seen from even further away, except that the curvature of the earth made it disappear. Years later he was quoted as saying the whole experience was a "peep into hell."

Van Kirk looked down at the city whose every detail he had memorized on two-dimensional maps, and saw nothing left; Tibbits turned the plane for a better view after the shock waves passed. All was gone. Only the fires that continued to be stoked by the city's 90% wooden structures remained. There was only wreckage, burning and dust.

The *Enola Gay*, now 11 miles from the drop zone, at 29,000 feet, began the first of three orbits around Hiroshima. Tibbits circled the mushroom cloud, 60,000 feet high. Parsons later said it was "like a mass of bubbling molasses, a mile or two wide. It was very black, but there was a purplish tint to it. The flames and smoke were billowing out, whirling into the foothills." The crew's comments were later paraphrased. One said it was like a huge hot bed of coals, like a barbeque grill miles wide, with flames shooting out everywhere. Caron, in the tail gunner's spot, took photos that would be shown around the world. Somehow, in the confusion, the recordings of the crew's thoughts and conversations during the historic flight vanished. As they headed home most of the crew thought, and some said, that "this day and event would be the end of the war."

Tibbits, according to Van Kirk, "crawled back through the tunnel of the plane on the way home to tell the men what the whole mission was about, although he never used the word "atomic." Tibbins and Parsons, the only ones to have witnessed the Trinity explosion, did their best to explain what had happened. The mission's success was best summed up by Lewis, the co-pilot, who said that "the Japs would throw in the sponge, probably even before *Enola Gay* had landed at Tinian."

The whole mission went according to plan. Van Kirk recorded the time of touch-down at Tinian in his navigation log at 14:58. The mission had taken 12 hours and 13 minutes and covered over 2960 miles. Little Boy was dropped just 16 seconds behind their projected schedule.

Van Kirk describes the Hiroshima mission as "Letter perfect." But "the Nagasaki mission was one of the mostly fouled up things you ever saw in your life." According to Van Kirk, "they should have delayed the mission, but they were anxious to get it done, as the Japanese thought we only had one bomb, and they needed to be convinced to the contrary, and that they should surrender now."

Even hours before the *Enola Gay* arrived back at Tinian, reports were circulating around Tokyo that Hiroshima had been completely destroyed, even though the total communications network had been destroyed. For those who survived, it was a nightmare. The entire city became a place of death and decay, with no hope of rebirth. It was left to rot and die.

A few days after returning, Tibbits and Van Kirk had a meeting with Curtis LeMay, the commanding officer, who turned to Tibbits and asked if any more bombs were left. Tibbits replied that there was one more, stateside. According to Van Kirk, LeMay said, "get it out here, and you guys are flying it."

So, three days after Hiroshima, the crew of the B-29 *Bockscar*, under the stewardship of Captain Chuck Sweeney, dropped Fat Man over the city of Nagasaki, situated in an industrial valley. They released a devastating force of 22,000 tons of TNT, about one and a half times of that dropped on Hiroshima. The original target was the city of Kokura, but cloud cover saved the day for her. The target this time was the large Mitsubishi arms complex, and about 70,000 were killed.

I found the names assigned to the two atom bombs interesting. The original bomb was named "Thin Man," after President Roosevelt, and was later changed to "Little Boy" when the overall size was shrunk. "Fat Man" related to the fact that it was not a uranium but a plutonium bomb—it was more powerful and bulged at the middle.

As the second bomb was being dropped, the Japanese Supreme Council for the Direction of the War—the Big Six, as they were known—began contemplating the unconditional surrender that the Allies had called for weeks before the dropping of the two bombs. The end was in sight: the day before Little Boy was dropped, the Soviets had declared war on Japan, and millions of Russian troops were crossing the Manchurian border in China. Not many wanted the Soviets to invade Japan, including the United States, since Stalin's appetite for power and conquest was all-encompassing, worldwide in scope, and becoming more obvious with each passing day.

The six members of the Supreme Council met at a meeting chaired by the Prime Minister. The hours passed away in complete deadlock, as three dissenting members attempted to gain more concessions from the Allies. Finally, an "Imperial Conference" was called, and the Emperor was brought in to sift out the opposing arguments. He finally rose and gave his blessing to those who would accept the Allied terms. Emperor Hirohito broke the tie on August 10th at 2:00 a.m. and departed, saving his own skin in the process: one of the concessions the Allies granted was that the Emperor would retain his position and power during the reconstruction of Japan after the war.

The war was over.

On the same day that the Council capitulated, another B-29 was dispatched to cross the Pacific for a 6,000-mile trip to pick up the third bomb, which was being prepared. The anticipated date for dropping was August 17th or 18th, and the target was Tokyo, although Van Kirk said that "nobody really knew the destination" and he should have known since he would have been the navigator.

But it all became academic. On August 14th, the final declaration of surrender was hand-delivered to the State Department just five days after the Big Six conference, and nine days after the crew of *Enola Gay* dropped Little Boy on Hiroshima. It certainly got the attention of the world, and of those in power in Japan as well as the Allies, especially Stalin, who took great notice as the war efforts came to a sudden conclusion.

So, what about the other players on the scene?

Truman, of course, stood by his decision for the rest of his life. And many thought, like Truman, that the Japanese experiment would be the end of nuclear confrontation. But a few did anticipate that a nuclear arms race would ensue with the Soviets—one, it seems, that our *own* military promoted, not Stalin's military machine, as the propagandists would like us to believe. Henry Simson, then-Secretary of State, had many reservations about the entire atomic bomb mission and its ramifications, and the fact that it might trigger an arms race, a fact confirmed by his heart attack two days after Hiroshima and a day before Nagasaki. A month later, he resigned. He instinctively knew the dangers of what this weapon might do, even in the right hands.

Part of the reasoning behind the *use* of the nuclear bomb in Japan was the perceived threat that the Soviets were intent on moving into the void that the Germans had left behind in defeat. The Allies needed the Soviets to defeat Germany, and especially to take Berlin, but that was all. They knew that if Stalin were awarded the spoils of the war, he would create havoc and destruction, which of course he did in the Iron Block—not to mention the millions of his people who were interned in slave camps and died after the end of the war.

But what escaped our mentality at the time was that the American military was not content to end the hostilities and retire. They needed a reason to continue with their war machine, and so they used Little Boy as a vehicle to perpetuate their very existence. They needed a future target, even though it was halfway around the world and in shambles, and "Uncle Joe," as Russia was known, was the bull's eye on the target. They needed an ongoing enemy, as the rest of Europe posed no immediate threat, since it lay in ruins.

After many decades of declassification, the plot was revealed, reflecting the sinister mentality of the military. The Chief of Staff of the Army Strategic Air Force, in a top-secret, three-page document, spelled out its intent in a document known as "Estimated Bomb Requirements for Destruction of Russian Strategic Areas." It outlined 66 Russian cities, including Moscow, to be destroyed by the use of nuclear weapons, and it specifically outlined the targeted areas, measured in square miles, as well as the total number of weapons needed to do the job. The memo was released around September 15, 1945, about a month after the Japanese surrendered. That is quick work for a military with only one atomic bomb remaining in its arsenal.

Not even a month had passed, and many of the Japanese bodies had not even been buried. But the American military was already focusing on the next target, the Soviet Union. What a sad commentary. It reflects what many, like Oppenheimer, had predicted would happen if the powerful took control of the program.

Oppenheimer, credited with being the father of the atomic bomb, violently opposed the development of the subsequent hydrogen bomb, first tested in 1952. It was a thousand times more powerful than the ones dropped in Japan. He was so vocal and adamant that finally, in 1954, his top security clearance was revoked, which somehow sent a signal that if you opposed the program you could be mistaken for a Russian spy. He died a broken man a dozen years later, knowing, as many did, that the escalation of the atomic race would lead to no good. "In some sort of crude sense," he said, "the physicists have known sin; and this is a knowledge which they cannot lose."

Like most of our WW11 heroes, not many of the *Enola Gay* are still aboard. Tibbits is frail and uncommunicative in his waning years. He once said that as time wore on, he became an "expendable victim" of the changing public attitude towards what he was ordered to do at Hiroshima, especially as the nuclear arms race unfolded with the Russians. Only Van Kirk can talk about the mission today with any authority. After the war, he returned to college, obtained a degree in chemical engineering, and worked for DuPont Chemical until his retirement. Parsons, who armed the bomb, went on to become a Rear Admiral, but died in December 1953. Ferebee stayed in the air force, and retired after a stint in Vietnam; he recently passed away. As for Tinian, it obtained Commonwealth status. There, the jungle has all but erased any signs of the war. Some seven hundred people live there, in tin shanties in San Jose, the island's only occupied city. Hiroshima has weathered the fateful event, and is now a city of 900,000, almost three times what it was before the bomb. The A-Bomb Dome was left standing as a reminder of the tragic events that took place.

The A-bomb changed the world, and the devastation it caused will never be forgotten. Every year on August 6, people around the world attend memorial ceremonies involving origami cranes and paper lanterns. The lanterns in this Japanese Buddhist ceremony represent the souls of the ancestors; they are set adrift on water, helping the souls return to heaven. The lantern tradition has now become symbolic of world peace and the abolishment of nuclear weapons. Nevertheless, the events of 9/11, a day similarly drenched in terror and loss, evoked the horror of Hiroshima once again, bringing to mind the words of the poet George Santayana: "Those who do not learn from history are doomed to repeat it."

THE TRAIL OF TEARS:

THE VICTIMIZED AMERICAN INDIAN

The American Indian and his lifestyle were doomed as the last half of the 19th century came into play. The demise of this once-proud, self-sufficient people is tragic, especially in light of the fact that they never took much from others, never wanted to possess material goods, and never wanted to own the land, but just to use it while they were there. Their ingrained philosophy was rooted in the concept that it was not right to claim anything that belonged to nature, unless it was necessary for survival. Thus it would not take long for them to become at odds with the white men, whose objectives were diametrically opposed to those of the Native Americans when they began to occupy their sacred space in ever-increasing numbers. It was a short downward spiral, a period of about thirty years from 1860 to 1890 that, interesting enough, immediately followed the tragic conclusion of our Civil War.

The Great Plains of the Midwest were theirs for hundreds of generations, by some accounts. Each season they followed the deer, elk and buffalo into the tall grasses, and their every need was amply provided for. At the start of the Civil War, there were thought to be about 300,000 Indians in the West, as opposed to about 30 million people of European descent in North America.

For a while they lived in harmony with their newly discovered rivals for the territory west of the Mississippi. The Oregon and Santa Fe trails provided a common and disruptive thread through their sacred grounds. But the final spike into their very hearts and souls was the later expansion of the transcontinental railroad. At first it seemed that things would remain the same, since everything was so plentiful and the wide open spaces offered freedom of movement to all. At first, the two opposing cultures benefitted from each other's intrusions: for instance, Lewis and Clark and their fellow desperate settlers were saved when the Indians found them and provided them with food and shelter, enabling the success of their later expedition to the great Pacific Ocean..

However, as more and more white settlers sought out the freedom associated with the new frontier, their needs and ambitions began to reflect what has been called over the centuries "Manifest Destiny." In short, the phrase meant that the white European race was destined to rule "all" of America, and after the end of the Civil War, our politicians in conjunction with our military decided that we should settle the west and become caretakers of the Indians, their land, and their wealth in minerals, timber, and buffalo herds.

Most Indians on the Great Plains were peaceful at first, contrary to the accounts in some of our history books, written, of course, by pale-skinned scholars from the eastern part of the United States. But others had become hardened by then, such as the Apache and Pueblo Indians of New Mexico; the Spanish, in their quest for gold, brought with them their brutal forms of religion and warlike ways, such as burning at the stake and scalping the enemy, a horrible practice that found its way into the warlike culture of the Plains Indians, as a way leaving a lasting message that they, just like the Spanish before them, were not to be taken lightly.

For those who remember their history, the closing days of the Civil War were tragic, with events like the final march and destruction of Atlanta, so vividly portrayed in the book *Gone With the Wind*, and General Sherman's implementation of the term "scorched earth" after the death of Lincoln, referring to the looting and plundering of southern plantations and their people by him and his troops. Once this mission was completed, the big guns in Washington, including President Grant, decided that the military must "re-invent" itself in order keep a presence on the contemporary scene–a concept that has not changed much since those days, as we see today in Iraq, where justifications for the war dwindle daily and the truth surfaces about why we invaded Iraq in the first place.

In other words, the mandate was to victimize the American Indian just as they had the Confederates after the war, and to reap the benefits of the scorched earth policy. Except here, the scale of the conquered land and its riches was enormous. The mission seemingly went unchecked by a Congress and a series of Presidents who looked the other way as the settlers took more and more. They simply rubber-stamped, through treaties, these atrocious acts, under the auspices of "the end justifying the means."

So, with that prevailing attitude, and after the surrender at Appomattox, Congress in 1860 passed what became known as the Pre-emption Bill, which gave free land to those wanting to settle in the west. The Bill triggered a great exodus from the eastern part of this country, one that brought about the total devastation and the symbolic end of the Indian and his God-given rights, which gradually eroded, and by most accounts terminated at Wounded Knee in 1890.

The white settlers moved westward in alarming numbers. The advent of the railroad, with its ability to move large quantities of people and material great distances, expedited the process and was aided by the military, as part of the grand scheme for implementing Manifest Destiny. Often, huge amounts of corruption involved, and railroad barrens and politicians became wealthy virtually overnight.

The idea was to establish a series of government forts along the prime access areas into and through the Indian territories, areas formerly used by the Indians for grazing, hunting and fishing. When things got too lopsided in the favor of the settlers, the Great White Father always had things to trade for the Indians' rights to the land; the deals were often sealed by written treaties that bore little resemblance to what the Indians, those most affected by the agreements, had understood verbally.

The military assured the homesteaders a degree of protection. The newcomers were given land-in- fee ownership for establishing themselves as settlers, in contrast to the Indians, who had roamed these vast lands forever, never claiming any rights or ownership. Their mindset, for hundreds of generations, focused on borrowing the land, without making a long-term claim on its ownership, and using it to provide shelter and food for their families. The settlers, however, were given perpetual rights of ownership, something that was established in the European courts of law.

It was not just the settlers who put down their stakes of ownership: other "white eyes" came for the gold and other minerals, and who craved the profits from the animal hides that were the very substance of those who had lived there for so many generations. The Indians had known the value of letting the soil and the animal population replenish itself so that future generations could benefit from the same abundance.

The settlers and the military had a total disregard for this long-established culture and appreciation of nature's bounty. The White Eyes pushed on, in the early days heading to the Black Hills of North Dakota for the glitter of the gold and silver, and then on to Colorado and California, all without giving much thought to what they left in their wake. They virtually took as much as was economically feasible and then pushed on, unlike many of the early settlers.

The great Plains tribes like the Cheyenne, Arapahos, Sioux, Comanche, and Kiowas, with their great leaders like Red Cloud, began taking up arms against this intruding force that had to be dealt with. The new buffalo hunters from the east now slaughtered entire herds for the skins only, depleting much of the Indians food supply by leaving the animal carcasses to rot on the ground. The military played a big role in annihilating the buffalo since the Washington politicians felt they could not conquer the Indians as long as they had ample food. They promoted the buffalo hunters and fed and housed them in their forts, provided ammunition and arranged for shipments back east on the railroads for the hides, all in an attempt to starve the Indians into submission.

The buffalo hunters were provided with long-range rifles from the military that could bring down an animal from a mile away, enabling them to pick off the leaders of the herds, and then slaughter the rest. Some of these marksman could kill thousands of buffalo in a season, so from 1868 to 1883, some 30 million buffalo were eliminated. Some commented at the time that there were so many decaying white buffalo bones on the plains that it looked like snow from a distance.

As the Indians took up arms against the invasion of their lands and the slaughter of their food source, the U.S. government set up a series of Indian agents in the disputed territories, appointed by the all-white Commission of Indian Affairs, a sort of watch dog group that created and unilaterally enforced one-sided treaties designed to remove the Indians to lands that were not nearly as productive or desirable as the ones they had occupied for generations.

The idea behind Manifest Destiny was to convert the Indians into settlers who could grow crops and raise livestock, like the white man, but in a separate environment. This was unlike the Spanish, who conquered the Pueblo Indians and then cohabited with them. If this isolation policy could not be accomplished, the Indians were simply to be exterminated.

Since the Indians were reluctant to give up their lands, the "treaty" was designed to facilitate the process. It was presented as a reward for relinquishing their land, and was usually combined with some superficial form of compensation, such as food or clothing, which the Indians badly needed given the rapidly disappearing buffalo.

In most instances, with the exception of the Apache treaties I discuss later on, the treaties were one-sided, not reflecting the tribe members' wishes. They were a sham. Treaties needed to be signed by 75% of the tribe's members before Congress would ratify them. Most of these bogus agreements never received the appropriate number of signatures, but Congress approved them anyway in their haste to conquer the west, always finding a way to bend the rules for their own benefit.

Those tribes who refused to sign were forced into submission by the Bluecoats as the military moved into the west in increasingly great numbers. They isolated the Indians, starved them, and pushed them off their productive lands with their powerful rifles, fast-moving horses, and railways. Often they would raid Indian villages, killing their horses and destroying their food with their superior weapons, simply in retribution for the Indians' refusal to sign the White Man's self- serving, misleading, English-structured documents.

As time went on, the Plains tribes attempted to fight back, but many became like helpless children when taken to the Bluecoats' forts. The women and young were domesticated, and lived off the government dole, while the warriors were often tried, kangaroo court style, by military tribunals and hanged. Often the children and the women were sold into slavery into wealthy Mexican families as punishment for the resistance movement, or were traded for weapons or livestock as a means of continuing the march to conquer the west.

The treaties eventually became somewhat obsolete, especially after California became the 31st state in the 1850s, and territories like Minnesota, Kansas, Nebraska, and Colorado came into being, through the legislation of those in power in Washington. The new states had the right to do virtually anything they desired in terms of granting land ownership and rights to the humans who fell within their jurisdiction. With territorial law now "gospel," the white man was no longer on a level playing field. They just rewrote their own rules, leaving the reservations under the jurisdiction of the federal government.

Many of the treaties were negotiated with half-breeds as interpreters, since they could partially speak both languages. However, many of these interpreters could not read or write English, so most of the documentation was a sheer fabrication of one-sided terms and conditions. The major elements that were important to the Indians were discussed verbally, but were conveniently left out when the signatures were added. Even the legitimate treaties lasted only a few years as the areas expanded and the white man needed more and more of the prime land for homesteading and mineral extraction. They simply pushed the

Indians on to less desirable places, with promises that were rarely honored.

And of course, the treaties stated that the Indians had to live under the white man's laws, which had little meaning to them. Thus they were often punished or incarcerated for not conforming. For instance, the Pueblo Indians of New Mexico usually did not fence in their livestock, as was their tradition; they let them roam free. But when the animals were found grazing on the white settlers' land, they were shot with no explanation.

It is hard for me to speak for the Plains Indians, since their culture has become extinct. This, combined with the fact that I have never had an opportunity to live in close proximity to what is left of their way of life, leaves me able only to speculate about their world.

But I can, with some authority, talk about the Pueblo Indians of New Mexico, those dozen or so tribes currently residing in communities that have traditionally drawn their life blood from the Rio Grande River. The River is used primarily for domestic animal grazing, human consumption and irrigation of crops. The Pueblos are uniquely different from the nomadic tribes such as the Navajos and the Apaches that co-existed in the same area of the southwest. The Pueblos have maintained their land and traditions for centuries, and have remained in the same location, even though they are under the physical and political control of others–the Spanish initially, and now those in Washington, at the Bureau of Indian Affairs.

Unfortunately, many charged with their care have categorized them as uneducated misfits and often as alcoholics living off the Bureau of Indian Affairs, or their gambling income. Such a statement can be made with some degree of legitimacy, at least until one delves into the reasons why they find themselves in their contemporary predicament.

Unbeknownst to most of modern society, the Pueblos have some great traditions, part of which emerged from their interconnection with the Spanish. The Cochiti, Laguna, Nambe, Pojoaque, Sandia,

San Juan, Santa Domiongo, Taos, and the Zunoi live along the Rio Grande Valley in central and northern New Mexico. Their relatively permanent nature was not only their salvation, but was also a reflection of the Spanish influence, which so dominated the southwest for many centuries.

The Anasazi Indians built great cities in the western part of New Mexico, in the Chaco Canyon area. Most were carved out of the limestone cliffs that overlooked the streams and tributaries and served as their lifeblood. However, due to some unknown event, most likely drought or a pandemic of some sort, they simply disappeared, like the Mayans of Central America, leaving no trace of their human whereabouts except their edifices. One of these, Pueblo Bonito, was their grandest city, consisting of over 600 rooms; it is thought that around 1275, the Anasazi simply gave up trying to survive in what had once been a fertile valley, and formed what is now the Pueblos along the Rio Grande. It is only speculation that Mother Nature refused to cooperate in the final years of their occupation of these great but harsh lands.

Several centuries later, around 1540, the Spanish moved into the Rio Grande Valley under Coronado, who was looking for the Seven Cities of Gold. He conquered and named the villagers the Pueblos, *the town people*. Although the two groups lived together, the Indians initially refused to be subservient. When the Spanish failed to find the Seven Cities of Gold, they often burned the Indians at the stake in retribution, although no "mother lode" of gold has ever been found in that area.

The Indians finally revolted around 1680. On a pre-arranged day, they took up arms, killing the Spanish friars, who were often more cruel than the soldiers, and leveling their churches. Many Spaniards fled; others found refuge in the Fort in Santa Fe where they were virtually prisoners, since they had no access to outside food. The Pueblos eventually freed them and the last of the Spanish disappeared. Some years later they returned, with a more conciliatory attitude: the friars now declared the Pueblo Indians to be "human beings" with souls. This great breakthrough in human

relations ensured that these villages would exist relatively
unchanged until today.

Once mutual respect had been established, these communities
prospered. The Pueblos often fought side by side with the Spanish
against the nomadic tribes that raided them, mainly the Apaches,
Comanches and, to a lesser degree, the Navajos. Many
intermarried after the reconciliation, forming a permanent
settlement of Indian and Spanish culture. Their numbers grew
until an outbreak of European disease, a pandemic some think was
related to smallpox, devastated many of those with Native
American blood. Since then, it has been a struggle to maintain
numbers of Pueblo Indians in these unique villages, but they are
truly a unique window into the past. I found their culture
irresistible during the dozen years that I lived in Santa Fe.

It was not until 1924 that the Pueblo Indians were granted
citizenship by New Mexico. They were only given the right to
vote in 1948–a shocking denial of human rights for those who first
occupied our land. In the 1970s and 1980s I set foot in every one
of the 19 remaining Pueblos. Often my visits would dovetail with
their ceremonial times of the year, when they truly open their
hearts to the public as a way of preserving their threatened
heritage.

Some of these ceremonial events are a bit of a facade for those of
us who know the true story behind their plight and their struggle
for recognition of their past contributions to this country's
greatness. They put on a happy face to the outside world for the
sake of attracting the tourist dollar, and sadly pull in a handful of
people from the outside world who, over the centuries, have cared
little for their feelings, culture, hopes and aspirations.

One thing that stands out, as one walks these sacred sites of the
past, is that their culture focuses on the common good, not the
individual. Even the tribal elders and chiefs, who have found a
new source of money in the gaming industry, use their absolute
power for the common good of the tribal members rather than for
self-glorification. Although not all the Pueblos share a common

language, their religious beliefs seem quite uniform, and revolve around the concept that their spirits have emerged from a lower world. This is reflected in their way of entering their dwellings and spiritual centers–they climb up a ladder that leads to a small hole at the top of the dwelling, one that leads to the sky. It is referred to as a Kiva, and it is the most visible aspect of their architecture. These ladders and the openings in the tops of their buildings are their entry into what they call the "fifth world," a plane that we outsiders can't fully understand.

All these pueblos are sovereign nations, as I learned in my business dealings. Their unique status is enshrined by their treaties with the federal government, which exempt them from state regulation. This is one reason why they are allowed gambling casinos without interference on the local or national level. In a way, it is a financial blessing for those who remain, since it gives them a degree of self-sufficiency in a world that spits out electronic checks from the BIA. However, it also makes them increasingly dependent on the white man.

Many pueblos retain signs of the Spanish influence, with the churches centered in plazas, buildings that were constructed by Indian slave labour, and fenced-in corrals and irrigated fields of crops that are such a treat to see in their original, unblemished form.

Most of these massive pueblos are directly accessible from the Rio Grande River. I have stopped often on white-water rafting trips to wander around and enjoy the tranquility that reigns in these quiet places. Many have nurtured thousands of people in the past by growing such things as wheat, corn, squash, tobacco, fruits and chiles introduced by the Franciscan friars. The villages were totally self-sufficient for over 600 years; many have tens of thousands of acres that feed off the tributaries of the great river. Unfortunately, today they are but a shadow of their past, with full-time populations of less than a hundred. The people are focused on the past, and have few thoughts about what the future holds in store.

Often I would wander past the now-fallow fields, leaving my raft on the banks of the swiftly moving river. The fields once produced great bounty and were a source of much pride and happiness to those who lived in this peaceful locale, a far cry from our cramped, stressed little lives with airports and Ipods and pollution and waste. Everywhere I saw signs of the man-made ponds that once held turtles and welcomed migratory birds like ducks and coots, but that are now mostly dried out, reduced to cracked mud. Back then, the lakes were loaded with trout and bluegill, and must have attracted the most unusual migratory wildlife known to mankind. One can just sense that the Indians knew the habits and patterns of the migratory birds and could calculate their movements and somehow lure them into their man-made lakes for their consumption.

The Indians have a "sixth sense" for what nature is all about and how it functions and how it can adapt to meet the needs of the inhabitants, especially those who take only what is needed. Here you can sense the harmony they had achieved with nature. They were not intruders or interlopers, and they respected the world far more than we have. We, the new kids on the block, have devastated our environment over the last two centuries. Rarely did we leave the land in the same condition in which we found it, as they did.

I often made weekly trips to Albuquerque from Santa Fe by car along the interstate that bordered on or cut through some of the northern pueblos. Here you can see the diametrically opposed values of the two cultures: ours is evidenced by all the asphalt and concrete that has sprouted up along the interstate corridor, while their landscape has remained unchanged in the last few centuries.

In the overall scheme of things, there is one pueblo that truly captured my attention over the decades, although each one is unique. The most breathtaking of all is Acoma, a settlement that goes back to 900 A.D., by most accounts. The "sky city," a feat of Indian ingenuity, is based on the idea of achieving closeness to the gods, or to the sixth world. It also acted as a defensive structure, occupying elevations that were higher than the invading Spanish. It is located on a plateau 400 feet above the plains, just west of

Albuquerque. Some say that a sacred vortex of energy surrounds
the village, like so many of the table-top mesas in Sedona Arizona.
This elevated location was considered impregnable for centuries;
the Pueblo Indians survived by bringing food and water supplies to
the top from the fertile valley below.

Small winding steps carved out of the massive stone mountain
were the only access, originally. Many of the steps can
accommodate only one foot at a time, and a small one at that. It
seems that each step has a corresponding indenture carved in
sandstone for one's hands to provide steadiness along the way. I
don't know if anything in this country parallels this unique way
into a fortress-like place where people gathered for safety.

These narrow passages, the only way to reach the top, were small
and not easily navigable by large numbers of invaders. They also
offered hidden places, or crevices in the rocks from which one
could ambush the outsiders. In the several visits I made there,
mostly for ceremonial functions, I could just imagine the war
drums beating and the sounds reverberating off these magnificent
two- and three-storey adobe homes perched on top as the enemy
approached. The visibility to the horizon is almost unlimited on a
clear day. There is virtually no way that invaders could escape
undetected into the flat, barren desert landscape below.

It was electrifying to think of thousands of warriors congregating
in the central plaza, chanting and building up their spiritual
courage as they prepared for battle, with the women and children
looking down from the rooftops as they do today for the important
tribal ceremonies they enact for the public. It challenges the mind
to realize that their war chants and their appeals to the spirit within
carried them through the difficult times.

In its heyday, the setting must have been nothing short of grand.
The Indians' cultural strength was drawn from the pride they had
in their lifestyle, the women and children living secure in a world
of love and peace, and the harmony among the group, with the
elders providing wisdom and the youth offering the energy
required to protect their way of life from outsiders. Our society

could learn so much from the way they embraced the common good, and how they pulled together in tough times to preserve their heritage. Acoma was especially was isolated from the brutalities of the Spanish because of its strategic location, so the Indian race here remained relatively pure while other groups intermarried more frequently.

The Spanish under Coronado eventually took the pueblo by force. Apparently, they built a wooden bridge from another mesa and made their assault to the sky city that way, a feat that is hard to visualize. They killed about 1000 inhabitants, mostly warriors and the elderly, and the rest, mainly women and children, were sold into slavery in Mexico. All Acoma males over 25 had one of their feet chopped off as punishment for not initially bowing to the Spanish.

The white man never had open access to the sky city until the 1940s, when a Hollywood film was made and a road was bulldozed from top to bottom. Since then, it has become a major tourist attraction due to its uniqueness. It is one of the most spectacular sites in the world, a place where man and the gods, if there is such a thing, came together. Even though it is less than functional as a city today, it was one of the most important cities in North America during its prime. Now a reservation, it is a true treasure of the past, even though only about two dozen elders are still in residence full time. Acoma still has no electricity or running water as we, in the western world, know it.

Now the drums beat only on ceremonial days, a great reminder of what things were like 600 years ago. Today they remain silent on other days, a reflection of the Spanish conquest and the changing lifestyle that we and others have imposed upon them.

A totally different type of spirit emerges when one departs from the Pueblos. If there was ever a group that fought to the death to preserve its heritage, in New Mexico it would be the Apaches. Even though they often lived side by side with the Pueblo tribes, it was not generally in harmony, especially after the Spanish settled in. The Apaches, more nomadic, lived in the foothills along the vast Rocky Mountain range. They extended as far as Mesilla, N.M. near El Paso and as far west as Tucson. Often they could be found settling or raiding parts of old Mexico like Senora, when the American territories bore less fruit, or the Bluecoats were in hot pursuit.

The Apaches were originally run off the Great Plains of the Midwest by the Cheyenne and into the mountains of New Mexico. Many ended up in the southern part of the state, but some lived in and around the Santa Fe, Albuquerque area as did the nomadic Navajos. The Apaches were the last to capitulate to the western settlements, the last on the so called "Trail of Tears" that began with the Seminole Indians, who were rounded up and shipped out of the Florida Everglades, along with other southeastern tribes, to "god-forsaken" reservations in the midwest. These early tribes that were relocated found out what life was like under the thumb of the white man's laws and customs. They came to know the true meaning of this incomprehensible world, with all its punishment, suffering and loss of dignity. The Apaches were unique how they seemed to stand alone in the face of the overwhelming odds they faced. The history books have never treated them kindly, passing them off as savages to be done away with, or as easy to domesticate and convert to the white man's way of life.

Often, during the decade of the 1980's that I lived in Santa Fe, I would ride into the mountains to the east, the Sangre de Cristo Range, on a horse that I purchased at an auction, in effect saving him from the slaughterhouse. Even though I only paid what it was worth to the slaughterhouse–not much more than a dollar or so a pound live on the hoof–he turned out to be a magnificent animal. He was medium tan in color, huge in size, with a wonderful gait that enabled me to ride him without a saddle. He was the kind of mount that an Indian chieftain would have ridden into battle, I am certain. Even though he was not a full-bred quarter horse, he just took command of the situation as things arose. His ingrained habits left little doubt as to his ability to meet the challenges that lay ahead, which was very comforting when I would drift into uncharted terrain, as I often did.

At the time, I was in the middle of developing several real estate projects in Santa Fe, and spent many an evening and weekend in rural Tesque at Barbara's home, where I boarded this great stallion. Barbara had bought a smaller version at the same auction, but even though she was from Lexington, Kentucky and a great patronizer of the Kentucky Derby, she rarely rode her mount. She and I often preferred the creature comforts of the notoriously elegant Rancho Encantada, an exclusive dude ranch a dozen miles north of Santa Fe, practically at our doorstep.

For several years I was active in a joint venture with Betty the woman who owned the ranch. I developed 36 condominiums on her property, sold mostly to her exclusive guest list. As time went on we became close friends, especially around the cocktail hour at her private table in the elegant bar. She and some of her ranch hands like Rick were great students of the ways of the Apache, and particularly their notorious chief, Cochise. It seemed that some of those in the stables lived and breathed the Old West and revered the Apache nation, the last holdout from the white man's trickery and treachery.

At first, my magnificent scrap value animal intimidated me with his size, speed, and calmness, so I stayed fairly close to Barbara's small ranch, racing across the open pastures at speeds I had never experienced before, especially without a saddle. Finally I reached a comfort level with my horse, and was able to participate in a lifestyle that was quite similar to the Indians who pioneered this region.

Soon I was going up into the mountains, into unchartered areas. I felt comfortable, always knowing that I could see Barbara's ranch, no matter how far I strayed. It was magical; it felt like flying, free as a bird. I don't think I have ever experienced this sensation since, with the possible exception of sailing the great oceans, where you can immediately bring yourself back to a charted course with a satellite tracking device. There is something very special about having unlimited freedom of movement in uncharted areas, and knowing that you have not a care in the world, and it doesn't matter when you get home.

Often I would undertake trail rides with some of the ranch's exclusive guests. Once I bid on and won a trip at an auction that included riding with Sam Shepard and Jessica Lange, enjoying spring in the snow- filled foothills. Just arriving on the verge of success, they mostly stayed to themselves, although they were quite cordial and added a great dimension to these already intriguing foothills.

For hours, it seemed, when I went into the mountains, the horses would labor chest-deep in the snow, moving slowly between the enormous pines. Occasionally I crossed a stream that was difficult to navigate because of the rapidly running water from the winter accumulation of snow at the higher elevations; one quickly gathers that this is not the place to be unless you are well provisioned for the long haul, or are with knowledgeable guides. Often I returned to these foothills on my own, or with Rancho Encantado cowboys in tow. Fall was especially lovely, with the changing colors of the aspen trees, and the ease with which one could portage the steams, now were at their lowest levels. The trout fisherman loved this time of the year, as I did. I usually traded my fly rod for a camera during this special, most photogenic season, and time to time I even hired a photography instructor or guide me, showing me the intricacies of using various lenses, film speeds and filters to capture the array of colors that defined the landscape.

But, setting all this beauty aside, somehow I was able to focus on how the Apache were able to become one with these unique mountain settings, clustered along the Rocky Mountain chain. I let my imagination run, vicariously putting my stallion and myself in their moccasins hundreds of years earlier. The Apache were reclusive, unable or unwilling to adapt to the changing ways of the west. They must have found solace in the great rocky mountain range that runs all the way from northern Colorado to El Paso at the south. They chose to live as recluses, even as the final curtain came down.

Being nomadic, unlike the Pueblo Indians who lived along the lush valleys below, it seemed almost inconceivable that the Apache could eke out an existence, especially when the heavy snows fell.

They were confined to their mountain villages, often devoid of any food for months on end, except for that which they had stored during the milder times of the year. But that was their tradeoff, it seemed: they paid for freedom with hardship, and their lifestyle was not destined to last much longer. Likewise, I was destined to move on from Santa Fe, and to continue my quest for whatever appealing adventure came along.

Based on my limited experience with the spring snows, the colder months were extremely difficult. Probably there was fresh meat to be had, as game was easily tracked in the snow, but not much else. I remember riding past large beaver dams in the early spring, a sign that the furry little animals were not far away, and of course all the colored berries and fruits were coming into being, signalling that it would not be long before fresh meat would again be available, when the animals again began to move. Much of the large game that was hunted, according to the ranch hands, simply lived off the fat in their bodies while movement was restricted because of the waist-high snow that accumulated between the shade of the large trees.

The Native Americans had dreams, just like we all do, individually and collectively, about how they would like to be remembered. Their heritage here went back a hundred generations or so, and much of it was unrecorded. Their traditions, religious beliefs, ambitions, mating patterns, conceptions of the afterlife, and, especially, their legacy to a land they cared for and respected so much, has simply vanished.

What was memorialized was not in their tongue, but penned by others, and subject to a twisted interpretation. Accounts were written to make the pieces fit the puzzle of the white man's aspirations and cultural upbringing. It was partially for this reason that those who worked the stables at Ranch Encantado, the trail hands, took such great interest in the unrecorded history of the tribes that occupied the upper Rio Grande Valley. Betty Egan, who owned the ranch, owned a library of books that supported their beliefs.

The ranch management and their underlings seemed fascinated by Cochise, the fearless, most famous Apache chief. One ranch hand in particular, Rick, was an avid student of the Apache and of Cochise in particular, even though Cochise, with his warlike ways, was somewhat unrealistic about the leadership role he played for his people. Those at the ranch seemed deeply connected to the Apaches; their perspective was a physical one, rather than being rooted in the spiritual aspect of this tribe, which fascinated me. Of course, this spiritual side rarely surfaced in the history books. The Apache were always portrayed as warriors and savages by those they came into contact with, just as the Mexican Aztecs, despite their great civilization, were portrayed bloodthirsty people who sacrificed their young at the altar to some fictitious god.

It might be impossible, today, to fully understand the Apache, their culture, and their dreams: towards the end they lived hand to mouth, in a world that was closing in on them, a world that no one wanted a part of. Thus much of their customs and lifestyle were distorted to fit neatly into the white man's history books, which did not record their long-lasting, orderly, civilized society.

Rick and his buddies looked up to Cochise as a natural-born leader who achieved freedom for his people, albeit with great hardship. Freedom was something the ranch hands, deep down inside, would have liked to have had in their lives as well. They were like many others in the world, longing for their dreams to come true, wanting to get beyond their position on the lower end of the economic rung. Rick's love of horses, his attachment to the ranch and his infatuation with Cochise kept him from participating in the contemporary lifestyle that Santa Fe had to offer. But nevertheless, he seemed at peace with himself, within this limited environment.

Rick and I would often ride through the trails in the national forest surrounding the ranch, staying on the marked trails, which was dictated by the ranch's insurance policies. But sometimes, when he was not obliged to look after guests, we would find our own off-beat trails; as evening would set in, we would sit by the campfire at the ranch, or on the trail with a beer or two, hypothesizing about what it must have been like over a hundred and fifty years ago in this same terrain, for those who originally claimed it by right of birth. It would have been unthinkable to ride freely across these sacred mountains back then, without being under the watchful eye of some native tribe.

One can just imagine how they must have blended into their mountain surroundings as they were pursued by soldiers from the large fort in Santa Fe. If one looks hard enough, one sees dozens of hiding places that could accommodate a hundred or more people tucked onto the wooded wilderness, until they needed food or other supplies such as weapons and livestock, which necessitated raiding the settlers and the pueblos below. The horse, brought to the area by the Spanish, became a great vehicle for the warriors' hit-and-run tactics for survival.

Of course, before the white settlers monopolized the flat fertile valleys of the Rio Grande, the Apache were free to roam the lower elevations, where game and crops were plentiful. With the ever-increasing arrival of the settlers, that option quickly came to an end. The handwriting, for the permanent occupation of these Indian lands, was on the wall, as the settlers became increasingly protected by the military, which established a string of forts along the densely traveled trails to the desirable points of settlement.

But back to my visions of how things must have been.

One can just imagine their chiefs riding down to the white man's settlement of Santa Fe to talk about peace and relocation, with white flag in hand; yet another round of disappointing talks would lead to the eventual extermination of the Indians. Cochise himself lived a bit south of this area, and drew on other Apache tribes for support for his war parties, Rick told me.

The Apache Indians were willing to put their life on the line in order that the White Man would not encroach any further into their territories. Cochise, having seen the broken promises and dreams of the other tribes, wanted no part of it. He believed he had to destroy the white man and his settlements so that he and his people could live in harmony. In the end, Rick told me, the Spanish, the

white settlers and the government soldiers were too much for his
band of warriors. Most think Cochise was fighting at a distinct
disadvantage, with only 1 in 4 of his warriors equipped with hand
guns or rifles. Those with weapons had few bullets to support their
efforts.

The end result, the capitulation just below Ranch Encantado with
the Tesuque Pueblo, led ultimately to broken dreams, little
meaningful education and dependency on alcohol. The domination
of the Washington bureaucrats was coupled with the later arrival of
the gambling industry, which stripped them of their dignity. Many
gaming operations are concessionaired out to non-Indian entities
who promise jobs and instant wealth to the tribes, but they rarely
materialize.

Lives, once again, were turned upside-down to satisfy the greed of
the white man. I lived on the edge of the Tesuque Pueblo for years,
and from time to time met their chief and their elders; sadly to say,
they became pawns for the white man's financial interests. These
interlopers operate risk- free casinos leased at rock-bottom prices
and exploit the tribes, many of which are exempt from the legal
traditions of our states.

Rick's stories were fascinating: he told of the broken promises,
and the constant shifting of the fort. Commanders were known as
Nantans, and it seemed that each new Nantans brought in new
rules from the Great White Father in Washington. With each
broken promise, the Apache were more defeated. Their hatred and
their raids accelerated as their lands were taken away. The
troopers, Rick told me, retaliated, often taking women and children
when warriors were out on their raids. The end result was that they
were forced to reside at higher and higher mountain altitudes so
they could spot the approaching whites from great distances. Often
separate camps were set up for the women and children and for the
raiding parties, who were gone for extended periods of time in an
attempt to level the playing field.

They were tricked into temporarily relocating, just outside secure
forts like the one in Santa Fe. They were promised rations, warmth

and comfort in exchange for arms and their willingness to fight–but these were broken promises. These arrangements were unsatisfactory to the Apache, and specifically to Cochise and his allies. Their demise was largely brought about by the blankets they were given, Rick explained: taken off soldiers who had died of smallpox, they were often disease-ridden. Rick mentioned that more Apache died from their association with the white men in peaceful proximity to their forts–from food poisoning and related diseases–than from all their battle encounters. Women and children were especially vulnerable to the white man's evil ways.

Cochise controlled only a small band of Indians, several hundred at the height of his career, but was so respected by the other Apache chiefs that he could raise raiding parties of thousands of warriors. With the ever-increasing number of the white man's horses, the Indians could raid and retreat to far distances, so they were quite effective, even as their numbers diminished. When the Spanish were driven out of the Pueblos around 1680, they left many horses behind, according to Rick. In subsequent decades the horses roamed free and multiplied, giving tribes like the Apache great mobility for the first time in their history.

As time went on, the Spanish returned and settled in the Pueblos along the Rio Grande River, this time being more condescending towards Indian culture. As the numbers of white settlers increased, the Apache were threatened; their seasoned warriors became far fewer in numbers. Occasionally, dissatisfied members of the tribes would slip away and surrender to the white men at the forts, especially young warriors who were out of step with their elders, and the women and children of those warriors who had no one. No longer did the Apache enjoy the vastness of the west. As time passed, they became weaker and more frightened, making it difficult for leaders like Cochise to keep the traditions of the "warrior state" alive.

There is a great myth about the west, both from the white man's standpoint and also from the native perspective. The white man saw it as his future, a place to possess that provided hope and freedom, and unlimited economic possibilities for a future. The

more land they could occupy, the more they would prosper.
However, for the Indian the land was the center of the universe, to
be shared by the community; it was not something that had to be
constantly exploited. The Indians, as they lost their land, also
began to lose their identity. Many tribes had been at the same
location for a hundred generations. They prayed to the animal
spirits, those that sustained them. The white man and the Spanish,
on the other hand, believed in a different god who seemed
disconnected from the land and to the preservation of the
environment.

The Indians talked in terms of we; the white man said 'I." The
inner voices for both groups were different. But only the old and
dedicated warriors seemed intent on keeping their traditions alive.
According to Rick, young warriors and their families were given
valuable goods as well as prestige among the settlers if they
became "turncoats." And the white man realized he could not
conquer these renegade tribes without their help and knowledge.

With the advent of these defectors, now used as scouts to seek out
the remaining Apache, it became increasingly difficult for Cochise
and his loyalists to survive. Turncoat Indians knew the back trails
and hidden places where the tribes camped. Finally, the white man
had invaded the inner secrets of the tribes.

The mountain range around Santa Fe, the Sangre de Cristo
mountains, is named for the blood of Christ, perhaps partly
because of the amount of blood shed in that area. They are over
10,000 feet high. It must have virtually been impossible to track
down the Apache raiding parties in this thick dense forest, so for a
while the Apaches survived, until the turncoat Indian scouts
threatened their survival.

As the Apaches became more and more isolated, the white settlers
banded together, preventing them from going down into the fertile
and settled valleys of the Rio Grands to raid. This was especially
prelevant along the mountain passes that carried the wagon trains
from the Midwest, which had historically proved to be easy
pickings in terms of food, horses, livestock and ammunition.

As more settlers came, the closer the forts became to each other. The Indians raiding parties became ineffective. Isolation of the Apaches, the word of the day, proved fatal, as the young warriors that were the future often opted for a more promising lifestyle.

From time to time, the Apaches negotiated truces, often bogus, with the white man, which promised food and shelter, but these promises, cloaked in obscure language, never materialized. When they became desperate, Cochise and his warriors often took their raiding parties into Sorona, Mexico to avoid violating the clauses of the white man's treaties.

Living at the lower levels of the Rio Grande Valley, as I did, it was easy to imagine the magnificent lifestyle they must have had before the whites arrived, residing in the lush valleys during the winters and relocating into the high mountain ranges during the hot, humid summers. They had the blessings of ample food and shelter, and no cause to worry about their future. For many generations this was a given; Native Americans did not have to look over their shoulders in fear. They existed peacefully with nature for hundreds of generations.

The southwest tribes thrived on positive energy, before the settlers arrived. Children were raised to be self-sufficient, and were groomed for a successful future. The women and the elderly were provided for. But then–everything changed. One by one they fell like dominoes to the white man's wishes, through disease, starvation, the battlefield, or the heartbreak of broken promises.

It seemed to me, after talking extensively with Rick, that the Apache were the most independent tribe, far more than the Pueblo Indians. In the final analysis, only Cochise was able to negotiate a reasonable peace treaty, allowing for a relocation to the Canada Alamosa Reservation. Historians will remember him as the only chief who beat the white men at their game. Other Indians ended up slaughtered at Wounded Knee, or herded into degrading captivity.

Cochise's death doomed the Apache. When he died, they were removed to the diseased San Carlos Reservation, clearly a second-rate facility. They did not have the fire in their bellies to hold onto his stubborn tradition of resistance. The Apache were known for their great spiritual powers, and Cochise, almost supernatural to his followers in this war of extermination, was unfortunately bound to lose. His burial marked the end of their independence.

THE POLITICAL GRAVEYARD

The year was 1962, the month October—the time of the nerve-racking Cuban Missile Crisis.

Not so coincidentally, only a few days before, an obscure, nondescript building went into service. It had a vital source of reconditioned air and miles of tentacles of wire, which were buried under a golf course. The wires reached out of the structure into a vast communications system in the adjoining mountains of West Virginia. The building, 100,000 square feet, had over 50,000 tons of concrete, some of which was submerged 100 feet below ground and clandestinely incorporated into this country's most elegant, oldest, high-profile, dignified five-star resorts.

The Greenbrier had housed 23 men who were or would be Presidents of the United States. Five of these were the Chief Executives prior to the Civil War.

The existence of the structure was shrouded in total secrecy. It was a place where food was accumulated in such vast amounts that the corridor in which it was stockpiled was the length of a football field and a half. There were endless supplies of food and water, not to mention the 50,000 gallons of fuel, changed regularly for 35 years. The resort served as a perfect front for this establishment, which used the resort's catering, security and maintenance staffs.

It was constructed in anticipation of a clientele that would occupy its 18 dormitories, with bunks whose name plates were revised every two years. But the clientele never showed up, and to this day the establishment serves only as a frightful and outdated $14,000,000 reminder of the Cold War. That works out to about $25,000 per bunk—a bit pricy by my estimation

As I recall from my youth, this period in our history was one where the doomsday scenario prevailed. That mood passed, and did not grip our country again until about half a century later, on 9-11. During the Cold War years, people were digging up their back yards and installing bomb shelters, storing large quantities of canned foods and potable water and a bit of whiskey. As teenagers, we were shown evacuation routes out of the metropolitan areas we lived in. We suffered through weekly air-raid drills to loud sirens, although we never did much except leave our classrooms and congregate on the sidewalks. It was, in a way, a welcome relief from the doldrums of our tedious high school studies.

Since then, entire generations have grown up not knowing what homeland security really was, or should be. The term was certainly not associated with a life-threatening, panic situation. During World War II, I am told, homeland security was taken very seriously: nearly every neighborhood had civil defense wardens who wore white helmets and armbands and ensured that emergency procedures, when needed, would go smoothly. Black curtains were installed in most houses, and were to be drawn during the evening, in order to make our cities more difficult to see from the air at night.

In the last half of the 1950s and most of the 1960s, fallout shelters were the rage. My mother and grandmother even went as far as to purchase a farmhouse in rural Wisconsin—about a half hour from Milwaukee—for our safety. The home had a concrete basement, formerly used for storing potatoes in complete darkness. It was converted for our protection in the event of a Soviet nuclear attack. But then, as quickly as the nuclear threat had come, it vanished. In the 70s, 80s and 90s the Atomic and Hydrogen Bomb scares fell into obscurity, and bomb shelters and homeland security, considered essential thirty years before, were now seen as merely silly.

However, today, as we move into unchartered waters following 9-11, one must ask the question, "am I going to be left out in the cold by my government, on the outside looking in again"? I would surmise that if biological and chemical weapons are deployed, adequate protection or inoculation will only be available to a few in our society—namely the politicians, key government employees, the military, and trained medical and hospital personnel, all of whom are under the umbrella during a constitutional crisis.

After all, President Eisenhower once left us out in the cold. In 1958 he rejected a commission's recommendation for an extensive, $22.5 billion national fallout shelter system. Likewise, today, we will likely be on our own, if the worst-case scenario occurs. Ever since the Civil War, the government has not found a means of protecting the populace in times of emergency, even though that same populace funds the government's very existence, through tax dollars.

That is why this "five-star bomb shelter," which was designed to be the new location for our federal government's legislative branch, caught my attention several years ago. We, the people, are not part of the survival program now, nor were we then. Our lack of protection against bio-chemical warfare leaves us in a similar situation to the one we faced with the Congressional Bunker—virtually defenseless outsiders looking in at the privileged, protected few.

But I'm getting ahead of myself.

I, like many, had heard of the world-renowned Greenbrier resort, but like most I had no knowledge of the secrets hidden underneath, in the Congressional Bunker. As we know, it is a place that reflects our deep roots and our heritage; a resort ever since 1776, it was established just a few years after our country gained its independence. It served the carriage trade, with the exception of a few years during the Civil War and World War 11, when it was closed to the public. The stately white hotel buildings, perfectly arranged cottages in rows, provide guest accommodations, and the outbuildings and recreational buildings catered to almost every conceivable human need. This Old-World setting, with room for thousands of guests, had the elegance and grace of yesteryear, and reflected the comfortable lifestyle of our European ancestors.

Greenbrier, with six thousand acres of lawns, its ancient oaks tucked away in the lush green mountains, and the soothing, healing waters of its many mineral springs, has protected and preserved the manners and traditions of the well-bred for centuries.

When one arrives, as I did quite unpretentiously in my twenty-foot motor home, or as others in the past have done by horseback, railroad, automobile, airplane or stagecoach, Greenbrier's stately presence immediately offers a haven from the hustle and bustle of the outside, often mundane, environment. The breathtaking mountain ranges stretch as far as one's imagination will let them go, it seems. Civilized America has always had an eye for luxury and elegance, and it has always been found at Greenbrier—with the possible exception of the time when the Shawnee Indians used it as their river settlements and hunting grounds for deer, elk and buffalo.

For countless decades, it was the summer capital of the Old South, drawing privileged cotton, sugar, and tobacco plantation owners from Virginia, Louisiana, the Carolinas and Georgia. The guests enjoyed traditional European diversions such as fox and hound hunting and elegant balls, where all donned their finest European outfits.

The earliest guests were household names—Daniel Webster, Davy Crocket, Francis Scott Key, Henry Clay and many others. Not all were assured of admission. Guests were greeted at the gate by the hotel's manager, and were either accepted or turned away, depending on their standing and credentials. Being an aristocrat, senator, cabinet member, prominent banker or judge often meant that you also had to pass muster at the front desk, in order to be permitted to mix with the Old South elite.

When I was there, I saw a copy of an old account book from 1816, when the going rate was $8.00 a week per person. Servants, children and horses were half price, $4.00. So, if you arrived solo with a servant and two horses, the bill generally came to $20.00, or about $3.00 per day—about the price of a glass of ice tea today, without the tip.

A bit later in history, the Greenbrier served as the headquarters and hospital for the Confederacy, at least until the Union Army took West Virginia as its prize. General Lee was in residence after the war, at which time the grounds and structures fell into disrepair. The Confederacy had paid for its occupancy with Confederate bonds that became worthless after the war, sending the resort into a struggle mode until the railroad arrived in the late 1800s and revitalized it. The gentry reappeared shortly afterwards. At that juncture the Chesapeake and Ohio Railroad took over its ownership and it again became the "in" watering hole for the elite from all over the country.

Before long, the social season at the Greenbrier lasted year-round, and was complete with elegant cotillions with chaperones and tasteful summer lawn parties. It reflected the fact that America had finally reached its Golden Age. Brass bands met the arriving trains at the station; patrons often arrived in their private railroad cars, where their every need was catered to. Many stayed in their railroad cars until the servants had inspected the rooms and unpacked their possessions. As the century turned, both southerners and northerners participated in the elegant balls, often held several times a week. The young, eligible guests in particular measured each other's success by the number of trunks they arrived with for the season. In the first half of the twentieth century, everyone who was socially prominent found their way to the Greenbrier, with its magnificent ballrooms, lobbies, entertainment rooms and sweeping verandas and terraces.

In time, it was favored by the who's who of the golf world, as well. Hogan, Snead, Player, Hope, Eisenhower, Palmer, Trevino and Nicklaus, to name a few, often enjoyed the well-manicured links. The prominent families that graced the upper echelons of society were also in residence. In the years leading up to the Second World War, people like the Vanderbilts, Pulitzers, Armours, Guggenheims, Rockefellers, Carnegies, Bloomingdales, Astors, Fords, DuPonts, and Chryslers, and members of the House of Windsor, could often be found socializing here.

Many think Eisenhower's affection for golf at the Greenbrier had much to do with the establishment of the Congressional Bunker, although he had also had a working relationship with the ownership during WW11, when the resort served as a hospital. This extraordinary, undisclosed, thirty-year-plus partnership was responsible for quietly establishing the operatives for the location of the bunker and overseeing its construction. It was a totally covert operation, and was practically unknown to the outside world until the *Washington Post* blew the whistle, revealing the location and the innermost secrets of "Project Greek Island," as it was called.

In 1992, after the article broke, headlines across the country read something like this: *Hotel Argamagenon, Secret Underground Capital Confirmed*, and *Wartime Hideaway Revealed* .

Of paramount importance were the resort's massive physical plant, its supporting facilities, and its impressive infrastructure, especially suited for maintaining and replenishing supplies. All of these features were incorporated into the routine operations of the hotel, without drawing attention to the nature of the covert operation. Additionally, the hotel had a proven track record for discretely working with the government. First it had housed foreign diplomats, and later it had functioned as a wartime hospital. Eisenhower, then an Army General, visited the Hospital on occasion and had developed a bond and a solid working relationship with the owners. Moreover, the rail service to the front door and the newly constructed private airport made Greenbrier accessible to the nation's capital. The fact that it was surrounded by 11,000 foot mountains that would make it a tough target for a nuclear strike must have been one of the deciding factors, too.

The more I consider a worst-case terrorist scenario in today's context, the more I have come to realize that the United States virtually has no solution or protection to offer the masses. That is especially true for those of us who are out of the Washington loop: and the Congressional Bunker at White Sulphur Springs is a case in point. Back then, according to Tip O'Neal, the former Speaker of the House who was actively involved in the project,

Congress could not even provide for themselves. He added that the whole Congregational evacuation program was "so far-fetched" that he "never mentioned it to anyone." This is a sad comment on our homeland defense effort back then, but even half a century later, we have not made a great deal of progress.

The whole idea was totally ill-conceived. Outside of the half dozen members of the leadership, none of the other congressional members was ever informed of the concept, let alone its location. Shockingly, no provisions were made for the leaders' families, although the time required to round them up and get them there would have been prohibitive anyway. They were not part of the privileged set who were to exist under the Greenbrier's tennis courts if and when the sky fell. But it was sheer lunacy to think that the Members of Congress would leave D.C. without their families for a point on the map nobody even knew existed. This, combined with the fatal flaw that the trip by train was considered, time-wise, more than the length of time it would take the Russian nuclear-launched weapons to find their targets in D.C., made the whole project unfeasible and impractical.

But again, I'm getting ahead of myself.

A short description of the Congressional "white elephant" supports my argument about just how absurd the whole concept was. The decades-long preservation of the bunker with a "ready alert" status, at least until the *Washington Post* blew the cover, was equally ridiculous. Since then it has become a museum—a Cold War monument to the absurd.

The Congress-in-hiding fiasco starts with the entry door. It's 12 feet wide and 15 feet high, and it weighs 28 tons; the hinges alone are a ton and a half. Next comes the "exhibit hall," 90 X 190 feet with 20-foot ceilings, all buried under twenty feet of soil. Today it serves as a convention center for the hotel. The rear of the hall had two auditoriums, one seating 470 for the 435 members of the House, and the other with a capacity of 130 for the 100 member Senate. Of course, there was also space for the Architect of the Capital, who designed the structure.

The strange part of the "exhibit hall" was the fact that they installed 110 urinals, I am told. This is probably more than one could find in any of our major football stadiums, which cater to much larger numbers of rapidly filling bladders.

All that being said, with the exception of several unique built-ins for communicating with the outside world, the design of the complex seems fairly straightforward.

There's an infirmary and an operating room, and dormitories with hundreds of metal bunk beds and ample shower facilities. The dining room has place settings neatly laid out; these were updated every two years, since the players went through the musical chairs of the electoral process with their constitutions back home. Interestingly, the concrete walls had false windows constructed inside wooden frames with country scenes painted on them so the congressional elite could enjoy their final days of entrapment in peace and serenity, with the illusion of having some connection with nature.

The architects incorporated a "waste incinerator" to cremate those who fell by the wayside.

Those who were radioactive upon arrival would be screened at the front door and rejected from the bunker. The rules were such that the door, once shut, could not be re-opened until it was all clear, whatever that meant. Even with the massive provisions, it is unlikely that those entrapped could survive for more than a few months. But those inside could have become the bunker's prisoners for whatever the remaining life of the nuclear fallout was—maybe decades, it was thought. That is a lot of time on C-Rations, especially for lobbyists who are used to the good life in D.C.

Of course, there were state-of-the-art communication facilities, replaced over time as things got more sophisticated. It was all provided by ATT and its subcontractors. A television studio was a must, so they could tell their constituents what a fine job they were doing—despite the fact that most of us would not be out there listening. The two chambers were duplicates of those in Washington, right down to the paintings of the Founding Fathers on the walls (duplicates, of course), to assure us all that our government-in-hiding was operative and functional.

Outside radio contact was also available, since it was possible to erect relay towers out of concrete bunkers in the event that the conventional means failed. For three whole decades, the whole underground system was staffed and overseen by a host of military and civilian employees working in total secrecy. They performed their jobs just in case a need for the bunker arose.

Let's return to Speaker of the House Tip O'Neill for some insight.

He was quoted as saying, "I just never thought it would work"..."especially since we were barred from bringing our spouses and children." This is an interesting statement, given that O'Neill was one of the less than half a dozen Members of Congress who knew of the bunker's existence and sanctioned it.

So, if the idea was totally off the mark from its inception, prioritizing only those privileged few who counted and would continue on with our democracy, we have to ask ourselves what hair-brained scheme they have in mind for the rest of us peons in the post-9/11 world. Are we again going to be on the outside looking in? I think so!

As a final parting shot to the bunker, the political big shots back then had airplanes and railroad cars set aside for three decades in order to move them there expeditiously. A bogus evacuation plan was also devised at our expense—a sort of civil defense cover so the "big boys" would not be detected. It went something like this.

The plan was to move 45,000 residents from Fairfax County to Greenbrier County in the event of a nuclear war. We were to be the lemmings going over the edges of the mountains, to divert attention away from Congress, to a a place where few shelters, food or potable water existed.

Now, let's think about the predicament we find ourselves in today. The options are as chilling as they were in the1960s. If you believe in the old saying that history repeats itself, we will once again be hung out to dry, just as we were then.

So what about the post-Cold War and 9-11 eras?

Keep in mind that the new players, the terrorists from third-world countries, must substantially downsize their financial thinking and planning, since they don't have the massive resources that Russia had, back then, at their disposal.

It seems logical, then, that the only way for the death-defying terrorists to compete in this new environment is to attack with weapons that are small in size, but still lethal, easily transportable, and of course, relatively inexpensive. They use weapons that are terrifying when deployed and that continue to demoralize us with time, as subsequent terrorist activities unfold.

Ironically, despite all of the monies spent on homeland security, we seem to have a one-issue President and White House staff. They seem unable to focus on a multitude of issues simultaneously; consider their preoccupation with the ill-conceived invasion of Iraq, and their futile attempt to create a democracy there. By diverting our energy and resources there and to Israel and Pakistan, we have done nothing more than add fuel to the fire of hatred for this country in the eyes of the Muslim population. In my estimation, these events have created dozens of terrorists for every one that existed before 9-11.

In other words, we conveniently find "avenues of diversion" when our government fails. Just wait and see, as we fail in rebuilding Iraq. What was a divided population under Saddam will re-unite against America if we continue to occupy Iraq and parcel out its oil reserves. The whole Iraq situation is a smoke and mirrors trick if there ever was one, for protecting our national interests.

For the terrorists, biochemical/ biological weapons might be their most realistic option. And they could be the weapons that we are most vulnerable to, as was the case with smallpox. It is a destructive weapon system that can be deployed effectively in areas of high concentrations of population.

The chink in our armor, like most of our shortcomings, is self-induced. At one point eradicating smallpox was a top priority in this country. We developed a vaccine that eliminated it altogether worldwide in the early 1970s, but not before 500 million people had died from it.

Unfortunately, we let our defenses down in the 1970s. At the ill-conceived suggestion of the World Health Organization (WHO), we destroyed most of our smallpox stockpile and put the rest into two WHO laboratories, which they assured us that they had control over. Atlanta was one, and for some strange reason, Moscow was the other. Talk about letting the fox into the hen house!

Immediately thereafter, knowing exactly what inoculations were available to the rest of the world, the Soviets went into a massive program of developing a destructive biochemical smallpox weapons arsenal, cultivating it in amounts that even the professional medical world could not comprehend. They used the WHO's supply of the vaccinations for the feed stock. Along with the lethal arsenal, they also developed methods of delivery that meant that even an accidental release of the smallpox virus could cause a catastrophic event of the greatest magnitude.

We have not had a smallpox outbreak in our country for over fifty years, and the Osama Bin Ladens of the world know this. They certainly have figured out that our medical people have not been trained to diagnose and treat the disease for the last half century. If they do their homework, and they surely will, they will come to the conclusion that anyone under the age of thirty has never been inoculated for this disease that historically kills one in three. What's more, nobody I know in the medical profession is willing to state categorically that smallpox vaccinations given thirty years ago would still be effective. Most speculate that after ten years, most of the protection is gone. In short, we as a population are without protection from this deadly killer.

What is even more critical, to my thinking, is that nobody at the highest political and military levels knows for sure what "modifications" the Soviets made to the "warfare germ," if any. These alterations could easily make the existing and limited supplies of vaccinations, based on "Mother Nature's" infection process, vulnerable or even useless. This is a terrifying wild card that I don't care, or dare, to speculate about.

We may well end up like the emperor with his new clothes—naked before the terrorists, who can easily purchase or develop devastating, inexpensive weapon systems, using the feed stock of the bankrupt Soviet Union. And many of our own scientifically inclined universities have trained those on the other side of the fence, making the situation even more frightening. Some of the top Iraqi and Iranian bio-terrorists were trained in our country; Iran's "top dog" also spent time at the Center for Disease Control in Atlanta, no doubt seeking out our vulnerabilities. And who knows about the others, from North Korea, Israel, and China.

I am troubled, also, by the biblical overtones of it all. So much religious literature reflects the idea that the world will be cleansed of its evils by a plague. Radical religious leaders could easily turn these historical teachings into, or conveniently translate them into, a justification for the use of biochemical weapons of destruction—which are hundreds of times more deadly than a naturally occurring plague. Third-world religious fanatics don't need much arm-twisting, especially when the method of choice is inexpensive, expedient, and sanctioned by the Bible or the Koran itself.

Certain biological and biochemical warfare techniques can be much more deadly than explosives, primarily because they leaves a wider "footprint" and come in waves, unlike bombs, whose initial damage is known or can be calculated or contained. The initial collateral damage caused by intentionally infecting a few thousand people with smallpox would be enormous. The numbers would quickly spread to the tens and hundreds of thousands, and even millions, within months, under the right circumstances.

What might appear to be a localized situation could engulf hundreds of square miles because of the light weight of smallpox particles and the long incubation periods prior to detection—a function of both the deadly nature of biological weapons and the transitoriness of our society.

For instance, if a biological weapon like smallpox were released into the air ducts of a major shopping center, where hundreds of thousands of people might congregate in a period of a week or ten days, tens upon tens of thousands could be subject to the disease after it raised its ugly head. It could then easily spread into adjoining cities and counties, and eventually engulf an entire state. Likewise, an open-air "aerosol" release would affect all parts of the country and spread to other continents as well.

The dry spores that are released are virtually undetectable until they find a home in the moist parts of the human body—lymph glands—where they begin once again to cultivate and grow, all the while emitting their deadly poisons. Sooner or later, the host's vital organs start to collapse. Immunity can be rendered useless if a dose of the vaccination is not applied within four to seven days of the exposure.

But I am getting a bit ahead of myself, once again.

Given how simple it is to understand the technology behind cultivating smallpox, and given the availability of the feed stock, the deadly process could very easily be set in motion. Any group with a makeshift laboratory with the proper oxygen, nutrients and controlling temperature, supported by the initial feed stock, could become a powerhouse in the field of mass destruction in a very short time. It is not uncommon for smallpox to multiply several times each hour by dividing itself; thus hundreds of millions of these deadly cells can quickly be produced a sophisticated laboratory.

The following is a simplified explanation of what could occur:

First, the spores would undergo the drying process; when the moisture is removed, several chemical changes occur. The dry, deadly, dormant spores can then be stored for decades. Of course, the real trick is to make the spores tiny enough that they can enter the membranes of the lungs.

When they are set free, as in my shopping center example, this method of warfare is so cost- effective that the results can be measured in pennies per dead person, rather than in the thousands of dollars needed for even limited editions of such things as "dirty bombs." And the method works very well in a controlled, enclosed area like a regional shopping center.

If we don't take immediate action, an attack of smallpox could be kept below the radar screen, and would be catastrophic to the vast majority of us. Health and Social Services Director Tommy Thompson assured us after 9-11 that within a few years there would be ample supplies of smallpox vaccinations available, even if it was the diluted kind. The big problem was that he and his cohorts failed to convince the medical community of the need. As a result, the vaccination program has virtually been scrapped. Most hospital workers refused to take it because it was not offered to members of their immediate families. So, when the day of reckoning comes, the hospital personnel will not be there for us.

Let's consider a hypothetical situation involving smallpox, which exemplifies its destructive capabilities and reveals the psychological and physiological effects it could have on us. (Keep in mind that most who do not die would be physically scarred for life). Imagine that the main targets were a dozen or so large shopping centers in or near major metropolitan areas, with no or few anti-terrorist programs in place, and no air purifying systems. It's easy to see the ramifications.

It's also a given that most of the lower-paying positions in this country often go to immigrants, many of whom are here illegally. They are the ones who sweep floors and do the chores we Americans find beneath us, including late-night maintenance in our shopping centers. Imagine a few hundred of these characters, under the direction and pay of a terrorist group. They could easily install the biological killer, smallpox, in the air ducts in dry powdered form; it comes in a small container, not much larger than a five-pound bag of sugar. It would be undetectable, invisible, and odorless.

Assuming that each of these shopping centers potentially caters to well over two hundred thousand shoppers in a fortnight or less—a conservative estimate—these twelve "time bombs"could infect about 1,000,000 people (half of those shopping there might contact the disease) without their knowing it, at least for the 7-10 day incubation period. The planted material could then be removed, and the maintenance men, inoculated beforehand, would be on their way to their next venture before authorities even knew what happened.

If these communities had populations of, say, over a million each, the demand for the smallpox vaccinations stockpiled by the government could well exceed the total supply within a few weeks.

In any event, in the first wave, 1,000,000 would hypothetically take sick, and be moved to our hospitals, doctors' offices and medical clinics. Unfortunately, many of these facilities don't have what they call "negative pressure areas," which insure that airborne diseases will not leave the infected room. So, the hospitals would inherit their own problems, and those already occupying their beds would also be subjected to smallpox, and would use up further supplies of the precious vaccination.

The infiltration of those infected then starts to paralyze the medical community—especially if the event takes place between January and March, which is the influenza season, when most medical facilities are fully booked. (Keep in mind that the early symptoms of smallpox are very similar to those of the flu; by the time the medical community could differentiate between the two and allocate the inoculations, many would be past the point of receiving any worthwhile treatment).

As the disturbing news dribbles out, the 24/7 news channels begin to sniff something that will sell bundles of TV time advertising, as 9-11 and the Florida 2000 Presidential election recount did. Soon, the affected cities and medical treatment facilities begin to see the bigger picture and start shutting down. Since the vaccine is not available to the public at large, people start to think about quarantining themselves at home, or at least not venturing out into public places, which only further plays into the hands of the 24/7 networks and the terrorists.

One in three won't make it, so the level of anxiety begins to rise, especially because the levels of vaccine are tremendously inadequate. And of course, the first doses go to those who are supposedly looking out for our interests—the politicians, military, police and medical personnel. I for one don't like the odds—to say the least.

Remember the lemmings going over the edge of the mountains near Greenbrier? That was the same concept, but in reverse order. They won't need us as a diversion when this happens because the vaccination potential is totally inadequate. The logical solution, assuming they had ample supplies, would be to re-inoculate the population prior to an outbreak—but that does not seem to be in the cards.

The federal government developed today's first line of defense, called the "ring theory." As they have explained, it focuses on the principle of containment, and on quarantining the infected and then vaccinating the rest of the populace. This is a bit of a sham, given the inadequacy of the vaccine supply and the extent to which the disease could spread in a matter of weeks.

It's like the Old West idea, seen in old John Wayne movies, of circling the wagons for protection, but the fatal flaw lies in the fact that the only effective way to contain it is to pre-vaccinate the entire population, given that our society is so large and so mobile.

When the hospitals reach capacity, which doesn't take long, the inexperienced police and National Guard will be left to herd people to "quarantine camps." The people will be subject to police powers that we have never experienced in a national emergency.

Needless to say, the 24/7 media will have a field day endlessly discussing the events, parading experts around in an attempt to outdo each other, probing for non- existent supplies of vaccinations, fabricating fill stories about who was responsible, confirming worthless leads on the terrorists, or speculating on their further activities. Mass hysteria will keep many glued to their TV sets. Meanwhile, everyone will ignore the issue of whether there is enough vaccination material to go around, and enough medical personnel to administer it. The message is beginning to sound familiar, isn't it? It certainly brings to mind the secret hidden in the bowels of the Greenbrier at White Sulphur Springs... does it not?

And so goes the first wave.... Now comes the second wave.

The hourglass of vaccinations is starting to empty, just as the epidemic starts to take on astronomical proportions. Each initial infection, if not checked, can set off as many as ten more cases in highly concentrated areas. So the 1,000,000 could become 10,000,000 in a few weeks, after the initial group has been discovered and diagnosed. Now, only skeleton crews are alert and available in our medical facilities. The cat is out of the bag, as far as the shortage of vaccinations is concerned. The politicians are now in complete control, as with the Greenbrier Bunker scenario. Tent cities pop up as the hospitals become a thing of the past. Police and National Guard are everywhere, and now the entire world starts to take notice and react.

What about those who have been cordoned off in their homes? They will need food and water, and might not be permitted to shop or leave their surroundings. So, the overworked police and National Guard will again be called on, this time to go to the stores, where the shelves have been stripped anyway.

As the second wave hits with it full force, only a few short weeks into the epidemic we begin to see the following.

Neighborhood groups begin to form, solving problems that the national leaders won't provide answers for. The medical community, our front-line defense, falls by the wayside. A large percentage of the vaccinations are spent, so we are told, but only a small percentage of the population has been inoculated People become confused and are in denial. They start to feel that the odds are totally stacked against them. The 24/7 crowd, now out of ammunition to keep viewers' attention, raises the issue that only 60,000,000 doses of antibiotics exist for 6 billion worldwide. People all over start to crunch the numbers. They see the writing on the wall and take to the high ground, whatever that might be.

Shopping centers, office buildings and homeowners start to default on their mortgages, even though the government assures them that relief is on the way. Stock indices plummet, life insurance companies head south, and retail sales become non-existent except for the necessities. Travel, both domestic and foreign, stops. Schools close; hotels are vacant. People stay at home: no one knows who is infected. There are too many unknowns out there.

By this time the confidence factor is gone. Then the third wave comes. Just like the surfers anticipate, the "big one" come in threes.

The old theory was that each wave of smallpox infections would be ten to twenty times the size of the previous one weighs heavily on those in the know, even though this theory was established when regular vaccinations were available to most, and most of the world was systematically being vaccinated. The out-of-pocket cost of this disaster is estimated to be in the billions. Some speculate that the cost is as much as $10 billion per 100,000 infections, and the economic impact can't be measured realistically.

Compared to this, if it ever happens, 9-11 will be like child's play.

Even though this hypothetical scenario may seem far-fetched, it really makes me wonder about our nation's priorities. I cannot help but wonder why we are devoting so much time, effort and over $150 billion to Iraq. Is it just that the politicians' egos will not allow them to admit to a mistake or to defeat in the long run? We won the war, it seems, but in the first ten days following the capture of Bagdad, we lost the peace. We know from the Greenbrier that those who lust after power really don't care about anybody else but themselves.

So, what can be learned from the Greenbrier adventure? Both situations remind us of how those in power don't necessarily care for their constituents as well as they look after themselves. Stalin, for instance, murdered 50 million people through his sacrifices of humans in the war and later in his political slave camps. But there's an important difference: he was not presiding over a democracy. We pride ourselves on the fact that we do live in a democracy.

However, even here, those in power won't relinquish it. The more powerful you get, the less you are willing to share your power. Those who get in the way and question the leadership often become sacrificial lambs. The egos and the elbow pushers at the top won't let anyone get in their way, no matter which way the system leans politically.

Possibly I have been watching too many James Bond movies, I don't know. But I find myself looking over my shoulder a lot these days, and asking a lot of questions that those entrusted with our safety and well-being don't have the answers for—just as they refused to give us the answers about the bunker at Greenbrier.

ABOUT THE AUTHOR

Charles Klotsche became interested in writing during the mid 1990's after achieving noted success in business with his real estate development entrepreneurial ventures having exceeded $100,000,000 in scope. His projects and personality have been featured in dozens of prestigious periodicals including The Smithsonian, Architectural Digest, People Magazine, Popular Science, Fine Home Building, Progressive Architecture, Travel and Leisure and the National Real Estate Investor.

He has appeared in hundreds of articles in national and international newspapers including The Los Angeles Times, The New York Times, The Australian, The Milwaukee Journal, The Dallas Morning News, The San Francisco Chronicle, The French Associated Press, The Christian Science Monitor and The Arizona Republic. His ventures have aired on The NBC Evening News, Lifestyles of the Rich and Famous, Dateline and Hardcopy, and have been televised by The Voice of America to tens of millions worldwide.

Mr. Klotsche holds an Undergraduate Degree in Economics; a Masters Degree in Finance. He has lectured on university campuses around the country, as well as to literary and travel groups and for nationally recognized bookstore chains. His in-print books are distributed by most major book store chains and through Amazon.com.

He has traveled extensively (six continents and over 80 countries) and has written travel related stories for The Christian Science Monitor and Gannett, and written financial articles for Cox Newspapers. He has co-authored two full length screenplays, Capture and Provenance.

Voyages is his 13th book, a consolidation of his travel adventures as they appear in his trilogy. He is President of the Palm Beach Chapter of the Circumnavigators Club and Founder and Executive Director of the Globetrotter Marathon Program, a worldwide program for Iraq amputees to participate in international marathons.

Mr. Klotsche is an accomplished blue water yachtsman, published photographer, ecologist, new age thinker, sky and scuba diver, and mountain climber whose professional accomplishments and philanthropic activities have been featured in several of the leading professional publications. He currently resides in Palm Beach, FL.

Printed in the United States
138319LV00003BB/3/P

9 780967 389042